# The Complete
# History of the SAS

**THIS IS A CARLTON BOOK**

First published by Carlton Books Limited 2003
20 Mortimer Street
London W1T 3JW

ISBN 978-1-84442-227-2

**Executive Editor:** Roland Hall
**Managing Art Director:** Jeremy Southgate
**Picture Research:** Steve Behan
**Production:** Peter Hinton

Printed in Dubai

# The Complete
# History of the SAS

## The Full Story of the World's
## Most Feared Special Forces

**Nigel McCrery**

**Consultant Editor: Barry Davies BEM**

**CARLTON**
BOOKS

# Contents

Introduction   6

Chapter 1: 2000s – The SAS Today   10

Chapter 2: 1990s – Central America to the Gulf   34

Chapter 3: 1980s – Northern Ireland to Gibraltar   52

Chapter 4: 1970s – Oman to Northern Ireland   82

Chapter 5: 1960s – From the Jungle to the Desert   120

Chapter 6: 1950s – Jungle Training and Desert Ops   142

Chapter 7: 1940s – The Early History of the Regiment   162

Chapter 8: After the Regiment   192

Appendix:
Weapons of War   208
Chronology   214
Roll Call   216
Index   218
Bibliography/Picture Credits   224

There have been many books written about the SAS, most without the Regiment's approval, yet the public desire to glean new information about any aspect of SAS operations continues unabated. Writing the latest stories of this unique regiment presents a problem, for the SAS has now gagged most of its members. However, wars have become part of the public domain, and every now and then a new tale will surface. During the research for this book I have visited Hereford many times, talking to members both past and present. Some have greeted me with smiles, while others have shown nothing but disdain. Notwithstanding, one characteristic bonded them all: they are normal, healthy human beings, and not the psychopaths many would have you believe.

The SAS is part of the British Army and, regardless of military disbandment, amalgamations and a steady erosion of service manpower, the Regiment has survived since its inception in 1941. True, it was reduced to little more than a territorial unit after World War Two, but its time in the wilderness was short. There has always been, and always will be, a role for those who 'dare', especially those who 'dare and win'. For this reason, and despite the Regiment's misgivings about publicity, its history is one worth writing, for it would be wrong to let such deeds and heroism go unrecorded.

Over the past 62 years the SAS has suppressed insurgencies, fought in major wars and confronted terrorism energetically. Yet, from the very beginning, its soldiers have remained hidden, often shrouded in myth and half-truths. In telling their story, I have started with their most recent operations in Iraq, going back through time to the first SAS operation in 1941. This reversal of time provides a better insight into the

**Early Days [above]: This group had to walk 100 miles to get back to their base from behind enemy lines. Special Forces: [right] Most armies now have an SAS-type unit.**

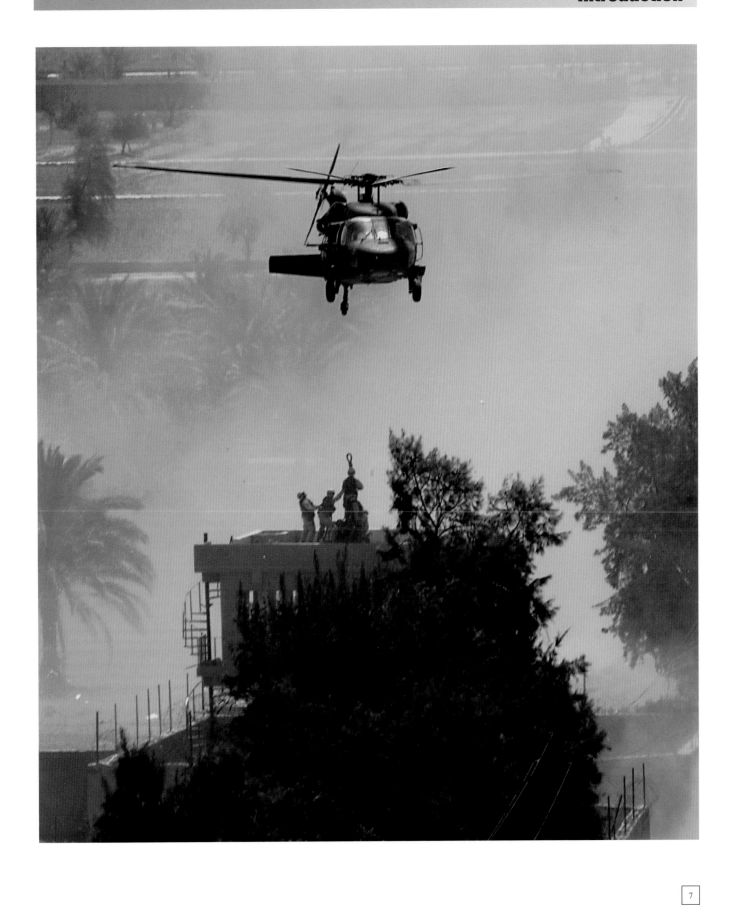

changes since the Regiment's origin.

The SAS family is truly a brotherhood of special men: for when men of the right calibre accept a common philosophy based on the individual spirit acting in tune with his brother-soldier to form a whole, then excellence can be the only result.

Research for this book has taken many forms and required the reading of more than 30 books about the SAS family. By far the best information was gleaned from SAS author and historian Barry Davies. Barry has amassed a huge database concerning all aspects of the Regiment and his picture library of the SAS is undoubtedly the finest in private hands. Many operations and individuals are mentioned more than once throughout the book, but where possible I have tried to keep repetition of stories to a minimum.

Unlike previous books, I have written this one using a familiar style, hoping to retain the original character of the conversations on which it was based. Inevitably, a number of personal opinions have crept into the book: should you discover these, please view them for what they are, as they do not reflect the official opinions or policies of the Special Air Service.

*Nigel McCrery, London*

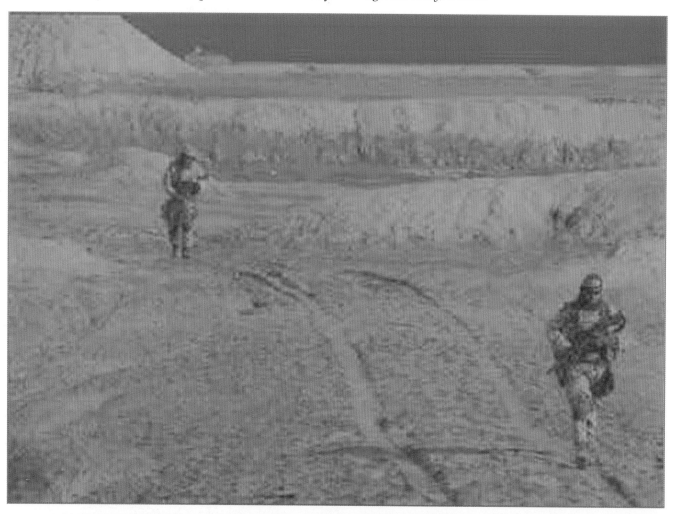

**It is said that the Taliban can smell British and American soldiers whenever they are approaching; night movement is essential.**

*The Fully-Rounded Regiment. The SAS have operated in all sorts of conditions around the world (jungle, below). They are highly-trained (sniping, above) and always ready (preparing for a door breach, top right). Right: The Iranian Embassy siege will be remembered for ever.*

# Chapter 1

# The SAS Today

**GROUND SUPPORT:** a small group of Special Forces land in the desert.

In order to appreciate the actions of the SAS, one must first recognize what makes the SAS so special. '22 Special Air Service' is the designation given to the present SAS regular regiment, now based in Credenhill, Herefordshire. The Regiment consists of around 200 men divided between four Sabre Squadrons, A, B, D and G. In addition to these, the Regiment also supports Training Squadron, 264 Signals Squadron and HQ Squadron.

There are also a number of smaller units, such as Operations Research, Demolition, Parachute Section, Boat Section, Army Air Corps Section and a host of sub-units responsible for the daily running and administration of such a large organization. In total, the new camp at Credenhill houses almost one thousand service men and women.

Many people often wonder why there is no C Squadron in the SAS. The answer is simple. During World War Two, a handful of Rhodesians opted to serve with David Stirling. In 1951 about 100 volunteered to serve with the SAS in Malaya; these were called C Squadron, Special Air Service. After the conflict the unit was disbanded, but in 1961 C Squadron was resurrected to fight on its own soil. For the next 17 years, Rhodesia fought a losing battle against factions of the African National Congress. (The courage of the SAS during its battles against ZANU and FRELIMO insurgents is best told in the book *The*

*Elite* by Barbara Cole). In June 1978, C Squadron became 1 Special Air Service Rhodesia.

The war ended in April 1980 when Robert Mugabe was elected Prime Minister of an internationally-recognized, independent Zimbabwe. In December of the same year the Rhodesian SAS was disbanded, at which time they received a telegram from the Commanding Officer of 22 SAS in Hereford: 'Farewell to a much-admired sister unit. Your professionalism and fighting experience has always been second to none throughout the history of the Rhodesian SAS. C Squadron still remains vacant in 22 SAS orbat (Order of Battle).'

**Walk up and run down is the only way to get to the RV (rendezvous) on time. At the end of Test Week comes the 'endurance march' - 40 miles with a 55lb Bergen in 20 hours.**

It should also be made clear that the SAS is not a machine; neither it is a clinical force cloned for warfare. It is what it has always been: a collection of dedicated soldiers. They are men who love military life, and wish to reach the pinnacle of their chosen profession. Above all, they are men who have found the true meaning of self-discipline. True, they seek adventure in the SAS, and thrive on the adrenaline rush, experiencing the same ecstasy as those who participate in high-risk sports. The standards for entering the SAS have been honed ever since the Regiment's conception and standardized since the mid-1950s. To reach this standard, every soldier must pass SAS Selection, possibly the most stringent military enlistment course in the world.

SAS Selection is hard; there is no other way to say it. The basis of the selection system is there to ensure that the valuable training time is only spent on the very best volunteers. Ideally, candidates for the SAS need to have had at least three years' service with a parent unit of the armed forces. This ensures that the basic training requirements and disciplines are already in place. In practice, most of the volunteers come from the airborne regiments and infantry units.

Selection is a funny word to use. The verb 'select' means 'to pick out the best or most suitable', while the adjective means 'chosen for excellence'. The problem is that nobody picks or chooses the volunteer; they must earn their place. It is more a case of the individuals selecting themselves. It is the single factor which makes the SAS so unique; a whole bunch of individuals, but with the capacity to act as one. All volunteers who pass selection must give up all previous rank held in their original regiments and revert to that of trooper. Each individual must then work their way back up the promotion line. In fairness, they keep their original pay, plus after a specified period they also receive additional SAS pay – something not to be sniffed at.

The physical side of Selection takes place in and around the Brecon Beacons in South Wales. Although not a high range of mountains, they are treacherous, exposed and battered by constant weather changes; death by hypothermia is seldom far away. Numerous SAS volunteers have suffered a slow death while lost and disorientated. It is therefore essential that a diligent, self-imposed training schedule be undertaken by the candidate prior to arriving at Hereford.

*The selection process to enter the SAS ranks as one of the toughest in the world. Preparation and skills such as excellent navigation help play a major part for those that wish to succeed.*

The overall course, which was originally devised in 1953 by Major John Woodhouse, has changed very little over the years. More emphasis was placed on safety after a series of deaths in the late Seventies and early Eighties, but the tests remain very similar.

Since the mid-Nineties, the SAS has run the Special Forces Briefing Course (SFBC) to ensure that prospective candidates are fully aware and prepared before they attempt Special Forces selection. It is also an opportunity for the Regiment to look at prospective candidates, making sure they like what they see.

Students will be given a series of briefings and presentations about the role of British Special Forces in general and specifically that of the SAS. This normally starts with a brief from Training Squadron OC, prior to being briefed on what Selection is all about and how best to prepare themselves. Those who return to attempt Selection must attain the required stamina and fitness; the ability to read an Ordnance Survey map also helps.

Test Week comes at the end of the first phase of SAS Selection. The week consists of a series of tests designed to push the individual to the very limits of endurance, hence the name of the final test: 'Endurance March.' Little prepares the volunteer for this. With a rifle and bergen (rucksack) weighing 25 kilos, they are expected to walk 40km in just 20 hours. No problem, one might say – until one realizes the route runs up and down the Beacons mountains. The endurance march starts early in the morning, and the volunteer needs to make good time by maintaining a steady pace; walk uphill, run downhill. Energy expenditure is high and food stops are required every three hours, but these rest periods last a maximum of 20 minutes. Most make a brew of tea and eat a small amount of high-calorie, light food. Eating too much food will cause the volunteer to vomit. Time during the rest break is spent checking the map and memorizing the route. During summer selection, the candidate must watch for signs of salt deficiency through sweating, while in winter they must guard against hypothermia. Simply being too hot or too cold will severely affect the individual's performance and overall route timings. Irrespective of what the weather looks like when you set off, the candidate should always carry a complement of clothing which will cater for all climatic conditions. The weather over the Beacons can change rapidly, from sunlight to thick fog. Accurate compass-work is needed in order to prevent the candidate from staggering around aimlessly when visibility is down to arm's length. In addition to map and compass navigation, the volunteers also require a working knowledge of the Global Positioning System (GPS). The lucky volunteers who find their way to the final RV (rendezvous) inside the allocated time can rest assured that, physically, the worst is over. Yet there is no time for relaxation: there is still a long way to go before the volunteer enters into the ranks of the SAS.

Continuation training follows, and all the necessary basic skills required of the SAS soldier are taught and practised. For many of the Paras and infantry guys it's back to basics: weapons training, patrolling skills, SOPs (Standard Operational Procedures), escape and evasion exercises, parachuting and finally five weeks' jungle training. Then, for those who cannot swim or drive,

there is a crash course in both before the volunteer is allowed to enter an SAS Squadron. Finally, before this is done, he will receive his beige beret with its famous winged dagger – and, as any SAS man will tell you, it is a special moment and a fabulous feeling!

There is an orbat of the SAS at the back of this book but, briefly, the SAS consists of four Sabre (fighting) Squadrons, R Squadron being held in reserve.

[Author's note: R Squadron is a Territorial unit directly attached to the SAS, officered and manned by a mixture of both ex-members of 22 SAS and volunteers from civilian life. These volunteers go through the same form of selection as regular soldiers, many having already served in the regular British Army. Members of R Squadron are highly professional and take their soldiering seriously, often training with the regular squadrons on various exercises. The aim of the Squadron is to add extra manpower support for 22 SAS. The Squadron was used operationally for the first time during the Gulf War, when 15 members volunteered. They fought alongside men of the regular squadrons, showing great courage. When one of the fighting columns was compromised by the Iraqis, they were

*Close Quarter Battle (CQB) skills range from hand-to-hand combat to refined shooting drills. This soldier (above) is using two weapons, an HKMP5 sub-machine gun and a SIG Sauer P226 pistol.*

forced into a series of shoot and scoot fire-fights, in which seven SAS soldiers, including a member of R Squadron became separated. With their vehicles destroyed, this group – whose number included a soldier shot through the stomach – were forced to exfiltrate themselves on foot. After two days of dodging the enemy, the R Squadron soldier managed to slip into the Iraqis' rear and steal a truck, in which the survivors made their way to the Saudi Arabian border. Days later, they were re-equipped and sent back into Iraq.]

## Organization

Each of the four squadrons is divided into four Troops, each with a small Headquarters section. The Troops are designed to operate in all terrains and environments, providing the different methods of insertion: Mobility, Mountain, Air Insertion and Boat. Each patrol within a Troop is made up of six men: this was increased in recent years from four, due to the amount of communications equipment and firepower carried by each patrol. Within each Troop, every SAS soldier will learn an individual skill such as medics, languages, demolitions or signals.

All SAS soldiers learn CQB (Close Quarter Battle). This is a standard requirement, the basics of which are taught during the final stages of continuation training. The wider role of the SAS demands that each man be proficient with the pistol and the sub-machine gun. These skills are the very essence of the SAS soldier – the weapon must become an extension of his hand, and feel as natural as holding a knife and fork.

In the old camp at Bradbury Lines these skills were practised in the famous 'Killing House': today, they use a highly advanced facility in Credenhill, to which many refer by the same name.  Due to the high number of personnel practising at any one time and the number of rounds fired daily, safety is of the utmost importance. Weapon training starts from the very basics of pistol work and encompasses all the problems of movement and weapons stoppages. It then progresses to the more advanced techniques using automatic weaponry. The famous SAS 'double tap' is learned; this involves firing two shots in rapid succession from the SIG Sauer P226 pistol. It takes several years to become comfortable with this method of shooting, but the results have proved themselves time and again. Two rounds stop a terrorist far better than one.

*A rare view of the 'Killing House', looking through night vision goggles in anticipation of the smoke about to fill the room. Prince Charles and Lady Diana are the guests of honour at this demonstration.*

Another favourite skill practised by the SAS is the famous hostage snatch. This drill forms part of the anti-terrorist hostage rescue scenario. The SAS plays host to an endless procession of VIPs who visit Hereford, and many are keen to view the anti-terrorist team in action. All VIPs are possible future terrorist targets, and the demonstration normally involves the visiting VIP sitting in the hot seat, surrounded by silence, not knowing what possessed them to volunteer in the first place. Abruptly, the door bursts open. A stun grenade explodes inches away. The VIP watches as laser beams of light penetrate the blackness. Those in the hot seat dare not move. It's not that they are doing as instructed, or fearful that any movement might bring them into contact with the hail of bullets now spitting within inches of their body. Seconds later, they are grabbed by the black-clad figures and literally thrown out of the room. Most VIPs are surprised to discover not a single hair has been harmed. Most – because when Princess Diana volunteered to sit in the hot seat, the odd bit of hair was singed.

*The Range Rover has been the backbone of transportation for the counter-terrorist teams since its inception. The first batch of white 'Rovers' were taken directly from the assembly line by SAS personnel at the express order of the Prime Minister.*

Apart from the Killing House, the SAS has a vast variety of equipment and training aids which are in close proximity to Hereford (called Camp 1). Most are in constant use. Several aircraft types are available to practice both aircraft entry and assault: there is also access to a complete two-storey building know affectionately as 'the Embassy'. Railway carriages are positioned to construct train hijack scenarios and there are plenty of roads to simulate coach and vehicle ambushes. Each move is practised time and time again, and to this is attributable the success of the SAS; there is no substitute for hard work, constant practice and attention to detail.

SAS training and operations are generally dictated by threats to the British sphere of influence around the world. For example, on September 5, 1972, at the Munich Olympics in Germany, eight Palestinian terrorists forced their way into the quarters of the Israeli team in the Olympic village. Calling themselves Black September, a name signifying the PLO's defeat and withdrawal from Jordan in September 1970, they killed two Israelis and took nine others hostage. There was an abortive gun battle to free the hostages between the terrorists and the West German Police. The nine Israeli athletes died, along with five of the Palestinian terrorists. This was seen as the climax of a whole series of hijackings and assassinations carried out by Palestinian militants.

Following the hijacks at the Munich Olympics, world governments became determined to combat this new breed of terrorism. At the G7 talks the following year, the various heads of government made an agreement to establish dedicated forces capable of dealing with any terrorist situation. In Britain, the SAS was tasked with equipping and training the new force, known by a variety of names including the Anti-Terrorist Team, SP (Special Patrol) Team and the Pagoda Team. New equipment was purchased and the SAS responded to the training with unmatched keenness.

Today, the SAS anti-terrorist team is housed at Credenhill, in a purpose-built building which is manned 24 hours a day by two teams, Red and Blue. Each team member is issued with an alert device and his movements are restricted, to allow for a quick response. On call-out, their vehicles are loaded with a vast array of weapons and equipment before a briefing is given on the operational requirement. The anti-terrorist team will only move into position when requested by the Home Office. The SAS anti-terrorist team is considered by most of its peers to be the best in the world.

At some time during the SAS operational cycle, all SAS soldiers have the opportunity to serve on the anti-terrorist team. Normally, the skills of the individual will dictate whether a soldier is to be part of the assault group or a sniper. All assault team members wear a black, one-piece, fire-retardant suit; on top of this go the body armour and the weaponry. This is normally a Heckler and Koch MP5 sub-machine gun, which clips flush across the chest. Additionally, a low-slung Browning Hi-Power pistol is strapped to the leg for back-up, or for use in confined spaces. In the past few years, the SAS has evaluated many hand weapons: the current model is the TK. Respirators are normally carried in their container strapped to the back, but it is more likely that during the actual assault the pack will be discarded and the respirator shoved up the left arm, held by its straps and ready for immediate use. Most actions now involve wearing the respirator, for it not only protects against gas but also presents an evil-looking, anonymous mask of menace to the terrorists. Boots are non-slip, similar to professional climbing boots.

Snipers' dress will frequently be identical to the assault teams, but excellent camouflage clothing is also used. Again, the same weaponry is issued, but additionally they will each have two sniper rifles, one for daytime use and one fitted with a night scope.

*Each of the four SAS squadrons rotate through the counter-terrorist team. When first founded in the mid-1970s, the snipers attached to it used the Tikka Finlander. The weapon was extremely accurate at ranges up to 300 yards.*

The main sniper weapon used when I was last on the team was a Finnish Tikka M55, but this has since been changed for the British Accuracy International PM sniper rifle.

Training for the team can be very exciting, but it is also exhausting. Abseiling down the side of a building in full gear is not as easy as it sounds. The entanglement of ropes, harness, weapons and stun grenades has to be cleared rapidly so that the soldier can close with the terrorists. The drills are very repetitious, but the end result produces a team which can challenge any terrorist act, from a hijacking to the seizure of an oil rig.

Most members of the general public see the SAS as a land operational unit, with its talents directed towards such things as embassy or aircraft assaults. They would be wrong, as a quarter of the SAS is trained for seaborne operations. That said, the SBS (Special Boat Service) takes on the primary role in tackling problems at sea, although if required the SAS will become involved in the actual assault.

# SBS

In 1975 the Royal Marines were given the task of providing Britain's Maritime Counter-Terrorist Force, and 1 SBS was thereafter dedicated to this role. In 1979, 5 SBS was deployed to Arbroath in Scotland in support of Comacchio Company, the quick-reaction force for the protection of nuclear weapon sites and convoys and for counter-terrorist operations on ships and offshore installations. Thereafter, 1 SBS concentrated on operations involving ships. In 1987, 1 and 5 SBS were amalgamated and located at Poole in Dorset, where they were redesignated M Squadron SBS and remained dedicated to the maritime counter-terrorist role.

In 1982, at the start of the Falklands War, 2, 3 and 6 SBS were deployed in advance of the task force, landing on the islands some three weeks before its arrival. SBS reconnaissance teams played a major role during the campaign, keeping enemy positions under constant observation and carrying out beach reconnaissance tasks.

In 1991, elements of the Special Boat Service (formerly the Special Boat Squadron, but redesignated post-1983) were deployed to Saudi Arabia during the Gulf War, carrying out Scud-hunting operations in the eastern sector of southern Iraq and attacking a major enemy

*The SBS has integrated with the SAS to the point where a section is permanently housed at Credenhill. Their role concentrates on shipping, oil rigs and all matters pertaining to operations at sea.*

line of communication. Two years later, SBS personnel were deployed to Bosnia on reconnaissance tasks and remained there until 1996 as part of the British Special Forces element serving with the NATO Allied Rapid Reaction Corps.

Today the Special Boat Service, together with the three SAS regiments and two SAS signals squadrons, forms one of the elements under the command of the Directorate of Special Forces, which was established in the early 1990s.

The current role of protecting shipping is likely to be increased as the threat heightens. Oil rigs provide the British nation with vital fuel and revenue. For the most part they are unarmed, poorly protected and isolated, leaving them vulnerable to terrorist attacks. Likewise, a cargo ship laden with explosives could access central London via the Thames. In such a scenario, dock areas such as Canary Wharf would suffer the same fate as the Twin Towers.

Both SBS and SAS divers have used a wide variety of diving equipment over the years, and have generally kept up to date with the latest technology. Divers are used in many roles, such as sabotage on shipping, covert entry to offshore facilities and underwater searches prior to VIP visits. The present diving equipment used by the SAS is the German-made Drager system, which is a lung-governed, closed-circuit breathing apparatus for use with pure oxygen. This small, compact unit is easily operated and maintained, giving the diver up to four hours submersion depending on the underwater activity. The Drager is ideal for covert operations, as it uses a semi-closed circuit with a soda-lime cartridge to provide air purification: this leaves no trace of bubbles either below water or on the surface.

Since 1970, the normal delivery system has been a Rigid Raider assault craft which replaced the inflatable Gemini. This facilitates speedier disembarking for the men on board. Fitted with four lifting-points, the craft can be transported by helicopter and is powered by one or two 140hp Johnson outboard motors, giving it a top speed of 37 knots. It is capable of carrying nine fully-equipped men plus a coxswain.

The Rigid Raider is claimed to be almost unsinkable, although one of the craft actually achieved this feat at the end of the Falklands campaign, when 1st Raiding Squadron planned a diversionary raid on Port Stanley. All four Raiders were hit, yet only

*'Hearts and minds' have always played a large part in SAS operations. This Arab dhow visited many isolated villages where the SAS medics would offer their services. Such simple acts did much to win over the local population.*

one sank, and even then not until the others had managed to limp clear of the danger. Both SBS and SAS have recently taken delivery of 16 new Rigid Raiders, which were specially adapted for them and are constructed of Kevlar, giving them a hull weight of less than 300kg. This means that a four-man patrol can carry the craft, even when it is fitted with twin 40hp motors.

In January 2002 the MV Nisha, a cargo ship inbound for London docks, was seized off the south coast of England. In a dramatic dawn raid by Royal Navy units, including the Special Boat Service (SBS), together with Customs and Excise officers, the ship was stopped and boarded. The ship, flying the flag of St Vincent and the Grenadines in the West Indies, was then escorted to Sandown Bay in the Isle of Wight.

Once in dock, Customs officers started their extensive search, but no explosives or ammunition were found; in fact, the vessel was carrying raw sugar to a Tate and Lyle refinery on the Thames. The seizure was due to an intelligence tip-off warning the British authorities such a ship could be carrying 'terrorist material'. The ship had called in at Djibouti on its voyage, so it is entirely possible that al-Qaeda was involved. The British Government played down the incident, claiming the search was part of the nation's tighter security measures since the September 11 bombings.

Many believe the SAS to comprise swift and deadly killers; and for the most part, it is. However, the SAS soldier must also learn skills which will teach him to prevail on the hearts and minds of a people. Although not new, this concept has been exploited by the SAS, which has refined the skill into a tool of warfare. The SAS 'hearts and minds' philosophy is the responsibility of all its members, but the practical side falls to the medics and linguists. The system is simple: befriend and win the hearts and minds of an indigenous people through communication and practical help. The following example is just one of many.

After the abortive raid on the northern coast of Oman and the Free-Fall descent into Wadi Rhawdah, some of G Squadron set off on a 'hearts and minds' campaign. The trip was to take them by Arab dhow (a small sailing ship) around the Straits of Hormuz, where they would visit the tiny coastal villages of northern Oman. The dhow was crewed by three Arab soldiers from the Trucial Oman Scouts (TOS) and three SBS Marines who operated a rigid raider. As many of the smaller villages had no docks, the Raider was used to put the party ashore. The story continues in the soldiers' own words.

"It wasn't until we reached our first village that the full term 'hearts and minds' really came home to me. I say 'village': it was nothing more than a few stone huts and half a dozen people. A party of eight SAS went ashore,

*This picture was taken as the Civil Aid Teams drilled for water during the Oman war. The teams would move in the wake of the SAS, producing quality water – always to the delight of the local population.*

two of them medics, of which I was one. I've seen poverty, but compared to this place poverty was the Ritz. Apparently, the family had committed some crime in the past and had been banished by the Omani Sultan to this remote and barren island. No one could remember the crime, or how long the family had been there, but it was several generations ago. They had one small boat – well, more a canoe – fashioned from a dead tree-trunk. The fish they caught, and a little rice, was all the food available. A well had been dug at the furthest point from the seashore, but due to the rocky features of this desolate place, this was no more than 50 metres from the water line. I tested the water: it was so salty none of us could drink it.

The head of the village, an old man who looked 80, yet I doubt if he was 40, welcomed us to his home. We were the first white visitors they had ever received on the island, and he celebrated with typical Arab hospitality: the best food in the house was offered. This turned out to be a 20-year-old can of pineapple; the label had long gone, and the contents had turned to mush. We sat there in our clean combat uniforms, healthy and well-fed; to a man, we were all humbled by the old man's gesture, and ate the fruit. I later examined one of the women who was complaining of toothache; she looked old, but gave her age as 25. I couldn't believe the state of her teeth: many were missing, and her gums were a rotting mess of blood and pus. Gripping one of her teeth with a pair of forceps, I was dismayed to discover that it was very loose – a gentle tug and it came out. In the end, I took out all her teeth and did my best to sterilize her mouth. We remained on the island for three days, and I continued to treat the woman. I have always been amazed by the speed with which penicillin injections worked on these people. Before we left for our next destination, all the ration packs were stripped of jam, butter and biscuits and presented to the old man – likewise, spare clothing was given to the children. A signal was sent requesting that the family be repatriated to the mainland.

"In a somewhat larger village along the coast, we found a worker who had fallen off the top of a building. His fall had resulted in a large, square piece of his skull becoming detached. Together with the medic, we removed the festering skin and the skull-bone from around the wound; the brain was clearly visible. In order to protect the brain, we took the lid off a large tin of beans from a ration pack. This was then beaten flat and placed in boiling water. Once it had cooled, it was placed over the hole in the skull and secured in place by healthy skin. Suturing the lid securely in place, we treated the wound with penicillin powder. Several months later, I had the opportunity to revisit the village. As I walked up the beach, the man was paraded in front of me; smiling, he bent his head and tapped the tin lid. The wound had healed extremely well, but a small section of the tin could still be seen: the letters 'ans' from 'beans' were still clearly visible.

"However, 'hearts and minds' is not just about water, food and friendship; it is also concerned with the enemy. If some of the enemy can be persuaded to change sides, there is much to be gained. During the Oman war, leaflet drops were made in an effort to explain what the new Sultan was trying to achieve. Many adoo (enemy) left the communists and returned to the fold. Likewise, many adoo were taken prisoner: these, too, were given the choice of being shot, going to jail or joining the *firqat* (Dhofari irregulars, formed from former insurgents into companies by SAS units, which operated in the country under the guise of British Army Training Teams). Those who joined us were quickly put in a chopper and flown over the territory of the *adoo*, or enemy: all the guy had to do was point to his old hiding places. These flights were know as 'flying fingers', as the chopper was normally followed by several jet fighters which would then bomb the indicated area with 500lb bombs."

When 'hearts and minds' tactics are used properly in warfare, a brotherhood and kinship with the indigenous people develops. The basics of life in most war-torn areas are always difficult; any effort to improve them is generally welcomed. The rewards for the SAS, are shelter, trust and information.

# Sierra Leone

The dawn of a new millennium did not change the world; for the SAS, it merely added to their burden. The Regiment continued to operate in major wars and conflicts which surfaced around the world, the majority of which were inspired by various terrorist organizations. On August 25, 2000, the SAS found themselves involved in Operation Barras, which took part in Sierra Leone.

Soldiers from the Royal Irish Regiment were sent to Sierra Leone as part of the 200-strong British training team assisting the country. On August 25, for reasons unknown, 11 of the solders in two vehicles left a safe road and entered rebel territory controlled by a renegade militia known as the West Side Boys. As they drove along an isolated jungle track, the soldiers were stopped and taken hostage. Once it became obvious that the men were overdue, other British forces in the country launched a search operation using helicopters, but failed to locate the missing soldiers. Two days later, an exchange offer was received from the West Side Boys asking for the release of their leader General Papa from prison, along with food and medicine. One of the soldiers was allowed to meet and negotiate on behalf of the rebels. He assured the British commander that they were being well treated and that no one was injured. On Wednesday, August 30, the situation looked somewhat better when five of the British soldiers were released in exchange for a satellite phone and medical supplies. The remaining six soldiers would not be released until the demands were met.

As negotiations continued, the British Government, not keen to show weakness, ordered 120 soldiers from the 1st Battalion, The Parachute Regiment, to Sierra Leone. It was also rumoured that a small force of British SAS had also been sent to the region some days before; both units were there as a possible military solution to the problem. The SAS unit supplied deep penetration patrols which located the West Side Boys' camp in the area known as Rokel Creek. It was there the six remaining hostages were being held. One of the patrols witnessed several mock executions of the hostages where they were lined up in front of firing-squads. This prompted the British Government to sanction a rescue attempt.

At dawn on September 11, the plan was put into operation. Three Chinook helicopters and two Westland Lynx gunships headed directly towards Rokel Creek. By 06:30 they were overhead, and the two Lynx helicopters began strafing the banks of the river. Moments later, one of the Chinooks landed, dropping the paratroopers directly in the rear of the rebel huts. A firefight broke out immediately with rebel guards who had been alerted by the approaching helicopters. As these were taken care of, a special hostage rescue unit of SAS men ran to the hut which contained the hostages. At that moment, a heavy machine gun opened up on the assaulting forces, killing one of the paratroopers. This served only to rally the British, who moved forward, overrunning the position and forcing the West Side Boys to retreat. By this time the SAS had located the hostages, who were hustled into one of the helicopters; it immediately took off and flew directly to the warship Sir Percival, which was anchored off the coast at Freetown. As the hostage rescue was taking place, the remaining two Chinooks landed at a secondary camp south of the first position where, with support from the Lynx gunships, the paratroopers engaged in a vicious firefight with the rebels. The fighting continued for several hours, but by mid-afternoon mopping up operations were complete and the rescue party was airlifted out.

The British had lost one man, with another seriously wounded and 11 more slightly injured  In addition to the six rescued  hostages, the British had captured one of the rebel leaders, Foday Kallay, killed 25 West Side Boys and captured a further 18.

*The terrorist attacks on September 11, 2001, shocked America and the rest of the world. This picture clearly shows the damage to the Pentagon, a building that epitomized America's military strength.*

# Afghanistan

On September 11, 2001, two hijacked airliners crashed into the twin towers of the World Trade Center in America. Soon after, a third struck at the Pentagon. A fourth hijacked plane, suspected to be bound for a high-profile target in Washington, crashed into a field in southern Pennsylvania. Almost 3,000 US citizens and other nationals were killed as a result of these acts. The prime suspect for these attacks was the organization al-Qaeda, headed by Osama bin Laden.

Al-Qaeda has bases and supporters in many countries, and embraces and supports radical Islamic movements worldwide. The organization was formed in 1988 by bin Laden, a radical Islamist from a wealthy Saudi Arabian family. Travelling to Afghanistan in 1979 to support the resistance movement against the Soviet invaders, he saw that the Muslim fighters were ill-equipped to carry out a sustained conflict against a technically superior enemy. Not only were they lacking in numbers and skills, but also the infrastructure necessary for the fight. Using his wealth and influence, he brought both workmen and construction plant to Afghanistan and, together with the Palestinian Muslim Brotherhood leader, Abdallah Azzam, began

to organize an international program of conscription through a newly-formed recruiting office: Maktab al-Khidamet (MAK – Services Office). As new recruits from such countries as Saudi Arabia, Yemen, Algeria and Egypt arrived, their transportation paid for by bin Laden, he began to build training facilities. Specialists were brought in from around the world to coach the men in guerrilla warfare tactics. Ironically, bin Laden was probably aided by the Western powers in his struggle.

By the end of the war, with the Russians gone, bin Laden was left with around 10,000 well-trained, well-equipped and war-hardened veterans under his command. Some dispersed back to their former lives and families, deciding they had done their duty and could now live in peace. Others had become so fanatical about Islamic fundamentalism they returned to their countries ready to organize their own terror groups and overthrow what they saw as secular governments.

Bin Laden's new fight started with his own country of origin. After the Afghan war, he returned to Saudi to raise an insurrection against the government there. This plan, however, was thwarted, and bin Laden was thrown out of the country and his citizenship revoked. Undaunted, he moved his centre of operations to Sudan, using his wealth to create farms and factories, supplying

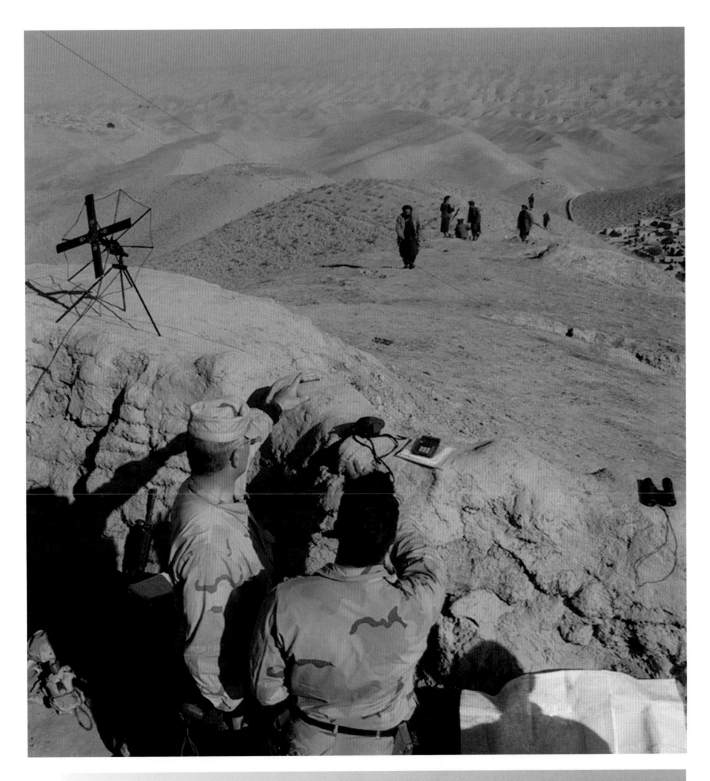

*Special Forces working with the Northern Alliance spot Taliban positions for the Air Force in Afghanistan. The SAS worked closely with American Special Forces.*

# Theatre of War: Afghanistan

11 men from Special Forces units were operating behind enemy lines. Numbers 1-5 represent their route - a trail of destruction including joining native forces (1) airstrike (2), and large firefight (4).

Tora Bora: in the mountains on the border with Pakistan, UK and US Special Forces units were helping native troops to rid the area of al-Qaeda personnel. Spotters were used to radio in air strikes (as below) from Bagram air base to great effect.

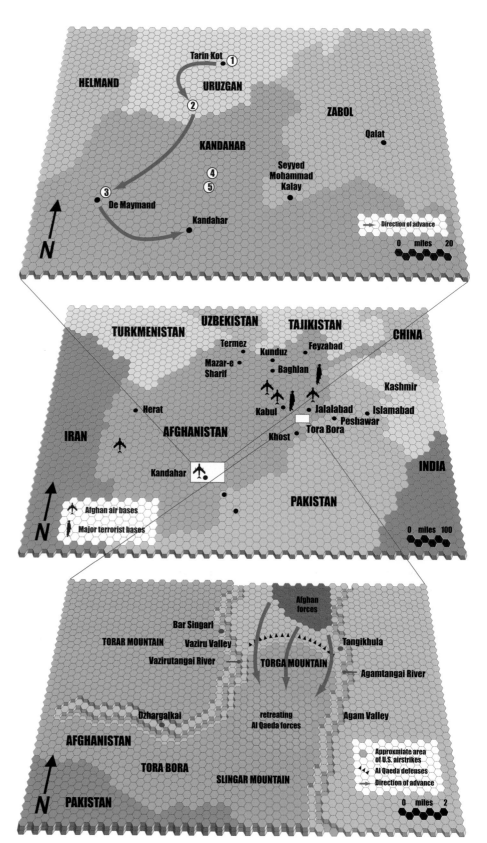

First map labels:
HELMAND, Tarin Kot (1), URUZGAN, ZABOL, Qalat, KANDAHAR, Seyyed Mohammad Kalay (4), (5), De Maymand (3), Kandahar, N

Direction of advance
0 miles 20

Inset map labels:
Kazakhstan, Turkmenistan, China, Iraq, Iran, Afghanistan, Pakistan, Saudi Arabia, India

Second map labels:
UZBEKISTAN, TURKMENISTAN, TAJIKISTAN, CHINA, Termez, Kunduz, Feyzabad, Mazar-e Sharif, Baghlan, Kashmir, Herat, Kabul, Jalalabad, Islamabad, IRAN, AFGHANISTAN, Tora Bora, Peshawar, Khost, INDIA, Kandahar, PAKISTAN, N

Afghan air bases
Major terrorist bases
0 miles 100

Third map labels:
Bar Singarl, Afghan forces, TORAR MOUNTAIN, Waziru Valley, Tangikhula, Vazirutangai River, TORGA MOUNTAIN, Agamtangai River, Dzhargalkai, retreating Al Qaeda forces, Agam Valley, AFGHANISTAN, TORA BORA, SLINGAR MOUNTAIN, N, PAKISTAN

Approxmiate area of U.S. airstrikes
Al Qaeda defenses
Direction of advance
0 miles 2

*Back to Basics: Special Forces ride into battle with units of the Northern Alliance. In this harsh and barren country horseback has long proved to be a most suitable form of transport.*

Special Activities Staff (SAS). These teams were staffed by retired members of Delta Force and Seal Team 6, all experienced field operators. They arrived on the ground in Afghanistan at the end of September 2001 in order to prepare for a major Special Forces operation.

A squadron of Special Air Service troops arrived soon after and began operating in the mountainous country. Their first task was to concentrate on finding Osama bin Laden and Mullah Mohammed Omar, the Taliban leader. Later they would help train and lead the soldiers of the anti-Taliban Northern Alliance in their push south towards Kabul.

It is also widely believed that the SAS took part in an incident at Qala-i-Jangi where hundreds of Taliban soldiers were killed. On Saturday, November 24, some 400 Taliban soldiers had surrendered to the Northern Alliance a few miles to the north of Mazar-i-Sharif, having fled the American bombardment of Kunduz. The prisoners were then shipped by lorry to a holding area in Qala-i-Jangi. This is a sprawling 19th-century prison fortress to the west of Mazar where the Northern Alliance warlord, Dostum, stabled his horses.

None of the Taliban soldiers were searched until they were inside the prison, at which time one of the prisoners produced a grenade and pulled the pin, killing himself and an Alliance commander called Nadir Ali. A second incident occurred later the same night when another prisoner killed himself and a Hazara senior commander, Saeed Asad. Despite these attacks, the Alliance guards did not seem too disturbed; neither did they arrange any extra security.

Around 10:00 the next morning, two CIA officers entered the prison with the purpose of identifying any al-Qaeda members. The senior of these two Americans, Johnny Michael Spann, 32, had operated in Afghanistan since the beginning of the war; his colleague was identified only by the name 'Dave'. They were taken by Alliance guards to an open area outside the cells where a group of Taliban prisoners had been assembled. As they were being interrogated, one prisoner leapt forward to grab at Spann's neck. Spann drew his pistol and shot the man dead. A fight then broke out, resulting in the two Americans and the guards firing at the prisoners. One prisoner managed to grab an AK-47 from an Alliance guard and opened fire. With this, Taliban fighters launched themselves at Spann, knocking him to

jobs for his followers. He also improved the infrastructure of the country – building roads and an airport. His many business interests included a bank, a construction company and an import-export business. More training camps were set up and former Afghan comrades were encouraged to move to Sudan.

However, Sudan's friendliness towards its guests soon began to crumble when its government started to bow to pressure from the United States. Not wishing to be subject to sanctions or other methods of persuasion, the Sudanese asked bin Laden to leave. This he did in 1996, returning with his followers to Afghanistan.

While many terrorist acts were attributed to al-Qaeda, bin Laden's involvement in the bombings of two American embassies in Nairobi, Kenya and Dar-es-Salaam, Tanzania, on August 7, 1998, was incontrovertibly proved. At the time, it seemed as if al-Qaeda could commit any atrocity it liked while hiding under the protection of the Taliban rule in Afghanistan – that was, until the attacks on America.

America fought back. However, armies take time to assemble and intelligence needed to be gathered. The Afghans had a ferocious reputation for fighting, especially in their own country. The first people to enter Afghanistan were a special unit of the CIA called the

the ground. Spann continued to fire his pistol, killing two more before he disappeared under the crush. Dave beat a hasty retreat as the Taliban overpowered the remaining Alliance guards, taking their weapons in the process. This group then ran to free the other prisoners before assaulting a nearby armoury where they obtained AK-47s, grenades and a mortar. A firefight then ensued, with the Alliance soldiers holding the south-east quarter of the fort while the prisoners held the south-western quarter. Some three hours after the incident had started, two vans and a pair of SAS Land Rovers arrived at the fortress gates. This force consisted of nine American Special Forces and six British SAS. There was a quick conference with the Alliance commander while one of the newly-arrived Americans talked to Dave on the radio. Dave outlined the position: he was stuck with a German television crew and had run out of ammunition. He confirmed that the Taliban prisoners were armed and Mike Spann was missing in action (MIA). Dave was told to stay put while they dealt with the Taliban, assuring him that he would be rescued. While the fighting continued unabated, the Special Forces called for air cover. Shortly afterwards two American fighter aircraft arrived overhead. At 16:00 the first missile hit, sending shock waves around the whole prison. The fighters continued to fire missiles for the rest of the afternoon, reducing much of the prison to rubble. Later that night, Dave and the German journalists managed to escape over the north wall.

By Monday morning, most of the Taliban had been

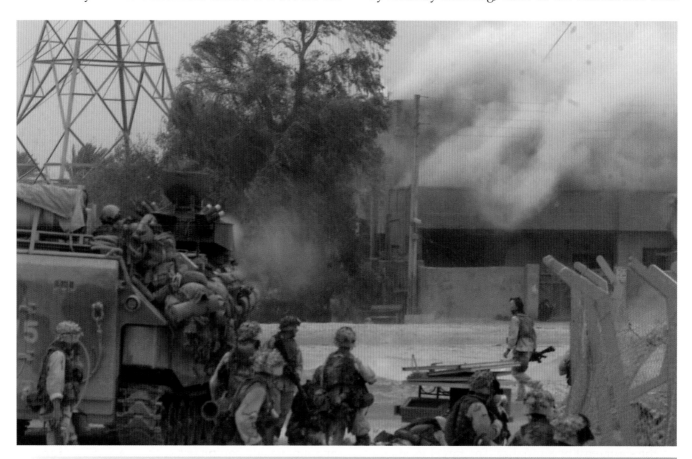

*Outside the prison at Qala-i-Jangi where an old fortress to the west of Mazar was used by the Northern Alliance to hold Taliban prisoners. A riot started while two American CIA members were carrying out an interrogation. This escalated into a major battle into which the SAS found themselves entangled. The man in the background on the extreme right is a member of the SAS.*

killed or wounded and the Alliance had retaken much of the prison. Then disaster struck. At around 11:00 another air strike was called and, while the previous strikes had been close, this one was too close. The explosion killed a number of Alliance soldiers as well as wounding several Americans and members of the SAS. The firefight subsided as the casualties and walking wounded were loaded into makeshift transport, which sped off to the US base. In all, nine men were airlifted out. Next day the Pentagon said that there had been no military deaths but that five US service personnel had been seriously injured and had been evacuated to Landstuhl Regional Medical Centre in Germany. Four SAS were also reported wounded, but the British Government never comments on its Special Forces.

Towards midnight, an American AC-130 gunship arrived over Qala-i-Jangi. Having identified points of Taliban resistance, it proceeded to strafe the area: at some point, one of its cannon hit an ammunition dump, creating a massive explosion which could be heard 10 miles away.

By Tuesday morning only a handful of Taliban were continuing to offer resistance and the Alliance started to move in and clear the prison. One prisoner who had escaped during the night was caught by local residents and hanged from a tree. The rest lay dead or dying in their hundreds, some still with their hands bound behind their backs. In one of the basements, five Taliban fighters were trapped alive. The Alliance soldiers threw in grenades before entering under a barrage of AK-47 fire. In the end, 86 filthy and hungry prisoners emerged; one of them was an American who had converted to Islam. Mike Spann's body was recovered, but only after a specialist team had been flown in to remove the booby trap which had been set under it.

There are two opposing views of the incident; some say the Taliban at Qala-i-Jangi fought to the death, while others say they were massacred.

The SAS had been in Afghanistan for several weeks when they were ordered by the American Central Command in Florida to raid an opium storage plant to the south-east of Kandahar. The target location was said to hold pure opium worth some £50 million and to be heavily guarded. In addition to the opium, it was believed, due to the large number of guards on-site, (estimated at 80-plus) that al-Qaeda might have some interesting intelligence documents at the location.

Unfortunately, maps of the area were virtually non-existent and the SAS were forced to rely on aerial photographs which had been taken by an unmanned US spy drone. The American command requested that the site be attacked almost immediately, leaving no time for a CTR (close target reconnaissance). This would have enabled the SAS assaulting forces to better determine the strengths and weaknesses of the al-Qaeda position and refine their strategy accordingly. Timing also meant that the attack would have to go in during daylight hours, abandoning the element of surprise and the use of their technically-advanced night vision equipment.

The SAS mustered two full squadrons: almost 120 men, the largest force it has fielded in a single operation for many years. The final assault was to rest on firepower. To this end, the SAS used some 30 'Pink Panthers' (Type 110 Land Rovers especially made for desert warfare), all armed to capacity with ferocious weaponry. The Pinkies carried both front- and rear-mounted GPMGs (General Purpose Machine Guns), while the role bar was mounted with either a Milan anti-tank rocket system or Mk19 automatic grenade launcher. These were supported by big 2.5 tonne ACMAC lorries acting as 'mother' vehicles. Just prior to the assault, the US Air Force would carry out two precise air-strikes. These would be close enough to destroy the drug warehouses, but leave the headquarters building intact.

The journey to the target started long before dawn; it was a long one over dreadful, rocky terrain. As the area was hostile, the column was forced to stop at regular intervals and send out scouts. For this, they used off-road bikes, just as they had done in the Gulf War.

Dressed in light order, which means no rucksack, each SAS man carried his personal weapon, which was either a Colt with an under-slung 203 grenade launcher or a Minimi. During such an assault the SAS prefer to forego any body armour, depending instead on speed of movement. However, in this case both body armour and Kevlar helmets were used. Belt equipment consisted mainly of grenades, ammunition, food, water and emergency equipment such as a SARBE (Surface-to-air Rescue Beacon) with which to call for help.

By 10:00 the force was within two kilometres of the al-Qaeda camp but the going was slow due to soft sand. This meant an on-the-spot change of plan.

Midday saw the start of the action, as half the SAS

lined up their Pinkies and started to lay down covering fire ready for the other half to assault. The ground was not suited to a direct assault and the al-Qaeda rebels had chosen their defensive positions accordingly. By 13:00 a serious firefight had developed, but the assaulting squadron continued to push forward. The assault was helped at this stage by the arrival of US F-16s. The first pass caused massive explosions in and around the compound, but, as requested, didn't touch the building serving as the headquarters. The second air-strike came close to wiping out the assaulting force. However, since by this time the air was thick with the drug-laden dust resulting from the destruction of the warehouses, nobody really cared very much.

Despite the horrendous fire put down by the SAS, the al-Qaeda fighters refused to give ground preferring to die. However, by 14:30 most resistance had been overwhelmed and the headquarters were raided for laptops, computers, papers and maps. The ground was absolutely covered with dead al-Qaeda fighters, with those who were only wounded screaming for Allah. On the SAS side, several men had been hit but, thanks to the body armour and Kevlar helmets, most of the wounds were to the limbs. That said, several were extremely serious and required all the skills of the SAS medics to keep them alive.

Finally the word was sent to 'bug-out'. Everyone jumped back into their vehicles and headed south. The first port of call was a rendezvous at a makeshift airfield where a C130, complete with doctors and medics, evacuated the wounded, flying them directly back to Britain for treatment in the Centre for Defence Medicine in Birmingham. The worst hurt of the four was hit in the stomach, arm and the top of one leg. He was in a stable condition but still faced with the prospect of losing his leg. This aside, the mission had been accomplished without the loss of a single SAS soldier.

Following the Afghan war, the papers reported that a dispute had developed between the Government and the SAS over the award of gallantry medals. Senior members of the Government are said to want the names of the decorated SAS men to be made public, along with detailed citations. The Regiment is fighting this, maintaining its veil of secrecy in order not to compromise its soldiers. One problem the SAS faces is that it was the only British unit to fight in Afghanistan, and hence any military award for gallantry in the country would be automatically linked to it. Additionally, some members of the Regiment would like two NCOs whose bravery was outstanding to receive the recognition they deserve. So far, the only praise the SAS has received has come from US Secretary of Defense Donald Rumsfeld:

"American Special Forces are on the ground, helping the Coalition, serving alongside the British Special Forces – some of the toughest, smartest troops in the world.

"Special forces in the US and Britain are not comparable," the US Defence Secretary said. "There are huge numbers of Special Forces in the States. In Britain, they are an élite force, able to put down an astonishing level of firepower, allowed to think for themselves and with incredible intelligence-gathering skills, prepared to hide up for days."

Although there is no record of it anywhere, one other story has vented out of Hereford. It is believed that an SAS unit saved the life of an American CIA agent who had been captured by the Taliban. The agent was moved to a house surrounded by a high wall and protected by at least 30 Taliban fighters. According to the story, the American military were pondering the problem when an SAS officer happened to hear of the situation and chimed in, "We can do it!" The surprised Americans were asked for a helicopter in order to perform the rescue.

It is rumoured that about eight SAS men then boarded the helicopter and flew directly to the building in question. Landing on the roof, half the team then proceeded to terminate any Taliban stupid enough to show his face, while the other four entered the building in order to carry out the rescue. They found the CIA agent strapped to a chair, suffering after a serious bout of physical interrogation. Again according to rumour, the SAS dispatched everyone in the room, grabbed the agent and made their way back to the roof. The area was fairly secure at this time, as just about every Taliban within sight had been killed. The extraction went off without anyone getting injured.

This story has never been validated, but shortly afterwards several members of the SAS were invited to visit the White House where they received medals. Additionally, the CIA, whose praises for the SAS know no bounds, have sought to use them in other operations.

## The Second Iraq War

On Thursday, March 20, 2003, at approximately 17:35, the first salvo of missiles fell on Iraq. After the Gulf War of 1991, when Saddam Hussein was left in change of Iraq, he failed to comply with UN resolutions to destroy weapons of mass destruction. The process of monitoring by UN weapons inspectors had come to an embarrassing end and America, together with the Untied Kingdom and its other allies, decided to invade. It was not the war the world expected: the UN and NATO failed to support the Americans and took no part in the conflict. In the end, the task fell to American and British soldiers alone.

The SAS were deployed on several operations into Iraq prior to the main air campaign, with small teams being infiltrated to ascertain information. The *Telegraph* disclosed in January that a team of 35 SAS men was operating in and out of western Iraq as part of a 100-strong allied force looking for Scud missile launchers which could be used to attack Israel. However, most of the teams were operating inside Baghdad in support of CIA and MI6 operations. These teams were intent on locating Saddam Hussein and confirming the satellite imagery by taking a GPS fix directly at the actual target. This accounts for pinpoint accuracy during the first wave of bombing, when Saddam Hussein was the target. SAS teams also monitored the oil fields, making sure they were not being prepared for demolition by the Iraqis and that they could

be quickly seized intact once the war began.

It is also believed that an SAS unit captured Watban Ibrahim Hasan al-Tikriti, Saddam Hussein's half-brother. Watban was included on the deck of cards issued to each soldier showing the 55 most wanted members of Saddam Hussein's regime. He was apprehended close to the Syrian border, where SAS units had been waiting in ambush. Watban, a presidential adviser, is accused of overseeing executions, deportations and torture. However, he fell out of favour when he argued with Saddam's son Uday – it is rumoured that Uday shot Watban in the leg at a party back in 1995. The SAS handed him over to the Americans, where he remains in custody at the time of writing. It is hoped that he can be persuaded to impart information as to the whereabouts of other Iraqi leaders.

Other than the odd report by journalists who stumbled across SAS units, there has been no information concerning SAS operations in the second war against Iraq. The only story which relates to British Special Forces is one concerning the SBS. The story first emerged showing two SBS men as heroes, when a captain and a sergeant trekked hundreds of miles through treacherous countryside in order to reach the Syrian border. On the surface, this looked very much like a replay of the Gulf War story of SAS patrol Bravo Two Zero. It is thought that two groups of about 30 men were inserted into Iraq, their mission to carry out reconnaissance and sabotage operations around Mosul. They were to operate using Land Rovers similar to those used by the SAS. One of the patrols is reported to have been lying up waiting for a resupply when it was spotted by an Iraqi Republican Guard reconnaissance unit. The Iraqis were quickly reinforced and a firefight broke out. Although the SBS were only outnumbered two to one, they decided to abandon the vehicles and make a run for the emergency RV. All the men made it to the ERV, where a Chinook helicopter picked them up. However, the captain and sergeant in question are reported to have taken a quad bike and made their way to Syria. The Land Rovers, which were left behind, contained a wide variety of sophisticated equipment and weaponry. These were later destroyed by an American A10 Tankbuster. Although this story was reported in the Mail on Sunday and various Internet sites, there has been no confirmation from the Ministry of Defence as to its authenticity.

## Sangin

Sangin, a small town in the northern part of the Helmand province of Afghanistan, has been an area of operations for the British Army on more than one occasion. The town itself was Taliban controlled as well as a haven for drug trafficking warlords. In an attempt to further efforts to take control of the area, a unit of SAS soldiers was tasked to snatch four senior Taliban leaders from a stronghold just south of the town. Along with some soldiers from 3 Para, the 'snatch squad', under the cover of darkness, successfully apprehended the four men, all of whom were on the Most Wanted list.

The plan was to rendezvous with a nearby quick-reaction force consisting of troops from 7 Para, the Gurkhas and the Royal Artillery. However, as the two units met, they were ambushed by around 70 Taliban fighters who had obviously learned of the assault. The Taliban had a firm advantage. Familiar with the terrain, they had chosen well-hidden positions from which to launch an attack with AK47s, machine guns and rocket-propelled grenades.

The British forces suddenly found themselves in the middle of a fierce battle, during which two of their four prisoners were killed while the other two escaped. Hemmed in by enemy forces, the men held their ground, with a bit of help from the artillery's 105mm light guns. During the firefight, which lasted more than an hour, two un-named members of the SAS were killed defending their positions. The assault ended when an

*Members of the Parachute Regiment providing back-up support to SAS deep undercover teams which have been compromised.*

Army Air Corps Apache attack helicopter and an RAF Harrier GR7 from Kandahar responded to a request for air backup and targeted the Taliban positions. It is thought that the Taliban sustained up to 30 casualties.

## The Rescue of Norman Kember and Members of the CTC

On Saturday, November 26, 2005, Professor Norman Kember (74), a British peace activist and member of the Christian Peacemaker Teams (CPT) was kidnapped in Baghdad along with three colleagues: American Tom Fox and Canadians James Loney and Harmeet Singh Sooden. The group responsible, calling itself the Swords of Truth, claimed the men were spies and threatened to execute them unless all Iraqi prisoners were released by December 8. Despite pleas to release Professor Kember due to his age and frail health, the kidnappers refused to relent, instead sending several video-taped messages showing the hostages to the al-Jazeera television station. In one of them Kember called for all British troops to be pulled out of Iraq.

On December 8, the day of the kidnappers' deadline, Kember and Fox were paraded on another video broadcast blindfolded and chained and dressed in the orange jumpsuits made infamous by Guantanamo Bay. The deadline was extended by two days. This passed without incident and the Swords of Truth continued to provide more footage of the men over the following weeks, repeating their threat that the hostages would be killed unless demands were met.

On March 10, 2006, the body of Tom Fox was found in the city. He had been executed. It was at that point that it became clear that negotiations had failed and the only choice was to set up a multi-national rescue mission and go in by force. The unit tasked with the actual rescue consisted of SAS troops, backed up by 250 men from the British, American and Australian counter-kidnap group as well as 100 soldiers from the Special Forces Support Group. Huge resources had already been poured into intelligence efforts to locate the men and finally on the night of March 23, the SAS were able to storm their way into a building within Iraq where they were being held. The kidnappers had already fled, leaving the men tied together in a ground floor room. The rescue was completed without a shot being fired or any casualties taken. Although Kember later thanked his rescuers privately, the peace activist resisted a public display of gratitude as a forced rescue had been against his principles of non-violent action.

## Ethiopia

The SAS were called in for another hostage rescue, this time in Ethiopia in March 2007. Five British nationals, connected with the British Embassy in Addis Ababa, together with their Ethiopian guards were overpowered and kidnapped by members of the rebel Afar Revolutionary Democratic Front in a remote area close to the Eritrean border. Their landrovers were left where they were stopped, still full of personal possessions and riddled with bullet-holes, while the hostages were marched across the region's salt lakes and into Eritrea.

Fearing a possible compromise of national security, the British Government convened an emergency COBRA meeting, deciding to have an SAS troop on standby in the UK in case they were needed for a rescue mission. Meanwhile, as negotiations continued, two SAS soldiers flew to Ethiopia in a liaison role and to reconnoitre the ground in case of action. However, in this case, negotiations proved successful and the hostages were released by the rebels without harm.

## SAS Conspiracy?

While the SAS have been quietly getting on with their normal business there have also been some oddball stories that have made the news. In September 2005, two British soldiers, thought to be from the SAS were apprehended by the Iraqi police in Basra. The two men, dressed in Arab clothing and wearing black wigs, were driving a car and were about to be stopped by the police for a routine vehicle search. Instead of pulling over, they drove at the police and started firing weapons. The men were finally arrested, and, according to a BBC report, the car was found to contain radio gear, assault rifles, a light machine gun, an anti-tank weapon and medical kit. Another report also stated that explosives had been found.

The soldiers were taken to a nearby prison. However, the purpose of their mission was already being speculated upon, even that they were to stage a car bombing in the city that would be blamed on Iraqi separatists and thus cause further tension. Certainly this was the theory in most of the Arab world, which generally points the finger at the occupying forces for fomenting unrest for their own purposes. Another factor adding to the conspiracy rumour mill was the sudden reluctance of the British press to cover the story.

The incident, though, did not go away. Despite high-level discussions between government officials of both countries, the governor of Basra refused to release his prisoners. On September 20, the British took the matter into their own hands after receiving reports that the police were about to hand the men over to a militia group. Warrior Armoured Personnel Carriers broke down a wall of the jail, thus liberating the SAS men, as well as accidentally freeing 150 other Iraqi prisoners, causing a riot in which one Warrior was set alight.

There is another explanation. Although Whitehall has kept any details of the incident secret, it is possible that

*A meeting of local Afghans in a disused fire base; notice the sand filled protection which is made by the British company Bastian.*

the men were on a close observation mission when they were stopped. As they had been told not to stop when challenged, due to their undercover role, they attempted to escape. A gun battle ensued and they were arrested. It is also possible that some of the equipment 'found' in the car could have been planted. It is one of those situations that we may never know the truth about.

## Colin Berry

Colin Berry, an ex-SAS soldier, had been working undercover for the Afghan government when he was involved in a shoot-out in his hotel bedroom in Kabul in January 2003. Two Afghans were killed and Berry was wounded before being arrested and thrown into jail. Afghan television broadcast the event as a row between business partners.

Berry, however, claimed he had been providing intelligence to the Afghan government, as well as MI6, about illicit arms trafficking. His investigations centred on the CIA initiative to buy back the weapons it had supplied the Afghan rebels with in the 1980s in their fight against the Russian invasion. However, he found that some of them were being resupplied to anti-government forces in both Afghanistan and Pakistan. He also stated that he was not responsible for the two deaths in his room and that it was, in fact, a set up, the killings being done by US Special Forces operatives, who then covered their tracks.

He was released after six months by President Karzai in a general amnesty for foreign prisoners.

## Afghanistan

The SAS have proved invaluable in the fight against the Taliban and al-Qaeda in Afghanistan, both during the first phase of the fighting in 2001 and in the current day. As well as collecting intelligence, SAS patrols have also killed dozens of enemy fighters during search and destroy missions in the rebel-held mountains in the south-east of the country. The Regiment's strength in Afghanistan in 2001 was high, consisting of two squadrons, backed up by troops from the Special Reconnaissance Regiment (SRR), the Australian SAS, and members of the Parachute Brigade.

One typical incident occurred near Kandahar in November 2001. Two squadrons, A and G, attacked an al-Qaeda stronghold in a cave complex near Kandahar. Air Troop performed the Regiment's first ever HALO jump over enemy territory and established a landing zone for the C130s that were bringing in the rest of the soldiers. In the ensuing battle, which lasted four hours, four SAS were wounded - one seriously, but the operation resulted in twenty enemy casualties and the gathering of important intelligence.

The seek and destroy role of British Special Forces in the war on terror has been aided by the use of the latest warfare equipment. For example, during the invasion of Afghanistan, the SAS were equipped with a hand-launched unmanned aerial vehicle (UAV) the size of a toy glider, as well as laptop computers able to link to satellite imagery from the larger American UAVs, Predator and Global Hawk. Sophisticated signals equipment meant that enemy communications could either be intercepted or else jammed by remote electronic jammers.

Recent SAS activity in Afghanistan, although ongoing, has been limited due to the British commitment in Iraq.

*Looking like something out of the Napoleonic wars, this wall breaching cannon has proved very effective against the thick mud walls which offer the enemy shelter in Afghanistan.*

*A British SF patrol shelters under the protective power of an Apache helicopter. The Afghan rebels know just how long it takes for the British forces to call up American fire-power – then they rapidly disappear.*

## Conscientious Objection

Ben Griffin was a serving SAS trooper with eight years exemplary service when he was sent to fight in Baghdad. However, after three months, Griffin went to see his commanding officer to inform him that he felt he could no longer serve alongside US troops. The reason for this was that during his time there he had witnessed several human rights abuses by American soldiers against Iraqis. In particular he was disturbed that many innocent Iraqis were being arrested in night-time raids and either imprisoned in the notorious Abu Ghraib jail or else handed over to the Iraqi authorities. In both cases the Iraqis underwent interrogation and even, possibly, torture. He felt that these actions, and indeed the war itself was illegal and therefore he had to quit on moral grounds.

Despite expecting a court martial, he was discharged from the army with a glowing testimonial to his good character. Instead of being accused of cowardice, he was actually praised for having the courage to stand up for what he believed to be the right thing to do. Griffin's action has been seen as a damning indictment against the British Government's policies within Iraq.

## Protecting Iraq's Borders

An important role that the SAS has been increasingly involved with in Iraq is that of protecting its borders against Arab insurgents crossing from neighbouring Syria. These insurgents, trained in countries sympathetic to Muslim extremism, such as Saudi Arabia, cross into Iraq where they then collect weaponry for use against government and coalition forces. It is thought that most of the bombings in Iraq have been the work of these foreign terrorists as they fight what they see as a holy war against the West.

In one such encounter, the SAS battled with a group of 12 insurgents that they had tracked crossing the border from Syria. A brief fire-fight followed in which all 12 were killed. The SAS took no casualties. In another incident, an SAS patrol arrested two insurgents, who later gave details of their training under questioning, therefore providing valuable intelligence.

The important role the SAS have played in Afghanistan was awarded when 12 of them were awarded military honours. Although the men were un-named, it is thought that four of the awards of the Conspicuous Gallantry Cross were bestowed upon the SAS soldiers wounded in action against an al-Qaeda base in November 2001.

The increased need for Special Forces skills in Iraq and Afghanistan has led to a shortage of man-power, as the Regiment is stretched to operating capacity. In order to fulfil operational commitments, the SAS has been forced to call up reservists from its two territorial arms: 21 SAS (Artists') Volunteer, based in London and 23 SAS (Volunteer), based in Birmingham, making another 60 men available.

The territorial units receive the same training as those in the regular SAS, and their principle role in Afghanistan has been their traditional one of long range reconnaissance. US commanders, in charge of most of the operations in the country, have been impressed by their skill and dedication. However, what was originally seen as a short-term solution to the under-manning problem now looks set to stretch to an indefinite period.

There have been suggestions in the past from defence ministers that the SAS should expand in order to cope with the increase in counter-insurgency operations. However, SAS commanders have resisted this, worried that greater numbers might lead to a lessening of the standard required of an elite group. Instead, the Government has now set up a Special Forces Support Group, consisting of members of the Royal Marines and Parachute Regiment, and the Special Reconnaissance Regiment, to provide specialist operational back-up.

# Chapter 2

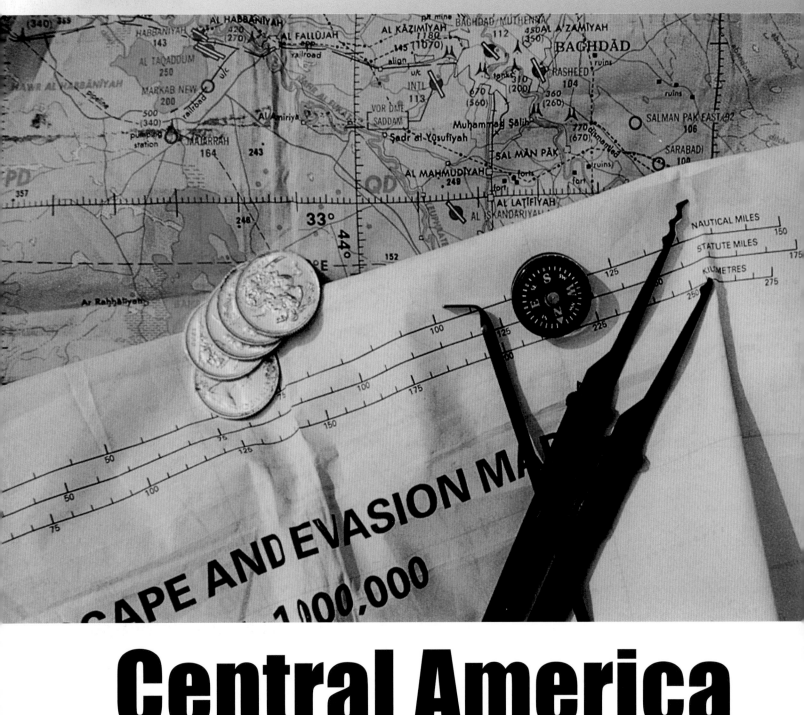

# Central America
# to The Gulf

**ESCAPE & EVASION:** *Some of the essential equipment needed for a period behind enemy lines.*

The decade started with David Stirling, founder of the SAS, being knighted for his services. Sadly, he died in the same year. He will never be forgotten – as long as there is an SAS unit, his name and legend will live on.

In August 1990, the SAS started its build-up training for operations in Colombia, where the drug cartels were seen to be the new enemy. The powers-that-be had decided a British force would help train the Colombian, anti-narcotics police. This would allow the Colombians to carry out their own special operations within a jungle environment. In all, soldiers from three SAS squadrons rotated through Colombia, each squadron teaching basic jungle tactics, plus a few counter-terrorist methods. The training force varied between 20 and 35 men; however, this was deemed to be overkill, as the SAS were not allowed to take part in operations.

The decision to use the SAS in Colombia had been instigated by Margaret Thatcher. She had publicly stated that she was going to send Special Forces to counter this problem, and that's exactly what happened. The Americans funded a large percentage of the operation, providing an overall budget of about £2 million for the two-year period. As well as training, this included such equipment as night-sights, waterproof equipment, bergens and military-type clothing.

Despite what all the other SAS books say concerning the role of the SAS in Colombia, in truth the Regiment carried out no actual operations against the drug cartels. True, they would go out on exercises, using the areas where the cartels were most active, but no direct confrontation was planned. The nearest they got to some real shooting was when the SBS, who had accompanied the SAS, reported that they were being threatened. Their task had been to train some of the police in boat work. This would allow the Colombians to intercept shipments of drugs being moved around by boat. During this training the SBS received news that members of a cartel were about to attack them. In response, the SAS set up an ambush using the SBS as bait; however, nothing materialised.

The only shooting which took place during the SAS operation in Colombia happened one evening in the

*As every SAS man knows, to win a firefight you have to use a lot of weaponry. These SAS soldiers are practising anti-ambush drills.*

*Colombia turned out to be disappointing for the SAS. Much of their time was taken up training Colombian troops to carry out bush operations against the drug cartels.*

training camp. Most of the SAS guys were getting ready to go down to Bogota for the weekend when one of the policemen shot a friend. Luckily, these guys were nothing to do with the training package: they were fully-trained police officers who had been messing about in the hallway playing Cops and Robbers. One officer pulled his pistol and had an accidental discharge; he shot his friend in the head. Two SAS medics tried administering first aid to the dying man, but the .45 calibre bullet had caused major damage to the skull and brain. It was obvious that the man would not survive unless he was immediately hospitalised. However, the Colombian police, who did not seem in a rush, bundled the wounded man on to a makeshift stretcher and ran off in the direction of the nearby medical centre. The staff there could not provide adequate treatment, so they threw him on to the back of an open vehicle and drove him 40 miles to a hospital. It came as no surprise when the SAS heard the man had died in transit.

# The Gulf War – 1991

In August 1990, Iraq invaded the defenceless, oil-rich state of Kuwait, creating a situation which resulted in conflict with the combined forces of the United Nations. Despite attempting to negotiate with Iraq, it became apparent that military action was inevitable and a huge task force began to make its way out to the Persian Gulf. The overall UN commander was the US General Norman Schwarzkopf, who was a veteran of Vietnam and had been involved in activity in Grenada, both theatres leaving him with little regard for unconventional warfare. As a result, it seemed unlikely that Special Forces and the British SAS, a unit originally created for desert warfare, were going to be used. Fortunately, the commander of the British troops, Lieutenant-General Sir Peter de la Billière, himself an SAS veteran and former commander of 22 SAS, managed to convince Schwarzkopf that the special skills of the SAS would be invaluable.

[Author's Note: There have been rumours that an SAS operation took place just hours before the Iraqis invaded Kuwait. It is claimed that a scheduled British Airways flight into Kuwait was used to infiltrate the SAS team.

Despite the situation, the flight went ahead, with many of the passengers, mainly French, taking note of the last-minute arrivals. Although there have been repeated denials that there were any SAS soldiers aboard the flight, British Airways was forced to pay £4 million damages to French passengers after a French court gave judgement against them.

Unsubstantiated information has since emerged that several leading Kuwaitis, together with senior members of the British Embassy staff, were spirited away by the SAS teams. This is not the first time such actions have taken place.]

Shortly after Christmas 1990 the SAS, on standby for action for months, left for the Gulf, activating the largest deployment of the Regiment since 1945, with men from A, B and D Squadrons in theatre. However, there appeared to be no immediate requirement for them,

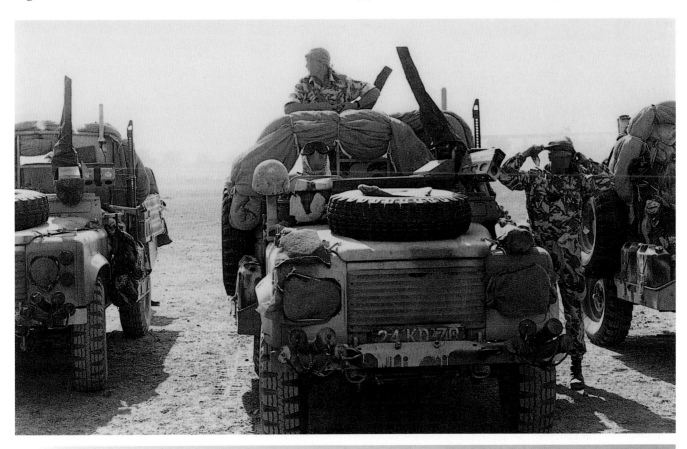

*An SAS fighting column prepares to cross the border into Iraq during the Gulf War.*

since the US Special Forces and SEALs had already taken all the border reconnaissance roles. It was proposed to use the SAS and Delta Force to rescue the hundreds of foreign nationals being held as hostages under Saddam Hussein's 'human shield' policy. However, this was a logistical impossibility, as the hostages were held in various locations all over the country, and too many lives, of both soldiers and hostages, would be lost, which would lead to bad press at home. After its previous experiences in Vietnam and Tehran the US, understandably, wanted to avoid detrimental press coverage at all costs.

By mid-January 1991, General de la Billière decided the SAS could be effective in creating diversions ahead of the main attack, destroying Iraqi communications facilities and tracking down the mobile Scud missile launchers which, so far, had eluded both satellite

reconnaissance and airstrikes. The SAS were to undertake these operations on the night of January 22-23, six days prior to the anticipated start of the main hostilities.

Many stories have come out of the 1991 Gulf War, in particular the fascinating story of the ill-fated SAS patrol Bravo Two Zero. However, there were many others which have not been so intensively documented. Those which follow are written from first-hand accounts. They convey the feeling, and something of the true nature, of SAS operations.

The patrol callsign Alpha Three Zero was one of the fighting columns which the SAS had inserted behind Iraqi lines. It consisted of a half-Squadron and was equipped with eight Type 110 Land Rovers, most of which were armed with a Browning .5 heavy machine-gun. Additional weapons included GPMGs, American

*Despite the vast load, the Land Rover performed well throughout the Gulf War. Note the motorbike, which was used as an outrider protecting the flanks as the column advanced.*

Mk 19 40mm grenade launchers and Milan anti-tank missiles. The night-sight for the Milan, which is called a MIRA (Milan Infra-Red Attachment), was mounted on the roll-bar of the leading vehicle. This proved to be an exceptionally valuable piece of technology, as most of the fighting would take place during the hours of darkness.

All the vehicles had petrol engines, which fed off two 10-gallon tanks. Additionally, they carried 16 jerry-cans, giving them an operating range of about 600 kms. Each wagon also carried six jerry-cans of water and rations to last 14 days. The normal allocation of ammunition per man was around 1,000 rounds, four high-explosive grenades and two white phosphorus. Each vehicle also carried several bar mines. Two cross-country motorbikes were allocated to each column: these would act as outriders. The mainstay support for the column was a Unimog which acted as the mother vehicle, carrying stores. The Unimog's great advantage is that it can be loaded to the gunwales and still go anywhere.

Alpha Three Zero drove from Saudi Arabia heading straight across the Iraqi border. It was as simple as that. The column moved in single-line formation with the Unimog in the middle for protection. The outriders used the bikes to scout ahead and check the flanks to prevent possible ambush. The column would drive only at night and lie up by day. They would stop about an hour before first light, usually in a depression, if one could be found, and camouflage the vehicles. Sentries would be posted, food cooked and eaten, before the men fell asleep on the desert floor.

Alpha Three Zero progressed some 100 kms from the Saudi border into Iraq during the first week. By this time the men had sorted out a routine, coming to terms with problems of moving by night and resting by day, although one problem had been overlooked – the weather. It was bitterly cold in Iraq, unlike anything one could envisage. Iraq at that time of year is a very hostile environment.

Late in the afternoon on Day Eight, while the men sat around happily, protected by the overhead camouflage nets and lazily passing the day away, the Iraqis appeared. A sentry had seen an Iraqi vehicle heading directly towards the SAS position. He was frantically pointing over to his right. Fist balled, with thumb pointing down, means only one thing – enemy.

This is what the SAS refer to as 'headless chicken'

*The Russian Gaz 69 captured by the SAS during the early days of the Gulf War. All but one of the occupants were killed. You can just make out the number plate under the comouflage net.*

time. They grabbed weapons, darting here and there tripping over each other while trying to find a good fire position. Then the professionalism took over. Weapons acquired targets and the adrenalin rushed through the body. There was nothing but the sound of the engine as the vehicle drew closer. The Iraqis had spotted the SAS position from some distance and drove directly into the camp area, stopping within 20 metres of the nearest camouflaged hump. Fortunately, they had assumed the SAS were Iraqi forces, unable to believe that enemy troops would be so close to Baghdad.

The SAS watched as both the driver and another man, who had been sitting in the front seat, got out. The driver then walked to the front of his vehicle, opening up the bonnet. One of the SAS men broke cover and walked out to meet the Iraqi, who turned out to be an officer. The Iraqi was a short, slightly chubby guy in his early to mid-thirties, tidy and clean-

*SAS members displaying the Union Flag as a method of recognition. This same ploy was used during the Second World War.*

shaven. He had dark hair and a very small moustache, characteristic of the Middle Eastern male. As the two men came together, a look of bewilderment came over the Iraqi's face. Suddenly the SAS man threw up his rifle and fired: nothing happened. He dropped to his knees, trying desperately to clear the stoppage – and at that moment a second SAS man shot the Iraqi dead. This burst was swiftly followed by several others, terminating the officer and the driver instantly.

The two SAS men then ran towards the vehicle, a Russian Gaz 69, only to discover two more Iraqis in the back. One had been severely wounded as the intense SAS fire ripped through the vehicle, but a second had survived without a scratch. He later also turned out to be an officer.

The SAS pulled the wounded Iraqi from the vehicle, dropping him to the floor. An incredible amount of blood gushed from his side and soaked into the sand. He had been hit several times, with the main damage just above his hip. While still in the truck, the man's body had been in a position which stemmed the flow of blood, but once he was moved the pressure of blood was released. The SAS knew he would die shortly. Other members of the patrol pulled out the only surviving Iraqi soldier, half-crazed. He wailed in Arabic 'In sha'Allah' (It is the will of God) and was obviously glad to be alive. When two SAS interpreters

interrogated the man, they soon discovered that he actually had both maps and orders clearly showing the battle plans for the area. It also transpired that these Iraqis were the lead element of a large column which would be materialising at any moment.

The SAS commander swiftly issued orders for everyone to pack up and be ready to move. By this time the wounded Iraqi soldier had died. Some of the SAS men placed him in a shallow grave along with the other two, but they had barely finished covering the bodies when their commander ordered that they be dug up and placed in the back of the Gaz. The POW was bagged and tagged, then thrown on the back of the Unimog. Then, some 15 minutes after the initial contact, callsign Alpha Three Zero started to move away from the position. As their aim was to get the prisoner and the information back to Allied Command, a course was set towards the Saudi border. They drove for two hours before stopping to send a radio message. It was then that they discovered an Iraqi position just 100 metres directly to their front. They moved back carefully and drove off in another direction. Two hours later, they stopped again. This time there was no sign of the enemy. While a full contact report was sent back to SAS HQ in Al Jouf, some of the men decided to bury the three dead Iraqis. The ground was so hard they could only dig down six to eight inches. In order to accommodate the three bodies they made the hole wider, covering it with earth and rocks. They had just finished when once more they were interrupted by the Squadron Commander, who came running up demanding an explanation of what they were doing. Somewhat surprised, they said, "We're burying the bodies!" Again, the commander ordered them to be dug up and put back on the Iraqi vehicle.

Once the contact report had been received the column moved off, continuing in a southerly direction. Their intention was to get to within some 25kms of the border where arrangements had been made for a resupply by the RAF.

Arriving at the pre-arranged RV, the column started camouflaging their vehicles and set about their normal administration. The resupply was due to arrive at their location at 04:00. The helicopter came in low and fast, the pilot flying literally 10-20 feet above the ground, using only PNGs to penetrate the darkness. As the chopper got closer it flared its rotors, kicking up masses of dust. Finally, it settled, with the rear ramp deployed. The SAS men rapidly transferred the resupply to their vehicles before putting the Iraqi prisoner on board. They were about to load the Gaz, with its three bodies, when the RAF loadmaster told them, "No way." The final act came when the commander of Alpha Three Zero was told to get on the helicopter; he was being replaced by an SAS Sergeant Major.

Under their new commander, the men mounted their vehicles and moved off in box formation; two groups of four with the Unimog in the middle. Between 02:30 and 05:00 they covered a distance of some 35kms, stopping only once – to place a bar mine under the Iraqi vehicle, which still contained the three bodies, with a timer set for 05:30. At exactly 05:30 there was a bright red glow on the horizon as the explosion went off. A few seconds later, there was a very dull thud. At last it was all over for the three Iraqi soldiers, who never knew anything about their demise, as they were vaporised, becoming part of the desolate landscape that is Iraq.

Alpha Three Zero was not the only SAS unit having fun in Iraq. Most of the other fighting columns and observation patrols had regular contacts with the enemy. One battle took place during the early hours of February 9, when an A Squadron team was carrying out a CTR (close target reconnaissance) on a communications installation. The team was commanded by an SSM (Squadron Sergeant Major). The SSM was standing on the back of a Pinkie, observing through the MIRA. The team had already cut their way through the barbed wire which surrounded the installation, leaving one Pinkie at their entry point to act as cover. Moving further into the Iraqi position, the SSM realised that the place was far bigger than he had originally thought. However, by this time they were committed, so he told the driver, Keith, to keep going. Suddenly, as they topped a small rise, he made out some shadowy movement through the TI. There were enemy all around, and it was just a matter of seconds before contact would be initiated. Making a snap decision, the SSM decided their only alternative was to brazen it out and drive through the Iraqi position as quietly as possible, hoping the dark would conceal their identity. Good way to do a recce! As they continued weaving their way through the Iraqi defences and accommodation, a soldier stepped out in front of the wagon and made a vain attempt to stop it

*After the prisoner had been extracted back to Coalition HQ the Gaz 69 was destroyed. An SAS demolitionist placed a bar mine under the vehicle, which still contained the dead Iraqi soldiers.*

by holding up his hand. John, who was sitting in the front passenger seat, aimed the GPMG mounted in front of him and opened up with a large burst of 7.62mm. The soldier disintegrated. Then all hell broke lose.

For some reason, even though it was dark, the Pinkie was pinged immediately by the Iraqis. Seconds later the three SAS guys were taking incoming from all directions. The SSM was hit in the first burst, a round going through the top of his knee, throwing him into the back of the wagon. At the same time Keith booted the Pinkie forwards, accelerating hard, hoping to burst through the position. They were going to make it. Swerving and driving like a maniac, Keith drove straight through the camp gates, with John blasting everything in sight with the GPMG. Then their luck ran out. Three hundred metres from the camp the Pinkie lurched to a sudden stop as it crashed hard into a tank ditch. Seconds before, the SSM had raised himself, hoping to get the rear gun into action. The sudden stop threw him over the roll-bar, where he landed half on the laps of Keith and John and half on the bonnet. His leg was lying on his chest. Shaking themselves, they immediately made to escape. Keith threw the SSM on his shoulders and started to run away from the wagon, which was now on the receiving end of the Iraqi fire. With John covering, they attempted to melt into the darkness. Those who know the SSM would describe him as a large, well-built man, with a mental strength to match that of his body, but the damage from the bullet and the vehicle crash had left him in a critical condition. Climbing a slight rise, the three hid among some rocks where they set to work to staunch the flow of blood from the SSM's leg wound. It looked bad. The Iraqis had regrouped and made an attempt to surround the three. Keith had left his rifle in the damaged truck, unable to carry both it and the SSM, so John kept the Iraqis at bay as they finally moved deeper into the darkness.

Slipping in and out of consciousness, the SSM commanded that the others should leave; he would provide what little cover he could. It was a dilemma which has had to be faced many times before – stay with a badly-wounded man, or try to take him with you and risk the whole group being captured. Even if the Iraqis did not find the SSM, he would die, but that could take several hours. Capture by the Iraqis would mean torture and possibly death – not much of a choice.

Keith bent over the SSM and whispered. "Shall I finish you, mate? It's your best option."

It was a tempting offer. One quick shot and no more pain. Again, this is not unique; several times during the Regiment's history the question has been asked. To my knowledge, this ultimate action has only ever been taken once. The SSM declined: "No, thanks Keith. I'll take my chances to the bitter end. Now go." As it was highly likely that the SSM would pass out, Keith and

John decided that they would be better off with the rifle. John had managed to grab a 66mm rocket from the damaged vehicle and this was left with the SSM. With the guys gone, the SSM slipped into unconsciousness once more. It was the sound of voices down in the wadi which snapped him back to awareness of his predicament. Several Iraqi soldiers were standing around a vehicle – a target too good to miss. He pulled out the 66mm rocket and aimed it at the truck. At the moment he was about to fire, two Iraqi soldiers jumped him.

"Who are you?" they asked in Arabic.

"English," the SSM replied. Although he was a fluent Arabist, he pretended he could only speak a few words. Surprisingly, an officer appeared and a stretcher was called for. Within hours the SSM was being treated by an Iraqi civilian doctor, who did a wonderful job of repairing the damage to the injured leg. Eventually he was treated in hospital, while his interrogation continued. One day, the two interrogators were standing by his bed deliberating a question to ask him when, as they turned to speak, he unintentionally pre-empted their question, giving away the fact that he spoke fluent Arabic. Despite protests from the medical staff, the interrogators ripped the drips and wires from his body and gave him a beating.

When the war ended, his reappearance delighted his next-of-kin, who had been advised of his status as missing in action, possibly dead. The SSM was awarded the Military Cross, a decoration normally only given to commissioned officers. This has only been done once before: in 1965, when another A Squadron SSM, Lawrence Smith, was awarded the decoration for his work in Borneo.

Next came the assault on an Iraqi installation known as Victor Two. This operation was given to one of A Squadron's fighting columns. They received their orders as they lay hidden in the vast wilderness of the Iraqi desert. It began when the two signallers started to decode long incoming radio messages from SAS HQ in Saudi Arabia. This feverish activity around the two signallers quickly spread to the rest of the men and soon the orders became clear: to launch an attack on an Iraqi microwave station that night.

The men began to prepare for the assault, with Mountain Troop putting together a model of the radar

*As the Gulf War ran into its second month the SAS fighting columns were in desperate need of resupply. This picture show a string of 3-ton trucks which drove into Iraq in order to RV with the columns. There were so many senior NCOs at the resupply RV that a special Sergeants' mess meeting was held.*

station from whatever kit they had lying around. They built it according to the intelligence coming over the radio, which seemed quite detailed on the set-up of the station but was confused where enemy strengths and dispositions were concerned.

At 15:45 everyone, except for the duty sentries, made their way to the middle of the LUP for a briefing. The sentries were to be briefed on their roles later; not an ideal situation as, in the rush, it was more than likely that they would not get the whole story and would go into battle not completely sure of what was happening. Nevertheless, ideal or not, the column was behind enemy lines and sentries were essential.

The briefing started with the men being formed up

in groups – the groups they would be in for the assault. Once they had settled, Brian, the RSM, and Paul, the OC-designate, joined them and the briefing began. Although Paul was a Major, and the new OC for the column, it was obvious to the men that Brian was still very much in charge (SAS rank structure has little to do with who is in charge).

The target radar installation was to be known by its callsign of Victor Two. The plan was for the column to drive to within 1,500 metres of it, place the vehicles in a fire support position and then send out a recce team. Once the location had been confirmed, these men would return to their positions with the assault team and close fire support before guiding them to the

*Alliance Commander, US General Norman Schwarzkopf, personally thanks SAS troops at the end of the Gulf War.*

target. The aim was to destroy the facility, which was the main centre for guiding the mobile Scud launchers to their targets. It had previously been attacked by Stealth bombers, but the problem was that most of it was underground and therefore safe from aerial attack. The only way to make sure it was taken out was by an attack from the ground. Once the column had achieved this objective, all vehicles were to make their way back to the present location. Brian made himself the overall commander of the operation. There were to be three assault groups, each of three men, plus close fire support and fire support groups. The rest of the

men were to assist with driving the vehicles.

The objective itself was a building complex with a microwave tower of about 45 metres (50 yards) in height. The outside perimeter wall was about five metres in height, while a three-metre-high internal security fence posed another obstacle. The main gate was guarded by a sentry position.

The plan was to fire two anti-tank missiles at the sentry position and the gate. An explosive charge would then be placed on the internal fence. Once this had gone off, the three assault teams were to enter the building, each taking a floor, including the floors below ground.

The floors needed to be cleared and then explosive charges laid before the teams got themselves out as quickly as possible.

The men, clear about their roles, soon got to work. They were enthusiastic about the operation despite the development of some internal politics within the group. The only piece of information which wasn't clear was how many Iraqis there were at the installation and how well armed they were. The intelligence coming through was vague, but suggested that there were more civilians than military personnel present, and so there was to be no indiscriminate firing on the part of the assault forces. A man needed to be identified as a soldier before he could be shot at. Of course, this was far from ideal in a situation behind enemy lines in the middle of a war. However, orders were orders.

It was suggested at the time that the column was being sent in because the Regiment wanted to 'blood' its soldiers; that is, it wanted to give them some experience of war and to be able to claim that one of its squadrons had led an attack in hostile territory. It was also rumoured that Headquarters knew exactly how many Iraqis were at the base and how well armed they were; after all, they knew all the other details about the location. Sensing that maybe they were not being told everything, the troops started to feel uneasy.

After a final brew-up, the men formed up in their vehicles and drove for a couple of hours until they reached a highway, or MSR, as they were known. Daylight was now fading. Having checked that it was all clear, the group moved off again. Before they got themselves on to the road, however, they needed to bridge a ditch so that the Land Rovers could cross over. This was done by Mobility Troop placing two sand channels, supported by sandbags in the ditch, so that the wheels could roll across them without the rest of the vehicle getting grounded. Within 17 minutes all the vehicles were over, the bridge dismantled, and they were on their way again.

Five kilometres from the target, the adrenaline started to flow. All senses were alert, expecting an enemy ambush at any minute; so far, it had all seemed too easy. Then the ground started to become more difficult to drive on, causing the column to make a 1km detour to the west. Here the ground became a mass of man-made slit trenches, but as the orders were to slow down or stop only if an enemy vehicle was spotted, the vehicles carried on at the same speed.

Closing fast now on Victor Two, the MIRA wagon came forward, needing to observe the area continually for enemy activity. When it was 1,500 metres away from the installation the column came to a halt, as planned. One of the men left his motorbike at the location, and it was logged in on the SATNAV so that the rest of them would have a position to make their way back to after the operation was over. The target was checked once more through the MIRA. It turned out that the site was huge – lots of buildings, vehicles and people; soldiers were positioned in both slit trenches and bunkers. There seemed to be little sign of the 'civilians' mentioned by RHQ.

At this point, Brian started to change the plans which had been made at the briefing. He decided that they should move forward immediately, without the services of the recce group. The column drove closer to Victor Two, internal politics changing the line-up as certain members of the group decided they wanted to take the lead, no matter what. Driving along a tarmac road, they soon found themselves right in the middle of the enemy position with hostile soldiers and vehicles all around. With the previous orders changed beyond any recognisable form, most of the men didn't have a clue as to what they were going to do next.

Without warning, the lead vehicles pulled over to the left side of the road and the others were obliged to form up behind them. They were now parked up alongside a small escarpment running parallel to the road. At last the recce party was sent out to do a CTR and discovered the magnitude of the site. In all, it was about a kilometre square, its focus being the massive control building and the microwave tower, bristling with communication dishes. They returned quickly, and a revised plan was put forward. Now it was proposed that the vehicles would split into two groups and give cover from the flanks. Meanwhile the assault teams, together with a cover party, would go on ahead on foot to carry out the process of demolishing the tower with explosives.

Their forward progress went unchallenged. On reaching the complex, 300 metres (328 yards) from the vehicles, the demolition teams went forward to lay their charges while the covering team hung back, keeping a look-out for any trouble. One of the cover party, while waiting near the back of an Iraqi truck, heard a sound from the cab. He went around to investigate and opened the cab door to reveal the sleepy face of an Iraqi soldier. The soldier, surprised, reached for his gun, despite efforts to stop him doing so. Then there was no other choice – within seconds he had been shot dead with a burst from an automatic rifle.

A firefight instantly erupted, and the column felt that every gun in the compound was trained on them. Even the Russian-made anti-aircraft guns were turned on their position. The Squadron fought back, giving it everything they'd got. By now the demolition teams had placed their explosives in the tower and were moving back to rejoin the rest of the column. The order was given to move out.

As the vehicles slowly regrouped and withdrew, they drew down a heavy rain of fire from all about them. Nevertheless, they kept going, punching a hole through the opposition with their own heavy guns. Finally, after an hour of battling their way through enemy positions, they disappeared into the night. Remarkably, despite the dangerous internal political manoeuvrings and the changes of plans, there were no casualties. A Squadron spent a total of 45 days behind enemy lines, during which time two men were killed and one was captured. Members of the Squadron received a DSM, two MCs, four MMs and four Mentions in Despatches for their bravery.

As a tribute to the SAS in the Gulf War, General Norman Schwarzkopf wrote the following commendation.

**Letter of Commendation for the
22 Special Air Service (SAS) Regiment.**

1. I wish to officially commend the 22 Special Air Service (SAS) Regiment for their totally outstanding performance of military operations during Operation Desert Storm.
2. Shortly after the initiation of the strategic air campaign, it became apparent that the Coalition forces would be unable to eliminate Iraq's firing of Scud missiles from western Iraq into Israel. The continued firing of Scuds on Israel carried with it enormous unfavourable political ramifications and could, in fact, have resulted in the dismantling of the carefully crafted Coalition. Such a dismantling would have adversely affected, in ways difficult to measure, the ultimate outcome of the military campaign. It became apparent that the only way that the Coalition could succeed in reducing these Scud launches was by physically placing military forces on the ground in the vicinity of the western launch sites. At that time, the majority of available Coalition forces were committed to the forthcoming military campaign in the eastern portion of the theatre of operations. Further, none of these forces possessed the requisite skills and abilities required to conduct such a dangerous operation. The only force deemed qualified for this critical mission was the 22 Special Air Service (SAS) Regiment.
3. From the first day they were assigned their mission until the last day of the conflict, the performance of the 22 Special Air Service (SAS) Regiment was courageous and highly professional. The area in which they were committed proved to contain far more numerous enemy forces than had been predicted by every intelligence estimate, the terrain was much more difficult than expected and the weather conditions were unseasonably brutal. Despite these hazards, in a very short period of time the 22 Special Air Service (SAS) Regiment was successful in totally denying the central corridor of western Iraq to Iraqi Scud units. The result was that the principal areas used by the Iraqis to fire Scuds on Tel Aviv were no longer available to them. They were required to move their Scud missile-firing forces to the northwest portion of Iraq and from that location the firing of Scud missiles was essentially militarily ineffective.
4. When it became necessary to introduce United States Special Operations Forces into the area to attempt to close down the northwest Scud areas, the 22 Special Air Service (SAS) Regiment provided invaluable assistance to the US forces. They took every possible measure to ensure that US forces were thoroughly briefed and were able to profit from the valuable lessons that had been learned by earlier SAS deployments into Western Iraq.

I am completely convinced that, had US forces not received these thorough indoctrinations by SAS personnel, US forces would have suffered a much higher rate of casualties than was ultimately

the case. Further, the SAS and US joint forces immediately merged into a combined fighting force where the synergetic effect of these fine units ultimately caused the enemy to be convinced that they were facing forces in western Iraq that were more than tenfold the size of those they were actually facing. As a result, large numbers of enemy forces that might otherwise have been deployed in the eastern theatre were tied down in western Iraq.
5. The performance of the 22 Special Air Service (SAS) Regiment during Operation Desert Storm was in the highest traditions of the professional military service and in keeping with the proud history and tradition that has been established by that regiment. Please ensure that this commendation receives appropriate attention and is passed on to the unit and its members.

H. NORMAN SCHWARZKOPF
General, US Army Commander in Chief.

# The Balkans

With the Gulf War behind it, the SAS once more settled down to a routine of training and servicing the numerous requirement of the British Government. One such role was to take the SAS into Bosnia. While the conflict was messy and many people were killed, the role of the SAS soldiers remained that of observers. As a result, the amount of information about SAS operations in Bosnia has been minimal, the main reason being the lack of action rather than security. Unlike other wars, the SAS were sent to Bosnia under a very different directive. Their mission was to observe the major forces in the area, with an eye to preventing trouble before it materialized. Individuals or small units were assigned to monitor the various Serbian units which sought to dominate the Muslim population. It was the role of peacekeeper, something not written in SAS doctrine; they are combat troops.

[Author's Note: It is not widely known that the SAS used its R Squadron, a squadron comprising a few retired regular SAS and civilians who are basically part-time soldiers, to fulfil much of its role in Bosnia].

The first public involvement of the SAS in Bosnia came when Major General 'Mike' Rose officially took over from General Briquemont on January 24, two days after a mortar shell had killed six children in Sarajevo. His first task was to ensure all information was channelled directly to him. Secondly, he made it clear that the aid convoys would no longer negotiate for passage. Days later, British soldiers fired back on the snipers who sought to prevent free passage of the convoys. Rose's attitude to the Bosnian Serb leaders was clear: "Back off or we will hit you hard." It was a policy which would have worked had it not been for the weakness of the UN and the indecisiveness of NATO. Agreements with the Serbs were full of lies, deception and intimidation, tactics designed to win time and ground against the disadvantaged Muslims. These stop-go tactics angered Rose and, although he had employed the correct measures in reply, the politicians failed to back his response. Thus the key

*Troops 'in and outs' mostly take place at airports these days.*

element of force was lost to him.

Towards the end of March, the Serbs started shelling the eastern enclave of Gorazde. The hospital was hit repeatedly and the wounded were forced to huddle in the basement. As the Serbs advanced with infantry and tanks, intent on taking the city, Rose called for NATO air support, sending SAS men in to act as forward air controllers. The bombing was remarkably accurate, and the Serb offensive was halted just as the town seemed about to fall. The air support was not sanctioned, but it had worked. The Serbs called for a local ceasefire while the wounded were evacuated.

The role of the SAS was to act as independent observers for General Rose. This they did by positioning themselves in close proximity to Serbian forces. It is rumoured that two members of the Regiment were spotted by the Serbs and fired on; as a result, one was killed and the other badly wounded. That night a second SAS team moved into Gorazde to assist the wounded men and also to extract a pilot who had been shot down during the bombing: this mission ended successfully.

# The Lima Embassy Siege

In many cases, the SAS are invited to the scene of a terrorist incident purely to give advice. Just such a case occurred on Tuesday, December 17, 1996. In this instance, 14 Peruvian rebels of the Tupac Amaru movement, known in Spanish by the initials MRTA, stormed the Japanese Embassy in Lima. The surprise attack occurred while the building was thronged with dignitaries as diplomats, Peruvian government officials and business leaders attended a party celebrating the Japanese Emperor's birthday. In all, some 600 people, most of whom were VIPs, were enjoying the party when the assault began. According to accounts provided by hostages who were later released, the guerrillas entered between 8.15pm and 8.25pm, as many of the guests were working their way down the buffet table set up in a tent in the grounds. An explosion, followed by a volley of gunfire, announced the takeover.

It has never been established exactly how the rebels gained access to the Embassy, but reports indicated that most of the attacking guerrillas simply stormed the high concrete walls which surround the Embassy compound. Other unconfirmed reports said that they

entered disguised as waiters, while one newspaper described how the rebels had spent three months tunnelling their way into the grounds of the residence. While this latter method may sound totally implausible, it did in fact have a grossly distorted basis in truth.

Whatever their method of entry, the MRTA rebels had certainly researched their target and timed their attack to perfection. The hostage list read like a Who's Who of Peruvian society and included the country's Foreign Minister, Francisco Tudela, Agriculture Minister Rodolfo Munante Sanguineti and the Speaker of the nation's Parliament. Also caught up in the assault were Peru's Supreme Court President, Moises Pantoja, and at least three of the country's legislators, as well as Japan's Ambassador, Morihisa Aoki, and 17 members of his staff. The ambassadors of Austria, Brazil, Bulgaria, Cuba, Guatemala, Panama, Poland, Romania, South Korea, Spain and Venezuela, together with seven Americans, were also unlucky enough to have accepted their invitations to the party. Without doubt the hostage list was the most prestigious ever taken in any terrorist action, although most guests managed to avoid being taken captive during the raid. Fernando Andrade, the mayor of the Miraflores section of Lima, escaped by sneaking into a bathroom and then climbing out of a window. US Ambassador Dennis Jett had attended the party but left around 7.45pm, about half an hour before the attack.

Those who were taken hostage were immediately divided into groups and ushered into rooms on the second floor of the residence. The various ambassadors were separated from the other guests and held together in one room, which was heavily guarded by the rebels. Despite a pitched gun battle during the takeover and the guerrillas' threats, by nightfall the siege had resulted in no deaths and only minor injuries. Once the siege had settled down, the rebels issued their demands via a telephone call to a local radio station. They were:

1. Release of some 300 imprisoned rebels, including Tupac Amaru's leader, Victor Polay, who had been in solitary confinement for the past four years.
2. Transfer of the freed prisoners and the hostage-takers to a jungle hideout with their hostages, the hostages to be released once they had reached their destination.

3. Payment of an unspecified amount as a 'war tax'.
4. An economic programme to help Peru's poor.

Although the demands centred on the release of imprisoned rebels, there was also strong reference to what the rebels called Japan's 'constant interference with Peru's internal politics.'

In response, the Peruvian Government and the President, Alberto Fujimori, who is of Japanese descent, reminded the world that they had sworn never to negotiate with terrorists. Fujimori, who was elected President in 1990, had managed to weaken severely the guerrilla movements, capturing most of the leaders and jailing thousands of militants and sympathizers. The takeover of the Japanese Embassy now put Peru's image at stake. It was because of President Fujimori's hard-line action in the past that Japan had invested so heavily in Peru, leading to the Tupac Amaru's resentment of Japanese influence on their country.

With so much in the balance, Fujimori spent most of his time presiding over a closed-door meeting of his Council of Ministers, including the chief of police, Kentin Vidal, a legendary figure who had led the successful operation to capture the rebel leader Abimael Guzman.

Twenty-four hours into the siege, when medicine was delivered to the Embassy, the rebels released four diplomats – the ambassadors of Canada, Germany and Greece and the French cultural attaché. The freed men read out a statement in which they said they had been sent to 'search for a negotiated solution' which would avoid deaths. During the next few days, the rebels released more hostages including President Fujimori's mother and sister. In return, Christmas turkeys were allowed to be delivered to the besieged embassy. Fujimori, however, rejected an opportunity to make a separate deal for other relatives trapped in the Embassy and flatly refused to release Peru's guerrilla prisoners. Instead, he offered the terrorists safe passage to some location outside Peru as an incentive for them to lay down their arms and free all their hostages. The rebels refused this offer and set several deadlines, each accompanied with the threat to kill hostages. All these deadlines passed without the loss of life. By January 6, 1997, the rebels were becoming agitated and refused to release any further hostages until the government started negotiations.

Within minutes of the attack, Peru's security forces had started flexing their considerable muscles, but they couldn't dislodge the guerrillas. They did, however, start to implement anti-terrorist procedures. All services were disconnected and the government refused to allow fuel into the residence for the generator which had provided power to the rebels and hostages after the electricity had been cut off. The Peruvian authorities ignored repeated demands to restore running water and telephone connections.

As the weeks went by, the Peruvian intelligence services started to monitor activities in the Embassy, setting up a series of listening devices. The CIA sent a US Air Force RG-8A aircraft with a forward-looking infrared camera to monitor the remaining 72 hostages and their 14 rebel guards. The 29-foot, single-engined aircraft makes very little noise and, in addition to its infrared camera, carries several high-resolution television cameras. The information gathered through these and other observation techniques was vital before any planned assault could take place. It is also believed that one of the hostages, a former military officer, was using a concealed two-way radio to supply information about the rebels.

While both the United States and Britain deny having had any direct role in the rescue operation, both have supplied experts in anti-terrorism training to Peru. And, remember, this was no ordinary terrorist incident. The taking of so many foreign nationals forced many countries to become involved. Some openly offered help. The British Ambassador to Peru, John Illman, voiced Britain's concern, saying: "We are ready to respond and are, in fact, making preparations in advance to respond to any such request. And we've made it clear that the experience that we have is totally at the disposal of the Peruvian authorities should they require it."

This response came in the guise of four members of the British SAS – four specialists whose expertise in the world of counter-terrorism was unparalleled. Their brief was to evaluate the situation and offer solutions. Ultimately, all of their solutions involved an assault of some form. In this case there was a choice of two primary actions:

1. Assault the Embassy.
2. Assault the rebels while in transit to freedom.

While the military planned and gathered information, the politicians tried to work out some form of compromise, one of which was to release the rebels and give them asylum in Cuba. To this end, President Fujimori had talks with the Cuban President, Fidel Castro. Some 11 weeks into the siege, a basic agreement was in place whereby a military aircraft would take the rebels to Cuba. Whether or not this was a deception or a plan to assault the rebels *en route*, we shall never know, for while these discussions were taking place another plan was being conceived by the shadowy figure of the unofficial head of Peruvian intelligence, Ivan Vladimiro Montesinos.

Montesinos is a cashiered army captain with a frightening reputation, and a figure who inspires fear

*The way in to the Japanese Embassy was through solid concrete floors.*

and fascination in Peru. He has not appeared before news cameras for several years but the fact that, wearing dark glasses, he strode victoriously into the liberated Japanese compound with the army Chief of Staff once the siege was over was an obvious indication of his involvement. In reality, it was Montesinos who had raised the 150-man commando unit which carried out the hostage rescue mission. Using his strong personality, he was able to recruit a combination of the best of the elite Special Forces units from the police and army and get President Fujimori's permission to use them in a daring plan.

Montesinos's plan was to tunnel under the embassy from several different directions. Then, at the right moment, the assaulting force would blast its way through the floor and walls. To facilitate the plan, 24 miners were brought in from the government-owned Centromin mining company. Over a period of several weeks they excavated several tunnels from nearby buildings, each running to a precise position under the Japanese Embassy. This was not an easy task, as the work needed to be done in secret, with both noise and vibration diversions having to be devised and put into operation. The end result was a series of tunnels, all equipped with electric light and ventilation. While the tunnels were being dug, the assembled group of élite commandos was undergoing painstaking training at a crude wooden replica of the Ambassador's home constructed in the hills outside Lima.

There remained, however, one small problem with the method of entry into the Embassy. The final flooring, which was solid concrete, had to be breached. If explosives were used, the blast in the confined space of the tunnel would leave none of the assault force in any fit state to jump out and close with the rebels, added to which was the great danger of a cave-in. The SAS have, for many years, contemplated such a problem and have researched and developed a wall-breaching cannon. This ingenious device not only creates a hole, but can do so with the assaulting force standing within a few feet. There is no violent shock-wave to tear the assault team limb from limb or cause a cave-in which would bury them alive.

Montesinos' plan was to make a sudden breach into the Embassy from five different directions. Twenty of the commandos would enter rapidly through the floor, while the remainder would enter at ground level through the compound walls. With the entire assault force in position, the plan was initiated.

On April 22, 1997, at 3.00pm, after four months of captivity, the hostages heard several explosions, rapidly followed by blistering gunfire. The rebels had become lethargic, and at the moment of the assault half of them had been playing football in the main hall, while some were sleeping upstairs. Those rebels outside the building were killed instantly, while those inside met their fate as the commando team carried out room-by-room clearance. In all, the assault took some 15 minutes.

During the assault only one man, Supreme Court Judge Carlo Giusti Acuna, died after being shot, and this was the result of a heart attack. Two police officers involved in the assault also died, one being a member of the security detail assigned to protect the President's son. In all, 25 hostages received minor wounds, with two others requiring surgery.

All 14 of the rebels were killed. Although at least two dropped their weapons and were seen by several hostages surrendering to the commandos, in the event the government reported that all the rebels had been killed during the assault. TV footage later showed that some of their bodies had been mutilated and even dismembered by the soldiers. The bodies of the rebels were buried in unmarked graves to prevent closer examination.

# Bosnia – Operation Tango

On July 10, 1997, the SAS were back in Bosnia, where they initiated Operation Tango. This action called for the arrest of two war criminals in Prijedor. Prijedor, which sits in the forested mountains, saw some of the worst ethnic crimes in the whole Bosnian war. The SAS unit was infiltrated into the area by Chinooks of Special Forces Flight 47.

The two men, Simo Drljaca and Milan Kovacevic, were wanted for war crimes and an arrest warrant had been issued by the International Criminal Tribunal for the Former Yugoslavia. Both are suspected of involvement in some of the worst excesses of ethnic cleansing in Prijedor, where thousands of Bosnian Muslims were imprisoned, starved and tortured in 1992.

The men were identified and tailed covertly before being challenged by the SAS, who were dressed in regular army uniform. Kovacevic, who worked as a director in the hospital at Prijedor, did not offer resistance when he was arrested. Drljaca, who was Prijedor's chief of police, pulled a pistol when confronted, shooting one of the SAS in the leg. The SAS responded, killing Drljaca. Drljaca's body, together with the wounded SAS man, was flown by an American helicopter to its base at Tuzla. Kovacevic was taken to the tribunal's headquarters in The Hague.

The SAS were also deployed to arrest General Stanislav Galic, the Serb commander who had rained down death and destruction on Sarajevo, killing thousands of innocent civilians. Galic, branded 'the Butcher of Sarajevo', commanded the Bosnian Serb army's Romanjia corps. This unit laid siege to Sarajevo for almost three years. From 1992, the Serb army simply used the city as a killing-ground. Snipers would shoot women as they queued for bread or children as they played. Whole families died as their homes were shelled or mortared. This was not a secret war: horrified viewers around the world watched the deaths on television. In February 1994 a mortar bomb hit the central market, killing 68 people and injuring 200. In all, the siege cost the lives of 10,000 people, most of them Muslims, with thousands more wounded.

Galic, who had left the army in 1997, did not expect to be arrested. He was not to know that the SAS had attached a sophisticated satellite tracking device to his vehicle and had been monitoring his movements for some time. On December 21, 1999, as he drove through Banja Luka, the largest city in the Serb part of Bosnia, he found his car boxed in by other vehicles. The box closed and he was forced to stop in a crowded street. Seconds later, his car was surrounded by two squads of SAS. As morning shoppers watched, bewildered, the windows of Galic's car were smashed. Strong arms dragged him to the ground while one soldier fitted Plasticuffs to his wrists. He was then thrown head-first into the back of a waiting car. As swiftly as they arrived, the SAS were gone. Two hours later, Galic was on board a NATO aircraft bound for The Hague. Galic, aged 56, was arrested on an indictment issued secretly by the UN war crimes tribunal. He will now stand trial for war crimes and crimes against humanity.

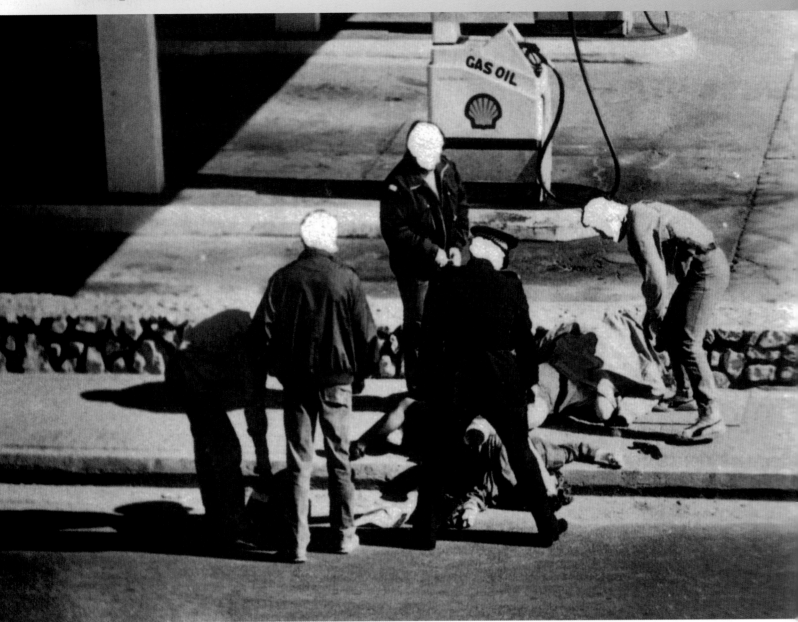

# Chapter 3

# Northern Ireland to Gibraltar

Sean Savage, Daniel McCann and Maraid Farrell were all shot dead by the SAS after a suspected bomb alert in Gibraltar.

The 1980s did not start well for the SAS, especially for those working in Northern Ireland. Special Branch of the Royal Ulster Constabulary (RUC) would occasionally get certain information which required the skills of the Regiment. Unfortunately, SB were always very tight-lipped on where initial information materialized. While this was good security practice, it didn't help those troops who carried out operations.

In one incident, SB requested the SAS Armagh unit take on three separate tasks. The first job was to watch two part-time policemen whom the IRA was planning to assassinate. The information from the SB clearly stated that they would be hit close to home. This was straightforward work for the SAS, who inserted an observation post (OP). All they had to do was sit and wait.

The second task was to protect a public house which the IRA had threatened to burn to the ground. This was another simple operation which, once again, involved inserting an OP and waiting for the IRA to turn up. Logistically, servicing two OPs with resupply and changing over men was not too much of a problem, until the weekend came around – at which time SB had an operation which required every man in the field.

It would seem that one of the local underlings in the IRA had seriously upset the organization. The punishment for his crime was to be knee-capped, with the job being carried out by a leading IRA member. SB were desperate to catch such a leading IRA figure in the act and employed a massive surveillance operation each weekend. This involved the SAS, E4A (an SB surveillance unit) and 14 Intelligence Unit in a huge stakeout of a particular Republican haunt which ran a disco every Saturday night. The problem for the SAS was one of manpower, and in order to commit themselves to the weekend operation they were forced to lift the OP on the public house every Saturday night.

On Week Two, the guys in the OP watching the home of the two policemen were spotted by a local farmer, and asked to be withdrawn. SB was informed of the dilemma and begged the SAS unit to stay in position. However, the final decision was down to the men on the ground, who opted to withdraw. Twelve hours later, as the two

*The SAS found working in South Armagh an easy task, however, their operations depended on good co-operation with the RUC Special Branch who provided most of the intelligence.*

police officers were returning from duty, their car was badly shot-up. The IRA had positioned themselves between the house and where the SAS OP had been. Had they remained in place, they would have had the IRA gunmen. As luck would have it, only one of the two policemen was injured in the attack.

The following weekend, every available man was committed to the operation around the disco, and as usual the OP on the pub was pulled off for the night. The surveillance operation went smoothly but, as with the previous two weekends, nothing happened. At around two in the morning, the operation was called off. One SAS car was to drop off the crew for the pub OP on its way back to base. They approached the public house, only to find it ablaze; the IRA had done their job during the brief moment the OP had been lifted. The SAS refer to this as 'the Paddy Factor' – needless to say, Special Branch was not pleased.

It was not just the SAS unit in South Armagh which was having bad luck; the Belfast unit was also getting

*Captain Richard Westmacott was sitting in the middle of the back seat as the SAS cars pulled up outside a house in Belfast. This meant he was last to exit the car making him the target for an IRA gunman who watched from a first floor window. Westmacott was killed instantly. He was a loyal SAS soldier.*

its share. In early April a number of IRA weapons were discovered. Although these had originally been under surveillance, the IRA had managed to move them to an unidentified hiding-place. Among these weapons was a 7.62mm M60 machine gun which had originally been stolen in America. It was vital that the weapons be relocated. Luckily, the weapons had been fitted with sophisticated location devices, but these only had a short range and limited battery power. After an intense search, a weak signal was discovered placing the weapons hide amid terraced houses in Antrim Road, albeit the exact location could not be identified. After an intelligence check by the RUC Special Branch, it emerged that the IRA had previously used one of three houses. Working on the 'best bet' principle, the SAS mounted an operation to recover the weapons.

On the afternoon of May 2, 1980, two cars containing SAS soldiers headed down the Antrim Road, screeching to a stop outside Number 367. Another vehicle, containing three more SAS, secured the rear. For security reasons, there had been no cordon or military activity prior to the raid, and the SAS team stormed straight at the house. Unknown to them, the IRA had mounted the missing M60 in an upstairs window of the adjoining house, Number 369. As the machine gun opened fire Captain Richard Westmacott, who had been sitting in the middle of the rear seat of the car and so was the last to move, caught the full blast. He was killed instantly. Realizing what had happened, the whole assault was quickly switched, but by this time the IRA man had surrendered. The sound of gunfire brought the Army and RUC to the scene; additionally, a Catholic priest suddenly materialized to see that the IRA man was allowed to surrender.

The tragic events of May 2 caused the SAS to drastically rethink its tactics. Today, in such a situation, the house would be put under surveillance before any direct intervention would be allowed. Captain Westmacott was the first SAS soldier to die in Northern Ireland, having joined the Regiment from the Grenadier Guards and served as a Captain in G Squadron. With curly fair hair, schoolboy looks and a love of poetry, his appearance belied his performance. He was a remarkably tough member of the SAS and in recognition of his achievements, was awarded the posthumous Military Cross.

# The Iranian Embassy Siege

Tragic though it was, Captain Westmacott's death seemed to end a run of bad luck for the SAS, as a few days later the anti-terrorist team successful stormed the Iranian Embassy in London.

The anti-terrorist unit had been in operation for more than five years, and now it had the opportunity to show what it could do. Some team members had been present when the Dutch Marines stormed a train which had been taken over by Moluccan terrorists, while others had assisted the German GSG9 unit throughout the Mogadishu hijacking. But now the SAS was to get its own venue, and to make it a real classic; moreover, it was filmed on national television and beamed around the world.

It all started when a group of terrorists arrived in London seeking accommodation. Almost inevitably they finished up in the Earls Court area, home to many recently-arrived foreigners. However, like so many members of the visiting Arab community, they found the pubs and clubs of the district a temptation too good to miss. This mixture of drinking and womanizing increased to the point where they were

forced to leave their accommodation and seek fresh lodgings. Eventually, the whole group finished up at 105 Lexham Gardens, where they remained until their departure on the morning of Wednesday, April 30. By 11:20, having mysteriously collected several weapons, two of which were machine guns, and a quantity of grenades, the group was standing outside 16 Princes Gate, home to the Iranian Embassy in London. They were terrorists, opposed to the regime of Ayatollah Khomeini and seeking the liberation of the oil-rich province of Khuzestan – which they called Arabistan – from Iran. At 11:25, the six gunmen entered and took over Number 16.

As they took control of the Embassy they gained 26 hostages, including the British policeman who had been on duty at the entrance. This was something which might have gone unnoticed but for the fact that, minutes later, a burst of machine gun fire could be heard. The police were on the scene immediately – swiftness initiated by the captured policeman, Trevor Lock, who had managed to alert his headquarters before being taken by the terrorists. Armed D11 marksmen soon surrounded the building and the siege negotiating plans were put into operation.

The anti-terrorist team in Hereford was at this time practising in the Killing House, but things were soon to change. By 11:47 Dusty Grey, an ex-D Squadron SAS man who now worked with the Metropolitan Police, was talking to the Commanding Officer in Hereford. His information contained the briefest details, but it was enough to alert the Regiment. Several minutes later, the duty signaller activated the 'call-in' bleepers carried by every member of the anti-terrorist team. Although the SAS had prior warning, there can be no move before official sanction from the Home Secretary, who at the request of the police will contact the MoD. Despite this red tape, it makes sense for the SAS to think ahead, and time can be saved by positioning the anti-terrorist team

*The SAS train for just about every emergency. Here they are being delivered by helicopter in order to assault a moving bus. The techniques were perfected at the secret training establishment known as Camp One.*

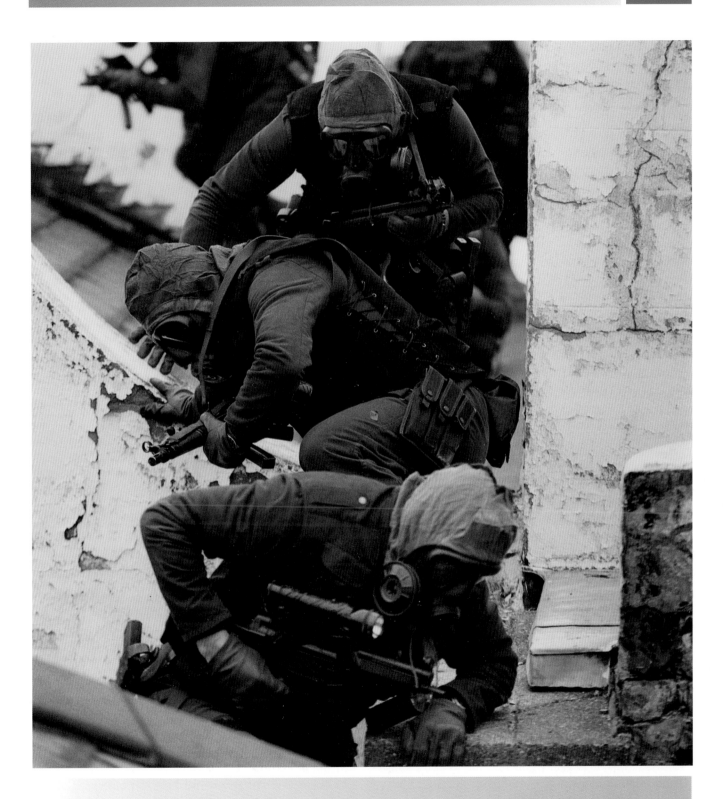

*Members of the assault team make ready to abseil down the Iranian Embassy in London.*

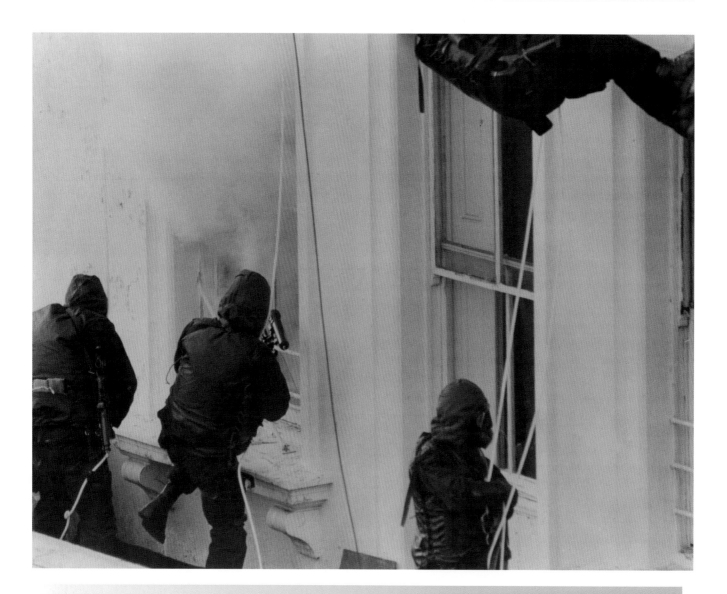

*The assault team make an entry into the back of the Iranian Embassy at Princes Gate.
All the teams were co-ordinated in order that the assault would take place simultaneously
on all floors.*

closer to the scene. Around midnight on the first day, most of the team had made their way to Regent's Park Barracks, which had been selected as a holding area. From here, information could be assembled and assessed. A scale model of Number 16, Princes Gate, was ordered to be constructed: this task fell to two Pioneers drafted in from the nearby Guards unit. Additionally, an intelligence cell was set up to gather and collate every snippet of information which would aid any assault.

By this time the terrorist leader, Oan, had secured

his 26 hostages and issued his demands. These included autonomy for, and recognition of, the people of Arabistan and the release of 91 Arabistani prisoners. The line taken by the terrorists was hard, but fair, and despite several threats to blow up the Embassy and kill the hostages, on Thursday, May 1, they released a sick woman. Later that same day Oan managed to get a telephone call through to Sadegh Ghotzbadeh, Iran's Foreign Minister. The conversation did not go well; Oan was accused of being an American agent and told that

***An SAS unit enter the front of Princes Gate after blowing out the window. This picture shows one of the first images the world saw as the assault on the Embassy was shown worldwide on television.***

the Iranian hostages held in the Embassy would consider it an honour to die for their country and the Iranian Islamic Revolution.

This lack of co-operation almost forced the terrorists to seek a mediator who was more sympathetic, but it also told them that the Iranian government did not care if the staff of its Embassy were killed or not. Another problem had also raised its head for the terrorists. Chris Cramer, a BBC journalist who was among the hostages, had become sick with acute stomach pains. His partner,

sound recordist Sim Harris, pleaded with Oan to call for a doctor immediately. This was done, but the police refused to allow him to enter the building. In the end, Cramer was released, stumbling out of the Embassy door and into a waiting ambulance.

Later that night, again under the cover of darkness, three Avis rental vans pulled up in a small side street by Princes Gate. Men carrying holdalls quickly made their way into Number 14, just two doors down from the besieged building. Within minutes they had laid out their equipment and made ready for an immediate action (IA). At first sight, this was very simple: if the terrorists started shooting, the SAS men would run to the front door of Number 16 and beat their way in – slow, primitive, but better than nothing until a clearly-defined plan could be organized.

By 06:00 on the morning of Saturday, May 2, the situation inside Number 16 was getting very agitated. Oan rang the phone which had been set up between the Embassy and Number 25, Princes Gate, the Royal School of Needlework, which now housed Alpha Control and the police negotiator. Oan's main complaint was that no reports of the siege had been broadcast by the media; how, he asked, could his cause be heard? He slammed the phone down in a rage. Late that afternoon, Oan was allowed to make a statement which was to be broadcast on the next news slot: in return for this, two more hostages were released, one of whom was a pregnant woman. The trouble was that Oan would not release the hostages before the statement was read out; likewise, the police wanted the hostages first. In the end, a compromise was reached and the broadcast went out on the Nine O'Clock News.

Two hours later, eight members of the SAS team had climbed on to the rear roof of Number 14 and were making their way amid a jungle of TV antennae to Number 16. Two of the men made their way directly to a glass skylight and after some time managed to get it free. It opened directly into a small bathroom on the top floor of the Iranian Embassy, and would provide an excellent entry point. Meanwhile, other members secured abseil ropes to the several chimneys and made ready for a quick descent to the lower floors, where they could smash in through the windows. Oddly enough, an enterprizing television director had managed to get a camera into a bedroom window overlooking the back of the Embassy: during the assault, he filmed the whole of the action.

By 09:00 on Sunday, things seemed to be heading for a peaceful settlement. Oan had agreed to reduce his demands, and at the same time Arab ambassadors had attended a Cobra Committee meeting in Whitehall; this had been chaired by Willie Whitelaw, the Home Secretary, who was to all intents and purposes in charge of the whole operation. For the SAS anti-terrorist team, events had become much more stable. By now, access

had been gained to Number 14 and efforts were being made to penetrate the wall. To aid this, various sound distractions – supplied by the Gas Board working in the vicinity – avoided the drilling being heard. On the far side, Number 17, which was the Ethiopian Embassy, had also co-operated. The basic plan had been formalized. This was to attack each floor at the same time and to clarify areas of demarcation to avoid over-shoot. Mock-ups of the floor layouts were constructed from timber and hessian sheeting and assembled at Regent's Park Barracks.

The police, who had adopted a 'softly, softly' negotiating approach, managed to drag the siege out for several days: time which was desperately needed for the SAS to carry out covert recces, study plans, build models and, more importantly, locate the hostages and terrorists within the Embassy building. They got a major break when they talked to the released hostage Chris Cramer, the BBC journalist. In releasing him as an act of faith because of his stomach disorder, the terrorists made a big mistake: in his debrief to the SAS, he was able to give them precise and detailed information about the situation inside the Embassy.

By the sixth day of the siege, May 5, the terrorists were becoming frustrated and the situation inside the Embassy began to deteriorate. All morning threats were made about executing hostages, and at 13:31 three shots were heard. At 18:50 more shots were heard, and the body of the Embassy press officer was thrown out. Immediately the police appeared to capitulate, stalling for time, while SAS plans to storm the Embassy were advanced. At this stage, the police negotiator worked hard to convince the terrorist leader Oan not to shoot any further hostages, and that a bus would be with them shortly to take them to the airport; from there they could fly to the Middle East. As the telephone conversation went on, the SAS took up their start positions.

A handwritten note passed control from the police to the SAS. Shortly thereafter, while a negotiator from Alpha Control was talking to Oan, the SAS moved in. Oan heard the first crashes and complained to Alpha Control that the Embassy was being attacked (this conversation was recorded, and one can clearly hear the stun grenades going off; Oan's conversation is cut short by a long burst of machine-gun fire). For the assault team, the waiting was over, and the words guaranteed to send their adrenaline pumping were given: 'Go. Go. Go.' At 19:23, eight men abseiled down to the first-floor balcony, on ropes secured to the Embassy roof. The assault came from three directions, with the main thrust coming from the rear. Frame charges – by now they had been perfected – were quickly fitted to the windows and blown. Stun grenades were thrown in advance of the assaulting men and the SAS went into action. Systematically, the building was cleared from the top down, room by room. The telex room on the second floor, which housed the male hostages and three of the terrorists, was of utmost priority. Realizing that an assault was in progress, the terrorists shot and killed one hostage and wounded two others before the lead SAS team broke into the room. Immediately, they spotted and shot two gunmen; the third hid among the hostages and was not discovered until later. As rooms were cleared, hostages were literally thrown from one SAS soldier to another, down the stairs and out into the back garden. At this stage they were all laid face-down on the ground while a search was conducted for the missing terrorist.

Breaking the siege took just 17 minutes. The SAS took

*Once inside the Embassy, the SAS swiftly dispatched five of the six terrorists. The terrorists managed to kill only two of the remaining 21 hostages before the event was over.*

no casualties, other than one man, who got caught up in his abseil and was badly burned.

With the operation finished, the problem was handed back to the police. Meanwhile the boys vacated Number 14 and went back to the barracks in time to watch themselves on television. Still dressed in assault gear, and clutching cans of Foster's lager, they crowded around, eager to see themselves in action. Halfway through Prime Minister Margaret Thatcher, who had left a dinner date, arrived to thank the boys in person. She circulated, as one man put it, "like a triumphant Caesar returning to the Senate", her face glowing with pride and admiration at her Imperial Guard. Then, as the news started to show the full event, she sat down on the floor amid her warriors – there can be no greater gesture of approbation from one's leader.

In total, 26 hostages were taken in the Embassy when the siege started. Of these, five were released before the SAS assault. Two died, but the remaining 19 survived. Of the six terrorists, only one survived.

## After the Siege

Back in Hereford, a few months later, the building of the new barracks at Bradbury Lines was completed. At the opening, the site was renamed Stirling Lines in honour of David Stirling, the Regiment's founder. A huge party

*Another photograph of Prince Charles and Princess Diana, this time posing with the full counter-terrorist team.*

followed, with many members of the original SAS in attendance. The buoyant mood felt after the Iranian Embassy siege continued.

Later that summer an SAS free-fall team took off from Brize Norton airbase in Wiltshire and jumped from the aircraft while over the south coast of England. Using the new High Altitude High Opening (HAHO) technique, all the team managed to make it across the English Channel, landing in France. Everyone was delighted, even though two were arrested by the French police for illegal entry.

## The Gambia, 1981

On August 1, 1981, Lieutenant-Colonel Michael Rose, commanding officer of the SAS, was out relaxing in the Welsh countryside, having had a busy time providing protection for numerous VIPs. A large number of Commonwealth heads of state had been in London, attending the wedding of Prince Charles to Lady Diana Spencer. The gathering of notables had presented a number of opportunities for terrorists; now that it was over, the SAS could return to Hereford and relax a little. Rose therefore arranged to take time off, enjoying the company of his children, something rare for the SAS commander. Even now, he wore an electronic beeper on his belt, which interrupted this much-anticipated interlude with an urgent summons. With all haste he made his way to the nearest telephone and made a call to Hereford headquarters. Diane, a telephonist of long standing in Hereford, switched his call to Major Ian Crooke, who was acting executive officer at the time. From Crooke, Rose learned that the small nation of Gambia, a former British colony, was in the throes of a *coup d'etat*. Launched two days earlier, it coincided with the absence of the nation's President, Sir Dawda Jawara, who was representing his country at the royal wedding. Senegal, Gambia's neighbour, with which is had a military assistance agreement, had already sent troops to combat the rebels. Additionally, Jawara had asked British Prime Minister Margaret Thatcher for help, and it had been agreed to dispatch a couple of SAS men to the scene. The Prime Minister warned of the need for secrecy; even this modest response, if it became public, could open her Government to charges of renewed imperialism in Africa.

Rose first told Crooke that he was inclined to take the assignment himself; always quick at making decisions,

*The main radio station of the Gambia. This was taken over by rebels who had opposed the government led by President, Sir Dawda Jawara. Jawara was in England attending the wedding of Prince Charles and Lady Diana.*

and ever politically-minded, his skills would prove very useful in Gambia. However, getting Rose back to Hereford would require him being picked up by helicopter, and he would need to make arrangements for his children; this would take time. Eventually Rose conceded that Crooke himself should choose another available man, select whatever weapons and equipment they would need and get to Gambia on the first available plane.

The Gambia covers an area of 11,295 sq. km of West Africa, and is the continent's smallest independent state. It is a narrow strip of land on both banks of the Gambia River, bordered by the Atlantic Ocean to the west and surrounded on the remaining three sides by Senegal.

The capital is Banjul, on St. Mary's Island, near the mouth of the Gambia River. A low-lying country, its terrain ranges from sandy beaches along the coast to a swampy river valley in the interior. The economy is overwhelmingly dependent on the export of peanuts, which provides most of the country's earnings. The population is primarily Muslim black African, of whom the Mandingo are the most numerous tribe; English is the official language.

English merchants won trading rights from the Portuguese in 1588, and in the early 17th century British companies founded settlements along the Gambia River. In 1816 the British purchased St. Mary's Island, where they established Bathurst (now Banjul), and in 1843 the territory became a Crown colony. The French, who controlled the neighbouring interior (now Senegal), failed in negotiations to acquire the Gambia River settlements which, in 1894, became a British protectorate. Gambia achieved self-government in 1963 and independence in 1965, under Dawda Kairaba Jawara; it became a republic in the Commonwealth of Nations in 1970. Independent Gambia is notable in Africa as a bastion of parliamentary democracy and political stability. It has maintained close relations with Senegal, with the larger neighbour being responsible for Gambia's defence.

By 1980, the average annual per capita income was only about £140, and this was on the decline because the peanut crop had fared poorly in two years of extremely dry weather. On the other hand, tourism was on the increase, and could have become an important source of revenue. However, such was the poverty in Gambia that the populace started to complain over escalating prices for basic foodstuffs; the problem was not helped by the high rate of unemployment. It soon became obvious from the number of anti-government slogans painted on walls that the government was in trouble. When slogans turned to actions and the President's private yacht mysteriously caught fire, the government

*The ferry which Ian Crooke and his group took to cross the Gambia River. Once across the river, they made their way directly to Banjul with the intention of putting down the rebellion.*

finally realized that a coup was being planned. President Jawara, however, discounted the information and flew to London for the matrimonial festivities.

The revolt was the work of the Gambian Socialist Revolutionary Party, which was headed by a young Marxist named Kukoi Samba Sanyang. His given name was Dominique, but when he became a communist he changed it to Kukoi, a word in the Mandinka language, native to Gambia, which means 'sweep clean.' Sanyang was also among the African radicals who had sojourned in Libya. The volatile Libyan leader, Colonel Qadhafi, envisaged a confederation of Islamic African states under his guidance. He attracted exiled African political leaders of Marxist persuasion to the Libyan capital, Tripoli, and plotted to reshape a number of African governments. Gambia, being 70 percent Muslim, lay within Colonel Qadhafi's fancied Islamic realm.

At 05:00 on Thursday, July 30, the coup erupted. Muscle for the attempt to overthrow Jawara was provided by Usman Bojang. A former deputy commander of Gambia's 300-man Police Field Force – a paramilitary organization charged with preserving order in the tiny country – Bojang managed to persuade or force the contingent based in the town of Bakau to join the coup. This group, which amounted to about one-third of the organization, disarmed most of the loyal police, then quickly took over the nearby transmitter for Radio Gambia and moved into Banjul, the capital. On the way they opened the country's largest prison and distributed weapons from the police armoury not only to the inmates, but to virtually anyone who happened along. Not long after daybreak, citizens and former prisoners alike began rampaging through the streets and looting shops. Soon, a free-for-all erupted. Within the first few hours of the coup, scores of bodies – policemen, criminals and civilians – littered the streets of Banjul. Arriving at Radio Gambia shortly after rebel policemen had seized the station, Sanyang closed the country's borders and its airport at Yundum, some 15 miles east of Banjul. Then he proclaimed a 'dictatorship of the proletariat' and charged the 'bourgeois' Jawara government with corruption, injustice and nepotism.

Most Europeans and Americans working in business or holding government posts stayed off the streets, while other foreigners and tourists remained in the capital or kept to their hotels in the nearby communities of Bakau and Fajara. Many rebel Gambian policemen, who saw no profit in harming Western individuals, guided anxious foreigners to the residence of the United States Ambassador, Larry G. Piper. The house was soon a haven to 123 nervous guests, 80 of them American citizens. A number of European tourists also sought shelter in the Atlantic Beach Hotel, on the outskirts of Banjul, along the nation's beautiful sea coast. During the trouble, two armed looters raided the hotel, ransacked the safe and took the manager hostage. As they fled the hotel, the two looters were shot dead in the hotel doorway. Fearing more looters would arrive, and hearing the constant firing outside, the hotel guests organized watches and posted guards, 'armed' with fire extinguishers.

President Jawara had made contact by telephone with his vice-president who had taken refuge in police headquarters in Banjul, where he was protected by loyalist troops. In London, Jawara wisely made himself accessible to the press; in doing so, he was able to downplay events at home. Because of this, the plight of the European and Americans trapped by the situation never reached the outside world. Had it done so, the coup would have attracted far more attention than it did. For the first few day of the coup, Jawara controlled all news of Gambia from London. Acting as if to resume control of the government, Jawara boarded a jet bound for Dakar, capital of Senegal. In a statement before leaving, the President talked about invoking a mutual assistance treaty which Gambia had signed with Senegal some 15 years earlier to fend off external aggression, yet at this stage no foreign agitator had been identified as having backed the coup.

By now, Ian Crooke and an SAS sergeant, Tony (not his real name), had chosen and assembled their weapons and equipment. These consisted of German-made Heckler & Koch sub-machine guns, Browning 9mm automatic pistols and a stock of ammunition and grenades. Crooke managed to pass his little arsenal through Customs and baggage checks and on to the first flight available. This plane happened to be an Air France commercial flight to Dakar. Although firearms can be carried in checked baggage aboard such aircraft, explosives are normally prohibited, but most anti-terrorist teams have direct contact with each other and after several phone calls the normal

channels are ignored. This is not uncommon: during the Iranian Embassy siege in London, the German GSG9 commander, Ulrich Wegener, had been allowed to observe the incident. Upon his return to Germany aboard a scheduled passenger flight, it was discovered that he was in possession of a weapon. Informal contacts within the British Diplomatic Service cleared the way in minutes. As always, Ian and Tony were dressed casually, bringing no attention from their fellow-passengers among whom were many reporters and television camera crews.

Upon arriving in Senegal, Ian Crooke encountered his first obstacle – British diplomats. Despite the brief from Prime Minister Thatcher directly to the SAS, the diplomats refused to allow them to get involved. With fighting going on between the rebel forces and Senegalese troops, and with a considerable number of British citizens in danger, officials in both Dakar and Banjul decided that it would only complicate their duties further if the SAS were to get in on the act. This would allow them to applaud the Senegalese if the intervention succeeded, or to chastise them if it failed. The SAS travel on many missions around the world, normally working close to their counterparts in VIP protection. Accommodation and reception in the various countries is normally handled by British diplomats, who generally shudder at the thought of having SAS men in their company.

With no word from Thatcher, in whose service he had come to Africa, Ian Crooke decided to go ahead with his mission despite the remonstrations of these relatively minor officials. Adopting the policy of 'out of sight, out of mind', the two men managed to get seats on a plane bound for Gambia's Yundum airport. Upon arrival, Crooke met the Senegalese paratroop commander, Lieutenant Colonel Abdourah-man N'Gom, who had established his headquarters in the confines of the airport.

Crooke also made contact with Clive Lee, a hulking six-foot-six retired SAS Major who was employed as a civilian adviser to the Gambian Pioneer Corps, a division of the country's Field Force which trained rural youth in agricultural and construction skills.

The SAS has a very loose connection with its ex-soldiers, most of whom are scattered around the world, mostly working in some security job or for a foreign government. In such circumstances it is expected that, should the need arise and their services be required, they are honour-bound to render all assistance to the SAS operation. As with David Bullig in Dubai during the Mogadishu hijack, so it was with Clive Lee in Gambia – and there are many other untold instances. The SAS brotherhood bond is extremely strong.

Hearing of the coup on the radio, Lee had rounded up 23 Pioneer Corps members, armed them and set off for Banjul (you can't keep a good SAS man down when he smells a fight). To get there from the Pioneer Corps base in the town of Farafenni, 60 miles east of the capital, Lee had to cross the Gambia River. Because of the hostilities, however, the ferry had suspended operations. As with Ian Crooke and the diplomats, this was no time to pussy-foot around, and soon the ferry captain had been persuaded to take Lee's band to the other side. Once across, they made their way directly to Banjul, where necessary moving through mangrove swamps to avoid rebel positions along the main road to the city. In Banjul, Lee's party made for police headquarters, where they reinforced a small contingent of loyalists and set about defending their enclave by barricading the nearby streets.

For the Senegalese troops, capturing Yundum airport had not been easy. During a fierce battle, almost half the 120 paratroops making the assault were wounded or killed. Once this task was completed, Senegalese soldiers entered Banjul; within a few hours, they had cleared the city of rebels. They had also gained control of Denton Bridge, across Oyster Creek, which would prevent insurgents from re-entering the capital from their concentrations in Bakau and Fajara. A combination of these actions secured the route from Banjul to the airport.

The Senegalese troops found the situation in Banjul little changed. Although N'Gom continued to strengthen his forces in Gambia and occasionally traded shots with the rebels, the military situation had reached an impasse. His troops were stalled outside Bakau because Sanyang had taken more than 100 hostages. The most valuable captives were Lady Chilel N'Jie – one of President Jawara's two wives – and a number of his children. In addition, Sanyang held several members of the Gambian cabinet. And although N'Gom had wrested Radio Gambia from Sanyang's rebels (the transmitter lay between the airport and the bridge), the coup leader had commandeered a mobile transmitter from which Lady Chilel appealed almost hysterically to Senegal, announcing that the hostages would be executed unless the paratroops withdrew. Sanyang repeated the threat himself. "I shall kill the whole lot," he warned, "and thereafter stand to fight the Senegalese."

On August 5, Crooke decided to make a reconnaissance. The blue jeans-clad SAS officer and his two associates slipped forward of Senegalese outposts and set out on foot. The weather was hot; during August in Gambia, temperatures routinely exceed 90° F. The three Britons, who were carrying sub-machine guns, could hardly escape notice in Fajara, but the outing was not as dangerous as it might seem. Although there was always the chance that an encounter with an armed insurgent could end in gunfire, the rebels did not seem inclined to harm Europeans. Furthermore, Crooke observed an unmilitary laxity among the troops staffing rebel positions. Unknown to both Crooke and the outside world, Bojang had been killed during the second day of the coup. His absence, and the resulting lack of leadership, probably accounted for the apparent decline in rebel vigilance. Crooke's sortie confirmed that the insurgents were now capable of little more than token resistance against well-trained Senegalese troops.

Crook persuaded N'Gom to begin an advance on Fajara and Bakau the same day. The British officer and his companions accompanied a contingent of Senegalese troops along the hot byways of the suburbs. Peter Felon, a British engineer employed by an American crane company, saw the party when they appeared at his hotel in Fajara. "Ten Senegalese troops and a British Army officer arrived at the hotel," the engineer recalled. The officer, probably Clive Lee, wore khakis with no insignia. "With him were two men whom I can only describe as the most vicious-looking professionals I have ever seen." Upon being told that rebels were hiding along a creek near the beach, the pair set off to find them. "There was sporadic, violent gunfire," said Felon, "then the two men walked calmly back to our hotel."

A US aid worker at the American Embassy was one of the foreigners who had taken refuge in Ambassador Larry Piper's house. It was early afternoon, he remembered, when a look-out they had posted announced that soldiers were coming up the hill. "The house", said the aid worker later, "was on a bluff sloping to the beach. I went out and saw a wave of Senegalese

*The clinic where the President's wife, Lady Chilel, and her children were held captive. Crooke and one other SAS man tricked the guards and managed to release the hostages before taking them to safety.*

come running up the hill in full camouflage-type gear led by three whites, one of whom had on an Australian hat, khaki shorts and a knife strapped to his leg. It was literally like living in a movie." After ascertaining that everyone was all right and leaving behind a dozen or so paratroops for security, the party disappeared.

Arriving at the British High Commissioner's offices, Crooke learned that armed rebel guards had escorted President Jawara's wife and her four ailing children – one of them an infant of only five weeks – to a British clinic the day before. Doctors at this tropical disease research facility, which stood only a block or two from the High Commissioner's office, treated the children and advised her to bring them back within 24 hours.

The interval had passed, and now Lady Chilel had returned for follow-up care. This information came by way of a telephone call to the High Commissioner from the British physician attending the children. The official told the doctor that armed SAS men would be there

within minutes, and Crooke and his two companions quickly headed for the hospital. Hearing that help was on the way, the doctor began to draw out his treatment: the wily physician even convinced the woman's armed escorts that they were frightening his other patients and persuaded them to put their guns out of sight.

As Crooke approached the hospital, he noticed two armed guards posted at the entrance. Handing his submachine-gun to his companions, the major gave them instructions to circle behind the guards, then walked up to the pair and distracted them in conversation as the other two SAS men crept up from the rear. It is difficult to imagine what Crooke could have said or how devious a plan he might have formulated in order to draw the guards' attention away from his accomplices. The SAS is mute on the topic; whatever Crooke's ruse, it worked. The two guards froze when they felt gun muzzles at the backs of their heads.

Leaving the captives in the hands of his able

assistants, Crooke slipped inside the clinic. He surprised Lady Chilel's weaponless escorts as they watched the children being treated and promptly took them prisoner. After conducting the President's wife and children to the High Commissioner's office, Crooke and his party retreated to N'Gom's headquarters at the airport.

A day earlier Senegalese troops, who now numbered about 1,500, had found and destroyed the mobile transmitter Sanyang had been using. Although Sanyang himself escaped, he was no longer a factor. With the silencing of its leaders, the coup's backbone was broken. Yet many hostages remained under rebel guns at a police barracks, and disorganized bands of turncoat policemen and criminals had to be rounded up.

N'Gom paced his advance slowly. Panic among the rebels might cause them to begin killing their prisoners. They had nearly done so a few days earlier, when a police officer who had been forced against his better judgement to join the coup began shooting some of the rebel guards. He was killed in a trice, but his brave act seemed to thwart the planned execution. The Senegalese paratroops edged up to one side of the barracks, leaving several exits unguarded for the rebels to flee. After a tense hour or so, the hostages walked free and the insurgents dispersed, to be captured later.

Eight days later the rebellion was all over, but it had caused more than 1,000 deaths. President Jawara was once again the unchallenged and elected head of the Gambian government. Kukoi Sanyang was eventually arrested in the neighbouring country of Guinea-Bissau, but the Socialist government there later released him, despite Gambian requests for his extradition. Senegalese troops captured more than 100 of the rebels and convicts, seven of whom were ultimately condemned to death. Libya was never connected directly with the coup attempt.

In Banjul, the President posed for reporters, hugged his baby son and announced: "I'm relieved and happy." His answers to questions about the rescue of his wife and children by European soldiers met with a cold shrug of the shoulders, and a comment that all such claims were much exaggerated. To make Jawara's political recovery as easy as possible, all official comment about the countercoup and rescue was reserved for African governments. The only confirmation of the SAS presence came from

a Senegalese officer, who told reporters that SAS personnel had, indeed, participated in restoring order. As always, the British Government remained silent.

The SAS party hung around Gambia just long enough to satisfy themselves that British citizens would be safe, and then made their way home. The operation in Gambia demonstrated how a few skilled and confident soldiers can influence an event far out of proportion to their numbers: additionally, they could disappear, as if nothing had happened, throwing yet another cloak over the SAS myth.

Ian Crooke gave a wonderful, detailed account of the whole incident to a full assembly of the Regiment. It was the highlight of an annual debrief, where other members of the SAS found out what everyone else had been doing around the world: as normal, it was for SAS personnel only. Although the British Government refused to admit involvement, it was recognized that the success of the action hinged in large measure on Crooke's initiative and good judgement. That he had a lot of help is undisputed. It came partly in the form of militarily incompetent coup-makers and partly from the presence of the Senegalese. N'Gom's troops supplied the manpower needed to fight rebels who were disinclined to surrender, and to maintain security in areas which had been swept clean. Nonetheless, Crooke was the one who tipped the balance. He chose to ignore the restrictions placed on him by British diplomats and acted as he believed the Prime Minister wished. Had he been wrong, he would no doubt have suffered severe consequences. However, in those days the SAS were very much Margaret Thatcher's blue-eyed boys.

Major Ian Crooke was a rare exception to the normal officer serving with the SAS; he was more at home drinking with the NCOs than in the Officers' Mess. Sadly, he suffered a terrible injury during a parachute jump in South Africa.

# The Falklands, 1982

The SAS continued its routine of sending soldiers around the world and manning the anti-terrorist team. That was until the Argentinians decided to invade the Falkland Islands in early 1982.

The Falklands are a group of islands in the South Atlantic which have been under British sovereignty

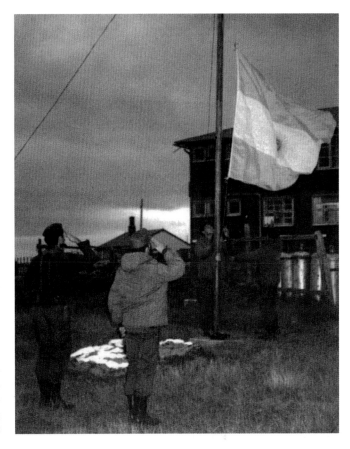

since 1833. When the Argentinians invaded the islands on April 2, 1982, the British Prime Minister, Margaret Thatcher, announced that Britain would win the islands back, taking them by force if necessary. Under Operation Corporate, a task force was immediately put together and sent on its way south. Both Peter de la Billière, then a Brigadier, and Lieutenant-Colonel Mike Rose, the Commander of 22 SAS, fought hard to have the Regiment included in the task force. By early April, members of D and G Squadrons were on their way.

It fell to G Squadron to get the ball rolling against the Argentinians. Teams from the squadron were inserted to observe the enemy in advance of the main task force arriving. Due mainly to the featureless terrain, it was a hard and difficult task. The guys were forced to conceal themselves in small clumps of outcropping rocks, where they would lie up during the day, braving the horrific weather conditions. By night, they would slip out of their hides and walk at least 10 kilometres in order to send their reports. This was to stop the Argentinians fixing their location when they used the radio. It was a testing time, but the SAS patrols remained hidden for three weeks before being relieved.

The weather was also responsible for an incident which occurred on the island of South Georgia. A decision was taken to land D Squadron's Mountain Troop on the island's Fortuna Glacier. A small island 500kms south of the main Falklands group, South Georgia housed a small Argentinian garrison. Retaking the island was seen by the British as a low-risk, high-propaganda value operation. The SAS would establish observation posts overlooking the town of Leith in anticipation of British forces landing to recapture South Georgia.

Wessex helicopters from HMS Antrim and HMS Tidespring dropped the troop, commanded by Captain John Hamilton, with their equipment and some pulks, on the glacier. The icy conditions hindered their progress and the situation was to deteriorate as night fell. One of the two tents was destroyed in a blizzard, increasing

the risk of hypothermia and frostbite, and Hamilton, knowing they would not survive another night, requested an evacuation.

The next morning, although still hampered by the blizzard, three helicopters, led by a radar-equipped Wessex, headed for the glacier in an attempt to retrieve the soldiers. They succeeded in rescuing the whole team, but as they took off again, one of the helicopters crashed into the glacier. Amazingly, only one man was superficially injured. The other two helicopters returned to help, dumping fuel and equipment in an effort to create room for the men aboard the downed helicopter. Suddenly the weather deteriorated even more and a second helicopter struck an ice ridge and also crashed. This left them no choice: the one remaining helicopter – named Humphrey ¬ would have to fly back to HMS Antrim. Piloted by Lieutenant-Commander Ian Stanley RN, Humphrey returned later in the day to the blizzard-bound glacier, where the remaining survivors were located and rescued. However, the helicopter was now dangerously

# Theatre of War: Falkland Islands

*The SAS were inserted into the Falkland Islands in advance of the main task force. They spent their days hiding and observing, their nights reporting back to base. This map shows SAS and SBS observation posts.*

*Fortuna Glacier, at the north-west of South Georgia was the scene of a serious Regimental disaster.*

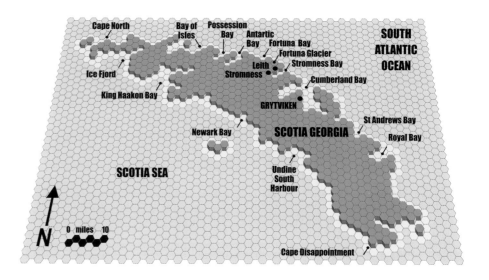

overloaded and struggled precariously back to the ship, eventually crash-landing on the deck. Stanley was awarded the DSO for his bravery and professionalism.

As the first attempt to land on the island of South Georgia had ended in failure, it was decided to try again. This time the SAS, SBS and M Company of 42 Commando went in by boat rather than by helicopter. Even this proved difficult: some boats developed engine trouble, missed the island altogether and had to be rescued. Eventually, however, they succeeded, and managed to carry out their task of setting up OPs

(observation posts) to gather intelligence about Argentinian strengths and positions on the island. According to one of the SBS OPs the main Argentine force, a group of about 100 Marines and the crew of the submarine Santa Fé, was stationed at Grytviken.

On April 25 a helicopter pilot returning to HMS Antrim reported the submarine leaving port and on the surface. Immediately it was attacked by helicopters from HMS Endurance and the frigate HMS Brilliant, using depth charges. The submarine was badly damaged and only just managed to limp back to Grytviken, its of several ships gave rise to some concern. To help balance the odds, the SAS were ordered to attack an Argentinian airfield known as Pebble Island on West Falkland. Previous reconnaissance had established that the Argentinians controlled the airstrip and that a number of ground-attack aircraft were based there. British commanders considered these aircraft a major threat to the main troop landings at San Carlos Water. The SAS were given their orders: to destroy all the aircraft and to kill the ground crew and supporting garrison on the island. The SAS forces were assisted in their task by HMS Hermes, Broadsword and also Glamorgan, which was to supply on-shore bombardment.

On the night of May 14, 1982, the helicopters, carrying 45 members of D Squadron, landed about 6km from the airstrip. The plan was that once the mortars and LAW rockets had been unloaded from the

appearance alerting the alarmed Argentines to the fact that British forces were not very far away and on the offensive. In fact, British forces were closer than they imagined: taking advantage of the enemy's confusion, a joint force made up of SAS, SBS and Royal Marines was about to assault the base. They were inserted by helicopter 3km away and slowly made their advance towards the port. When they reached the top of Brown Mountain, they looked down to see white flags being flown from every building. Despite the order to stop and hold their ground, elements of the SAS continued forward while the others covered from Brown Mountain. Cedric Delves, the SAS commander, arrived in the Argentinian position (having walked through a minefield) only to be greeted with a flurry of white flags. The Argentines had surrendered and the assault force had not fired a shot. 'Lofty' Gallagher walked into the base at last light. Around his waist was a Union Jack which he had carried all the way from England. In the time-honoured tradition, the flag was immediately raised by Lofty, giving the British forces their first victory of the Falklands War. By the next morning, a small detachment at the old whaling station of Leith had also surrendered. South Georgia was back in British hands. Tragically, 'Lofty' Gallagher was killed, along with many others, in a helicopter accident during a cross-decking operation towards the end of the Falklands War.

While the British fleet was a formidable force, the loss

*The SAS established themselves on the Falklands weeks before the main Task Force arrived. They suffered the weather and remained hidden from the Argentinian army while constantly sending back information on troop dispositions.*

helicopters, Mountain Troop would mount the main assault on the aircraft, while the other two troops were to form a reserve.

The attack on the airfield opened with a heavy bombardment from HMS Glamorgan, followed by the SAS using 81mm mortars, M203 grenade launchers, 66mm LAWs and small-arms. With the Argentinians forced to take cover, the SAS moved on to the airstrip and fixed explosive charges to the aircraft. The actual assault on the airfield was led by Captain John Hamilton, and destroyed in all six Pucaras, four Turbo-Mentors and a Skyvan transport, before withdrawing again. The Argentinians were caught completely unprepared and,

though they desperately returned fire, most of it missed. The only SAS injuries suffered were slight; in fact, the worst were caused by an exploding mine. It was reported that one Argentinian was killed in the firefight.

Aboard Hermes, the mission was hailed as a success. The aircraft had been destroyed, along with a great amount of enemy ammunition, and the Argentinians were now denied the use of the airstrip. The SAS returned to the pick-up-point, from which they were exfiltrated by helicopter and returned to the fleet.

With confidence running high, it seemed as if the war would not last much longer. Then, on May 19, just five days after the raid on Pebble Island, the Regiment

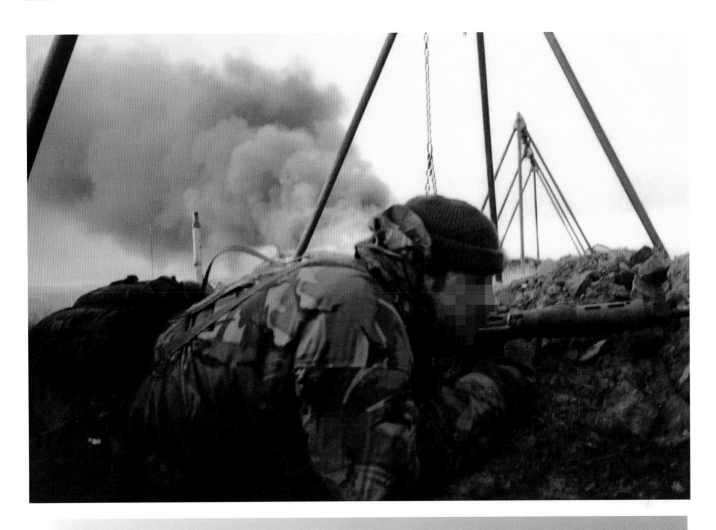

*A member of the SAS hugs the earth in the playground. The fire in the background is one of the town houses set on fire by mortar shells. The Argentinians were only a few metres in front of where the SAS man is crouching.*

suffered a tragic blow when a Sea King helicopter carrying a large group of SAS troops crashed. The helicopter had been cross-decking (moving troops from one ship to another) from HMS Hermes to HMS Intrepid when a bird strike caused the engine to fail. The helicopter plunged into the icy sea, killing 22 men. It was the heaviest lost the Regiment had suffered since the Second World War. Almost the entire senior ranks structure of G Squadron had been wiped out.

Undaunted by their loss, the SAS continued their aggressive actions, and at the end of May, D Squadron seized Mount Kent, some 40 miles behind enemy lines. Despite being heavily outnumbered, they held it until

relieved by Marines of 42 Commando. Although the war was drawing to an end, the SAS did not drop their guard, conscious that the Argentinians were still a formidable force.

On June 10, the SAS suffered another loss; this time, it was Captain Hamilton. He had taken out a patrol to recce Port Howard, on West Falkland. As they approached, they were spotted by the enemy, who engaged them in a firefight. Heavily outnumbered, the four SAS men tried desperately to fight their way out. Two managed to withdrew, while Hamilton and his signaller gave covering fire. Hamilton was hit, but continued to provide supporting fire. Some time later, the overwhelming force

*In order to stop any further loss to shipping during the Falklands War, a plan was put into operation that would destroy any remaining Exocet missiles held by the Argentinians. The plan was to land a squadron of SAS on the airfield at Rio Gallegos, in southern Argentina. The SAS were to destroy as many Super Etendard aircraft and Exocet missiles as they could find and then bug out. The mission was aborted in mid-air.*

of Argentinians killed Captain Hamilton and captured his signaller. His actions had allowed at least two of his men sufficient time to escape. Captain John Hamilton was awarded a posthumous Military Cross.

The last major SAS raid was mounted in East Falkland on the night of June 14. This involved an attack on the Argentinian rear while 2 Para assaulted Wireless Ridge, just a few miles west of Port Stanley. A total of 60 men from D and G Squadrons, plus six men from the SBS, used Rigid Raiders to assault Port Stanley harbour. They

succeeded in setting fire to the oil storage tanks and laying down heavy suppressive fire. The Argentinians retaliated with overwhelming force and the raiders were forced to retreat. One of the Rigid Raiders took more that 30 bullet-holes, but it refused to sink and managed to limp safely back to the mother ship. After a bitter battle, 2 Para finally took Wireless Ridge.

In the final stages of the war Lieutenant-Colonel Rose, along with a Spanish-speaking interpreter, used psychological warfare methods to persuade the

Argentinians of the hopelessness of their cause. Consequently, on June 14, Rose flew into Port Stanley by helicopter to commence talks with the Argentinians. It was after this meeting that Rose, together with Brigadier de la Billière, accepted the Argentinian surrender, thus ending the war. As a mark of the man, there is very strong rumour that Rose offered the Argentinian commander, Major General Mario Menendez, a Harrier fire-power demonstration as the Argentinian troops massed around Stanley. The same rumour also claims that he walked out of the building taking with him a prized statue of a horse which had reputedly been given to Menendez by a grateful government for his capture of the Falklands. But these were only rumours.

In May 1982, the discovery of a crashed Sea King helicopter near the Chilean port of Punta Arenas caused much speculation. Many versions of the story abound, but the one most commonly accepted is that the Sea King was taking a small reconnaissance party of SAS men to a point 40km from Rio Gallegos, an airfield in southern Argentina close to the border with Chile. The airfield was rumoured to be the main base for the Super Etendard aircraft which, with their Exocet missiles, were doing so much damage to ships of the British task force. Despite rumours that the helicopter crash-landed in bad weather, leaving the crew having to find their way to the nearest British Embassy in Chile, it is known that an SAS demolitionist placed a bomb under the fuselage to destroy the helicopter. Meanwhile, back on Ascension Island, two C130 Hercules transports were loaded with SAS troops from the recently-arrived B Squadron. Although never confirmed, it is said that they were equipped and prepared to assault the Argentinian airfield at Rio Gallegos – a one-way mission for which those SAS men on the helicopter had been the reconnaissance team. Political intervention by the Americans, who feared the direct intrusion into Argentina would only serve to escalate the war, finally called a halt to the raid and the aircraft returned to Ascension. The remains of the Sea King were discovered and the news flashed around the world. Fearing that surprise had now been lost, further such missions were aborted. The SAS advance party slipped quietly out of Argentina and a few days later had rejoined the task force. Had the raid been allowed to continue, the lives and equipment lost aboard the Atlantic Conveyor, hit by an Exocet a few days later, might well have been saved.

[Note: It is fact that an SAS demolitions man destroyed the Sea King helicopter, using a bar mine. It is also fact that almost a complete Squadron of SAS did board a C130 aircraft of 47 Squadron and take off from Ascension Island. It is also fact that the American President, Ronald Reagan, did not want Chile entering the war and risk causing a major conflict in South America.]

## Disaster on Everest

With the Falklands behind them, the men of the Regiment settled down to a more peaceful routine. In 1984 both 'Brummie' Stokes and 'Bronco' Lane made a second attempt on Everest, this time leading an all-SAS team consisting of soldiers from the Regiment's various Mountain Troops. The expedition was well planned, and by April 2 the front runners were already at 22,800 feet.

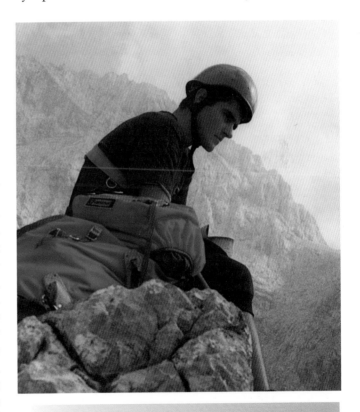

*Sergeant Andy Baxter, he was badly injured during an avalanche as the SAS made a second assault on Mount Everest. Andy died in August 1985.*

*This picture shows the SAS waiting in ambush. If necessary the soldiers could patiently wait for weeks at a time.*

Then disaster struck. A little after dawn on the morning of April 3 a huge avalanche, initiated by falling ice, swept down the mountain, heading directly for the base camp. It completely ravaged the camp, propelling it and the men down the mountainside. Corporal Swierzy was killed and several others lay badly injured, the worst being Sergeant Andy Baxter. He was returned to Hereford, but died of a brain tumour on August 12, 1985.

# The Brighton Bomb, 1984

By the mid-1980s, the IRA were becoming more audacious, and while most of their activities had taken place in Northern Ireland, they also brought violence to mainland Britain and the Continent. In October 1984, the IRA made a serious attempt to wipe out the entire British Cabinet at the Tory party's annual conference in Brighton.

The Prime Minister, 13 of her 20-member Cabinet and many of her senior advisers were staying at Brighton's venerable Grand Hotel, a 120-year-old Regency-style building on the seafront. In the early hours of October 12, many of the Party faithful were still awake, looking forward to Mrs Thatcher's address crowning the four-day gathering. She, too, was still up, having just put the finishing touches to her speech when at 02:54 the night's silence was shattered by a thundering explosion. Four floors above the cluster of suites occupied by the Prime Minister and her colleagues a powerful bomb had detonated, blowing out a section of the nine-storey building's façade 30 feet deep and 15 wide, and spraying broken glass and chunks of concrete through the halls and on to the street.

The gap extended from the roof to the fifth storey. Tons of plaster, flooring and furniture crashed from floor to floor, finally tearing through the Grand's elegant foyer where Tory leaders had gathered only hours earlier. Thatcher's suite, located only 30 feet below the source of the blast, was badly damaged; its bathroom was totally demolished. Miraculously, the Prime Minister was unhurt. "This conference will go on as usual," she declared firmly as she emerged from the wreckage, accompanied by her husband Denis. Thatcher was fully dressed, her face flushed with anger. "We were very lucky," she said, putting on a brave face. Inwardly, the Iron Lady was furious.

Others were not so fortunate. Four were killed, and at least 34 were injured. Among the dead were Sir Anthony Berry, a former Tory deputy chief whip; Eric Taylor, chairman of the Northwest Area Conservative Association; and Mrs John Wakeham, wife of the Chief Whip. Wakeham himself was injured, as were Alfred Parsons, the Australian High Commissioner to Britain, and Norman Tebbit, Thatcher's Trade and Industry Secretary. Wakeham lay buried for nearly seven hours before being rescued. Tebbit, who subsequently underwent exploratory surgery to determine the extent of his severe chest injuries, spent four hours under the rubble.

Some nine hours after the blast, the Irish Republican Army claimed responsibility. In a telephone call to the Irish state radio in Dublin, the group asserted that it had set off a gelignite bomb in an attempt to kill "the British Cabinet and the Tory warmongers." The IRA promised more violence in the future. "Thatcher will now realize", it said, "that Britain cannot occupy our country, torture our prisoners and shoot our people in their own streets and get away with it. Today we were unlucky. But remember; we have only to be lucky once. You will have to be lucky always." It was the boldest and most outrageous strike ever against public officials in Britain. The IRA had, in effect, tried to destroy the entire British Government.

The scene in the hours immediately following the Brighton blast was one of devastation. As Thatcher and her husband were taken to the safety of a police station the residents of a nearby hotel, including Charles H. Price II, the US Ambassador to Britain, were evacuated for fear of a second attack. Working with the help of television lights, and from time to time calling for quiet so they could hear cries for help, rescue workers used

axes to chop through the debris and brought in a crane to reach those trapped on high floors. Shocked delegates wandered along Brighton's seafront promenade in their nightclothes, while dishevelled Cabinet ministers worried about losing government papers. Lord Gowrie, Minister for the Arts, dragged canvas deckchairs from the beach for use as makeshift stretchers. Education Secretary Sir Keith Joseph, in pyjamas and silk robe, sat on his dispatch case by the shore.

Thatcher had a narrow escape. A Special Branch officer on the security detail in her hotel said she had left her bathroom two minutes before it was destroyed by the blast. Tory Party Chairman John Selwyn Gummer also had a close call. "I was just outside Prime Minister Thatcher's suite when I was thrown backward by the force of the explosion," he recalled. 'The Prime Minister came through the door and the first thing she said was. 'Is there anything I can do to help?' She was totally calm and looked very angry."

The SAS responded with a whole range of operations, requiring a full Squadron to be retained in the Province. The cost was high. On December 2, 1984, the SAS mounted an operation against the IRA in Fermanagh. Technical intelligence had indicated that several beer kegs containing 1,000 lbs of home-made explosive would be placed in a drainage culvert on a road leading to a local restaurant. The IRA was being continually monitored by the SAS who, due to the bomb misfiring, overheard a conversation between the bombers. When the SAS went to investigate a van parked nearby, they were confronted by an IRA member called Tony MacBride. As the SAS started to question MacBride, other members of the IRA opened fire from a nearby ditch, fatally wounding Al Slater. In the ensuing firefight MacBride was also killed and another IRA member, Kieran Fleming, drowned as he tried to escape by swimming the River Bannagh, which at the time was in flood. The police later arrested two more IRA members at a checkpoint as they tried to cross into the south. Slater had joined the SAS three years earlier, having served with the Parachute Regiment. He was posted to B Squadron's Air Troop where he was know as 'Mr Angry' for his impression of a comic character on Radio 1.

A classic SAS operation took place in Loughall on Friday, May 8, 1987. Intelligence had been received indicating that the police station at Loughall was to be attacked by the method used the year before in County

*The SAS waited in ambush when the IRA planned to bomb the police station in Loughall. All eight members of the IRA were killed during the action.*

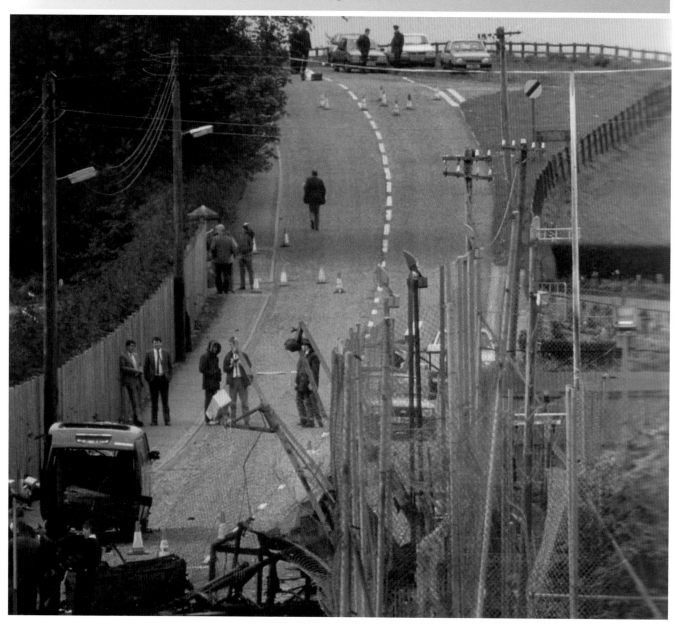

Armagh. In that incident, in April 1986, a stolen mechanical digger had been packed with explosives and driven into the RUC station at the Birches, causing extensive damage. A report that another JCB had been stolen in East Tyrone gave rise to the suspicion that an identical IRA operation was being planned. Every effort was made to locate the digger and identify the target.

After intensive covert searching, the weapons and explosives were located. Subsequently, the digger was also found, in a derelict building on a farm some 15km away. Surveillance by E4A provided more information, and eventually the target was identified as the RUC station at Loughall. This station was only manned part-time and consisted of one principal building running parallel to the main road, surrounded by a high wire fence. The time and date of the attack were eventually confirmed through a Special Branch telephone tap.

Two of the IRA activists were named as Patrick Kelly and Jim Lynagh, who commanded the East Tyrone active service unit. When masked men stole a Toyota van from Dungannon, Jim Lynagh was spotted in the town, suggesting that the van was to be used in the Loughall attack. Not long afterwards, the OP reported that the JCB was being moved from the derelict farm. At this stage the SAS, who had been reinforced from Hereford, took up their ambush positions. It was reported that some were in the police station itself, but this was not true – most of the main ambush party was hiding in a row of small fir trees which lined the fence on the opposite side to the station. Several heavily-armed stops were also in position, covering all avenues of escape.

At a little past 19:00, the blue Toyota van drove down the road in front of the police station. Several people could be seen inside. A short time later, it returned from the direction of Portadown, this time followed by the JCB carrying three hooded IRA terrorists in the cab. Declan Arthurs was driving, with Michael Gormley and Gerald O'Callaghan riding shotgun. The bucket was filled with explosive contained in an oil drum, which had been partly concealed with rubble. As the blue van charged past the station, the JCB slammed through the gate. One of the two terrorists riding shotgun – although at the time it was not clear which one – ignited the bomb and all three made a run for it. Back at the van, several hooded men jumped clear and opened fire in the direction of the RUC station. At this point, the SAS ambush was activated.

The sudden hail of SAS fire was terrifying. All eight members of the IRA fell under the hail of bullets. At the height of the firefight the bomb exploded, taking with it half the RUC station and scattering debris over all concerned. As the dust settled, the SAS closed in on the bodies. At that moment a white car entered the ambush area, its two occupants dressed in blue boiler suits similar to those worn by the IRA. They were unfortunately mistaken for terrorists, especially when, on seeing the ambush in progress, they stopped and started to reverse. One of the SAS stops opened fire, killing one of the occupants and wounding the other. It later transpired that the dead motorist, Antony Hughes,

had nothing to do with the IRA. Several other vehicles and pedestrians soon appeared on the scene, but by this time the situation was stabilized.

Loughall was one of the most successful operations ever mounted against the IRA, who were totally stunned by the loss of two complete active service cells. The Hughes family were compensated for their loss, and with no public inquest the matter was closed. The IRA, believing that there was a mole in their organization, went into a period of self-assessment, but they did not lick their wounds for long. Shortly after, on Remembrance Day, at a ceremony in Enniskillen, the IRA detonated a massive bomb. Eleven people were killed and more than 60 injured.

## Prison Assault

The same year saw the SAS involved in a rather strange operation on home territory. On September 27, 1987, a siege erupted in D Block of Peterhead Prison in Scotland. The block held some 48 prisoners, most of whom were serving long sentences for murder and rape. The majority of the prisoners gave themselves up after a short while but a hard core of five men, holding a prison officer hostage, refused to surrender. For the following week the rioters paraded on the rooftop, in full view of the world's media. Grampian Police responded with a specialist response team and, in addition, the Government ordered two SAS advisors to assist. A quick assessment of the situation indicated that the task would be better dealt with by an SAS team, who were well-versed in such assault tactics.

The Government finally gave its consent for the SAS assault on the morning of October 3. At around 04:00 a four-man team, armed with batons instead of submachine-guns, made their way from a skylight across a slippery roof to a hole which had been made previously by the rioters. They threw both stun grenades and CS gas through the hole before dropping in themselves to confront the prisoners. At the same time, back-up teams made an explosive entry through the lower-floor walls and proceeded to follow up the roof assault. The hostage was the first to be removed, too weak to help himself. The assault team hauled him through the roof hole and carried him back to the skylight, where he was lowered to safety. The prisoners were overwhelmed by CS gas and the black-clad figures bellowing commands to 'Move,' marshalled them back into captivity. The SAS assault team departed from Scotland less than two hours after their arrival, having successfully completed their mission.

Because of the Peterhead Prison riot, the Government set up a specialist team to deal with such incidents; these officers were initially trained in Hereford.

## 21 SAS Suffer

Around this time the unfortunate death of Andy Skrzypkowiak was announced in the national newspapers. Skrzypkowiak had been a cameraman, and part of a British film crew covering the war in Afghanistan – Skrzypkowiak was also a member of 21 SAS.

His death was due to a tribal dispute between two Afghan factions which were both fighting the Russians. The film crew was covering one group, irregulars commanded by Ahman Shah Massoud, as they attacked a Russian fuel convey on the Salang Pass. The rival party, Hezb-i-Islami (Party of God) was intent on capturing any Western journalists covering the Massoud raid.

Andy Skrzypkowiak was not the first SAS soldier to find himself in Afghanistan. It it rumoured that a small unit was infiltrated into the country in March 1981, its mission to extract samples of the titanium alloy the Russian were using for armour on their new helicopters. Although this was a CIA operation, ex-SAS soldiers were used to carry it out.

## Gibraltar: Death on the Rock

In Northern Ireland, the continuing war against the IRA had been relentless. When the opportunity arose, the SAS would hit hard. Most of these operations ended in the same way; a quick shoot-out, resulting in several dead terrorists. As well as operating against the IRA in Northern Ireland, the SAS could be called upon to work in mainland Britain, as well as overseas. Consequently, when in March 1988 information filtered through the security screen that a bomb was to be exploded in Gibraltar, the SAS was put on stand-by.

The IRA team consisted of three people: Sean Savage, Daniel McCann and a woman, Maraid Farrell. Each had a history of terrorist activity. The three, later acknowledged by the IRA as an active cell, had been spotted by British security services and trailed for months, and many conversations between the three had been recorded. This surveillance identified the target – the British garrison in Gibraltar – and the method of attack – a car bomb. As events became focused, the target was pinpointed as a ceremony at which several military bands would be parading. It was also known that the IRA had developed a new type of remote-control device which could detonate a car bomb from a distance.

In late 1987 Savage, a well-known IRA bomb-maker, had been located in Spain. With him was McCann, another IRA suspect. MI5 spent the next six months watching the two, gathering vital information which they were certain was leading to a bombing. When, on March 4, 1988, Farrell arrived at Malaga airport and was met by the two men, it seem likely that the bombing was on. At this stage the SAS was invited to send in a team (the SAS and the security services have had a good working relationship since the mid-1970s). The Gibraltar police were informed of the operation, and instructed that the IRA active service unit was to be apprehended. For a while, contact with the IRA cell was lost, but by this time the target had been defined. It was suspected that one car would be delivered on to the Rock and parked in a position along the route to be taken by the parade. This car would be clean, a dummy to guarantee a parking space for the real car bomb. It was suggested that the spot where the most damage would be caused was a plaza where the troops and public would assemble: this proved to be correct. At 14:00 on the afternoon of March 5, a report was received that Savage had been spotted in a parked white Renault 5. It was suspected that he was setting up the bomb triggering device. Not long after, another report was received to the effect that Farrell and McCann had crossed the border from Spain and were making their way into town.

The SAS men were immediately deployed, and once Savage was out of the way an explosives expert did a walk-past of the Renault. No tell-tale signs were observed indicating the presence of a bomb, such as the rear suspension being depressed: however, if they were using Semtex, 30lbs or more could be easily concealed. After consultation, it was considered probable that the car did contain a bomb.

At this stage the local police chief, Joseph Canepa, signed an order passing control to the SAS. Operation Favius, as it was know, was about to be concluded. The orders given to the SAS men were to capture the three bombers if possible but, as in all such situations, if lives are directly threatened – those of the SAS or anyone else – they have the right to shoot. It was stressed that the bomb would more than likely be fired on a push-button detonator.

The SAS men, dressed in casual clothes, kept in contact through small radios hidden about their persons. Each soldier was also armed with a 9mm Browning Hi-Power pistol. Savage met up with McCann and Farrell, and after a short discussion all three made their way back towards the Spanish border. Four of the SAS team shadowed the trio. Suddenly, for some unexplained reason, Savage turned around and started to make his way back into town. Accordingly, the SAS team split, two with Savage, two staying on McCann and Farrell.

A few moments later, fate took a hand. A local policeman, driving in heavy traffic, was recalled to the station. It was said later that his car was required; whatever the reason, to expedite his orders he activated his siren. This action happened close to McCann and Farrell, making the pair turn nervously. McCann made eye contact with one of the SAS soldiers, who was no more than 10 metres away. In response to this, the soldier – who was about to issue a challenge – opened fire. He later gave evidence that McCann's arm had moved distinctly across his body, and he feared he might be about to detonate the bomb. McCann was hit in the back and went down. Farrell, it is said, made a movement for her bag; she was shot with a single round. By this time the second soldier had also drawn his pistol and opened fire, hitting both terrorists. On hearing the shots, Savage turned, to be confronted by the other two SAS men. His hand moved to his pocket: this time a warning was shouted, but Savage's hand continued to reach into his pocket. Both SAS men fired and Savage was killed.

As the first news of the event hit the media, it looked like a professional job, but the euphoria was short-lived. No bomb was found in the car, and all three terrorists were found to be unarmed. Although a bomb was later discovered in Malaga, the press and the IRA had a field day. Allegations were made and witnesses were found who claimed to have seen the whole thing. The trio had surrendered; their arms had been in the air; they had been shot at point-blank range while they lay on the ground, and so on. Once again, the SAS were held up as killers: no matter that they had probably saved the lives of many people, and dispatched three well-known IRA terrorists. They would stand trial.

In September 1988, after a two-week inquest and by a majority of nine to two, a verdict was passed of lawful killing. Although this satisfied most people, the story did not end there. The SAS soldiers who took part in the shooting in Gibraltar were taken to court by relatives of the three IRA members killed. The European Commission of Human Rights in Strasbourg decided by 11 votes to six that the SAS did not use unnecessary force, ruling that the soldiers were justified in opening fire as the IRA members were about to detonate a bomb. However, they did refer the case to the European Court of Human Rights. Because of this court case, the British Government was forced to pay compensation.

In 1988, the SAS anti-terrorist team were sent to Cyprus where they prepared for an assault on a Boeing 737 aircraft. The commercial aircraft would be flying from Lebanon into Libya. Intelligence suggested that two British lecturers who had previously been kidnapped were aboard the aircraft. In the course of its flight, fighter aircraft stationed at a British RAF base in Cyprus would be scrambled. The fighters were to force the aircraft to land so that the SAS anti-terrorist team could assault it. In the event, the aircraft never flew, and after three weeks the plan was called off and the SAS returned to Hereford.

In 1989 Major Dare Newell died aged 71. He was a veteran member of the SOE in World War Two and Force 136 in Malaya in 1945. With his fighting and jungle experience, he was a welcome addition to the Malayan Scouts in the 1950s, where he assisted Mike Calvert in bringing a new professionalism to the force. He went on to become the Regimental Adjutant of the SAS and Secretary of the SAS Regimental Association, and was awarded the OBE for his services. Above all, Dare Newell is best remembered for his unswerving defence against those who would politically attack the SAS and frequently fought the Regiment's corner against its enemies in Whitehall.

# Chapter 4

# Oman to Northern Ireland

*The IRA in Belfast. This picture was staged for the press.*

The arrival of 1970 saw little or no change to the inactivity the Regiment had endured in the late 1960s. The period of relative peace which had reigned since the end of the troubles in Aden (1964–67) had not benefited the Regiment much. Despite the extensive training activities embarked upon by the SAS squadrons, many of the younger members had started to leave, tempted to become highly-paid bodyguards or by more active security jobs. Around this time, Colonel Johnny Watts took command of the Regiment and struggled to locate employment for his men. He found it in Oman. It was also a war the SAS desperately needed. Unfortunately, the minor exodus of personnel had by now taken many of the best NCOs, although some of them did return once the Oman War was under way.

The war in Oman (1970–76) stands out as the classic SAS operation. It was tailor-made to test the basic regimental skills which set the SAS apart from the rest. Both militarily and politically, the war had far-reaching effects on the whole of the Middle East. Moreover, the success of the SAS and the Sultan of Oman's forces helped stabilize the attitude of many neighbouring countries, pushing back the tide of communism which had threatened to engulf the rich oilfields on which the West depends. It offered a challenge which the Regiment eagerly accepted, and turned out to be a classic counter-insurgency campaign of modern times.

The size of the Omani conflict was small, yet it combined all the elements of modern warfare. Navy, air force and army were all combined with one goal: to win. It cannot be said that the SAS won this war on its own, for much of the fighting was done by the Sultan of Oman's own forces. However, one thing the SAS did undeniably do was to bond together the *firqats*, the Dhofari irregulars. These *firqats* and the SAS went on to become the lead elements in most battles in the early days. It was the trust between Dhofaris and the SAS which won the Dhofar war.

The SAS had served in Oman before, during the Jebel Akhdar campaign (1958-59), and now it was back. In the 1970s the war took place in the south, on a huge mountain massif known as the Jebel Dhofar (the repressive regime of Sultan Said bin Taimur had goaded the Dhofaris into rebellion). It was a strange refuge for wild tribes and 'freedom fighters'. In summer it is a place of great beauty, where lush green grass blows in the cooling winds and trees give homes to birds and other small animals. The problem was the People's Front for the Liberation of the Occupied Arabian Gulf (PFLOAG), known to the men of the SAS as *adoo* (Arabic for 'enemy'), which occupied most of the Dhofar region with the exception of the coastal towns of Salalah, Taqa and Mirbat. The rebels roamed free over the Jebel Dhofar, eating further into the beleaguered areas around Salalah. The base used by the Royal Air Force just north of Salalah was itself virtually under siege, and without outside intervention the Sultan's small defence force was on the way to defeat.

Although not a military man, the old Sultan had decided to send his only son Qaboos to the Royal Military Academy at Sandhurst, where he was commissioned into a British regiment. His stay in England was far from wasted, for with personal skill and the encouragement of his friends he had observed the workings of various councils and committees, and in general had familiarized himself with the intricacies of a modern state. His return home had not been a joyous one, though; the young Sultan could see the plight of his country and argued for change. His father's answer had been to further restrict his son's movements and accuse him of becoming a 'Westerner'. However, the young Qaboos bided his time. His chance came on July 23, 1970, when a palace coup took place. Aided by the young Sheikh Baraik Bin Hamood, Qaboos deposed his father in a bloodless take-over. Within weeks, men of the SAS had been sent to Oman to provide the new ruler with advice and assistance.

For some time Colonel 'Johnny' Watts, the commander of 22 SAS, and his second-in-command, Major Peter de la Billière, had been making preparations behind the scenes, and several secret reconnaissances had been undertaken by men of the Regiment. For the average SAS soldier, who was getting on with yet more training, the Oman War came as a bit of a shock, but was a welcome break from base routine. For the SAS, the first action started in the northern Oman peninsula, at the very entrance to the Straits of Hormuz. British intelligence had warned of a large arms shipment due to arrive at a small village on the Omani peninsula; this was to be accompanied by a group of Iraqis.

Barry Davies, a long-serving member of the SAS, recalls the event.

"I was walking across the square from the direction of the 'Kremlin' (the SAS Operations, Planning and Intelligence cell at Hereford) when a voice called out to me, and I turned to see a colleague running in my direction. Like me, he was dressed in a suit, as many of us were due to attend the marriage of a Squadron member in a few hours' time. 'Get your kit; we're going.' He didn't stop, but ran on past.

"'Where to?' I shouted at his receding back.

"Middle East" was all I heard before I, too, broke into a run, heading directly for the accommodation basha (a Malaysian word for a jungle home, used by the SAS to describe any form of shelter). There were a few guys still getting dressed for the wedding, but the bulk had already left for a few beers before the ceremony started. The sudden appearance of the squadron commander soon made me realize that this was not a drill. Quickly, he informed those present of the latest situation. It would seem that some Intelligence guy who had been lying low in a village off the Musandan Peninsula had picked up information on a huge arms shipment due to arrive at the tiny coastal village of Jumla. This arms shipment was to be accompanied by a group of Iraqis with communist persuasions. According to British Intelligence, this was translated

On 23 July 1970, Sultan Qaboos deposed his father in a bloodless coup at the Royal palace in Salalah. Within weeks, men of the SAS were sent to Oman to provide the new ruler with advice and assistance.

as the main communist head-shed moving into the area to take advantage of the turmoil within Oman. However, the SAS was going to snatch them and nip the whole thing in the bud.

"A few hours later, with most of the squadron still dressed in suits, we made our way to RAF Brize Norton. A day later, after a short stop in Cyprus, we landed at the British airbase in Sharjah. Without leaving the confines of the airport, we loaded our bergens and weapons on to several three-ton trucks and were driven out into the desert. To all intents and purposes this was done for security; in reality, the whole squadron was dumped in the middle of nowhere – yes, still dressed in our suits! Like all good SAS men, we dived into our bergens and changed into combat gear. A few of us then used the spartan scrub to put up some bashas for shelter before making the inevitable brew of tea. We waited.

"Later that evening, several choppers came in and we were ferried over to a campsite on the eastern coast. This was done for several reasons. First, the area was similar to the one we would attack, although it was minus a village. Second, a Royal Navy minesweeper, complete with several Rigid Raiders manned by the SBS, was due to arrive off our coastal campsite.

"The plan called for the SAS to be inserted by the SBS on to the small beaches both north and south of Jumla. This would be done during the hours of darkness and would allow enough time for us to scale the high, rocky peaks which towered out of the sea and surrounded the entire village. By dawn, with the SAS in place to stop any enemy running away, a combined force from local Arab states would assault the village and capture both the Iraqis and the equipment. On the surface, a sound plan: not only would it protect the Straits of Hormuz, through which half the world's oil passes, but it would stop a major catastrophe in the area. But the reality was rather different.

"The night before we left our training area to board the minesweeper, a priority signal arrived. By the light of our camp fire, Major Alastair Morrison read it to us. We listened with dread to his solemn words. It would seem that the Intelligence guy, whom we assumed was still in the village and still passing back vital information, had seen a ship docking at the small village port. He reported that heavy machine guns and mortars had been unloaded, together with several large boxes of mines. It was suspected that the enemy had received wind of our

*An SAS soldier in freefall. Dress and equipment is similar to that used for every freefall operation undertaken by the SAS.*

assault and planned to oppose it. The final words of the message were chilling: 'Expect to take up to 50 per cent casualties.' Silence fell on the not-so-happy group. Why do they have to tell you things like that the night before a mission?

"As if being blown to smithereens on the beach wasn't enough, the whole plan was delayed for 24 hours, but only after we had put to sea. The reason was bad weather. When the time came to leave the minesweeper and load our sea-sick bodies into the Rigid Raiders, I would have happily taken on the enemy single-handed rather than stay a second longer on that ship. However, as we approached the beach in pitch darkness all thoughts of sea sickness diminished, and I concentrated on looking through the night scope. There was nothing to see other than a few faint lights coming from the village. We hit the beach at full speed and I was actually thrown from the Raider in what looked like a spectacular, head-long dive. Somehow, I landed with a perfect para-roll and came up on my feet. Several of the

guys said the dive looked real gung-ho (I wanted to kill the stupid SBS boat handler!)

"Instantly we started to climb. It was steep and hard going, but Mountain Troop led the way, choosing the easiest route. An hour before dawn we were in position, looking over the village to the open sea beyond, our only casualty a broken finger. I should mention at this stage that some bright spark had come up with the idea of giving every SAS man at least six *shemaghs* (Arab headdresses) of various colours and design. The thinking behind this was simple. The assaulting Arab force was made up of several different local forces, all with a different-coloured *shemagh*. To avoid any possibility that we might be mistaken for the enemy, as the different units approached our positions we were to change headdress to comply with theirs. In reality, 40 SAS soldiers were all converted into Tommy Cooper look-alikes, as we frequently dived into our bergens looking for the correct *shemagh*.

"The light rapidly improved and suddenly, about a

mile out to sea, we spotted the landing force. It was heading at top speed for the beach. I have to say that from our position, high above the village, it looked impressive. The landing craft hit the beach and several shots rang out. This is it – here we go. Then slowly the villagers started coming out of their homes to greet the soldiers (visitors were rare in this remote area); tea and coffee were distributed and everything seemed very amiable. Then one of the white officers got tough: 'OK. Where are the Iraqi rebels? We know they're here in Jumla.'

'If they're in Jumla, why are you here in Gumla?' came the surprised reply. Yes, we'd invaded the wrong village! All that hype and planning gone to pot. There were no more than half a dozen villages along this hostile coastline, but Intelligence had picked the wrong one. By the time the head-shed had confirmed the fact, and sent us racing across the mountain-top, it was far too late. The rebels had long gone, and so had most of their equipment.

"We were all pulled back to the British base at Sharjah, where we sat around while a new plan was hatched. Apparently, according to intelligence, the enemy had taken refuge in a stronghold called the Wadi Rawdah. Even my best effort at explaining to anyone what that place looked like would not do it justice. It was a mighty bowl within the *jebel* structure. The sheer rocky walls towered up to 305m (1,000ft) even at the lowest point. On the seaward side there occurred a natural, narrow split in the rock structure, which allowed for entry and exit. The whole valley was the lost haven to a strange tribe called the Bani Shihoo. Reportedly a vicious people who had rarely seen a white man, their main weapon, apart from the odd rifle, was a vicious-looking axe. Like most rumours, it was false: they turned out to be a friendly bunch.

"The operation restarted with a parachute night drop carried out by two freefall troops. I think I'm right in saying it was to be the first operational freefall drop the SAS Regiment had ever undertaken. The rest of us would go in by chopper as soon as the boys had secured a landing position. I had time to go to the local base NAAFI for a drink, but just before I left I gave Paul 'Rip' Reddy, one of the freefallers, a hand with his kit. He was fairly new to the Squadron, but was a great guy with a real sense of humour. He joked about the amount of kit he was carrying on the drop.

"The aircraft took off around 03:00, and an hour later the men jumped from a height of 3,350m (11,000ft). 'Rip' Reddy was killed. Of all the deaths in the Regiment, this one stunned me. To this day, I can recall wishing him luck before I went off for a beer. He was so young, fit and full of life, but that would sum up most men who have died in the SAS.

"Before the news broke, the rest of the squadron had been trucked to a campsite closer to the wadi. Most of us were still sleeping when the Boss (Captain Morrison) came running round, shaking us awake and telling us to grab our kit and get on the chopper. He never said that 'Rip' was dead, but the speed of our move said something was up. This was also the first time I had seen a loadmaster sitting in the door of a chopper manning a fixed GPMG.

"Arriving from the air, the sight of the Wadi Rawdah takes your breath away. But we had more pressing things on our minds than taking in the spectacular view. As the chopper touched down we all jumped clear, fanning out in a defensive arc. That's when I saw two of Freefall Troop bring a body bag forward and place it on the chopper. As we started to relax, one of the guys told us what had happened. The drop had gone well, but the valley floor was dark and they had used beacon lights and SARBEs (Surface-to-air Rescue Beacons) to locate each other. Once they were all on the ground, it became apparent that 'Rip' Reddy was missing and a search was organized. They found him half-way up a gravel slope. His parachute had operated a fraction too late. This was established from the fact that his chute was fully deployed and he had been in the upright position on contact with the ground.

"We stayed in the area for about two months, using Sharjah as a base. I was pulled off to do psychological operations, an interesting task which gave me a good insight into the northern part of Oman. One of my tasks was to visit the small towns and villages prior to the arrival of the new Sultan. I would dispense a radio to most adults (a new Omani broadcasting service was being set up) and give T-shirts and flags to the kids. One of my visits took me back to the Wadi Rhawdah, where I came face to face with the Bani Shihoo. They were a strange community. They built small houses out of rocks which had been fashioned into uniform blocks, and

*The village of Taqa, southern Oman. The middle house on the right was home to the SAS team which controlled this area. The tree in the middle was the market place where slaves had been sold just a few years prior to the arrival of the British.*

enemy artillery fire to locate the guns), and this ensured that the *adoo* could not bring their heavy weapons in too close. The more distant towns of Taqa and Mirbat, which were manned by the SAS, were open to the full brunt of the *adoo*. In the days before the war was taken on to the Jebel Dhofar, these locations came under constant attack: hardly a night would go by without Taqa or Mirbat coming under fire.

Life for the SAS training teams, before taking the war up on to the Jebel Dhofar, was confined to village life and raising the *firqats*. Taqa, a small coastal village midway between Salalah and Mirbat, was the base and tribal home of the *Firqat* Kalid bin Walid. This firqat eventually mustered more than 80 men. They were also fearsome fighters. During the old Sultan's frugal regime, many young men had left the village and travelled widely within the Arab world. Fortunately, for the SAS, some had taken training with the Trucial Oman Scouts and had a very good knowledge of British military tactics. It was common to see the section commanders give the same hand signals which could be seen on the training areas of the Brecon Beacons.

The SAS normally lived in the village with the *firqat*, and in the case of Taqa occupied a two-storey building overlooking the village square. Daily life for the SAS evolved into a number of days training the *firqat* and a number of days defending the village. In addition, the SAS would do night penetration patrols and lay unmanned demolition ambushes.

The village was a collection of mud huts which seemed to have stood outside time for a thousand years. Some 200m (660ft) to the south was the sea, and to the north was the Jebel Dhofar. The bulk of the village sheltered under a small escarpment about 15m (50ft) high, on top of which stood an old Beau Geste-type fort. A troop of Baluchistani soldiers occupied the fort, which in turn was surrounded by a razor-wire fence in a half-moon shape. To the left of the fort was a mortar pit, with an artillery piece situated to the right. During the day, two mortar-trained SAS men would sit waiting patiently for the first distant 'plop'. This first indication of an *adoo* attack would normally bring the customary first two mortar rounds down the tube in reply. It was a kind of game. By day, the attack would normally be from a big gun fired from the tree-lined escarpment which lined the Jebel Aram and looked out over Taqa. The gun

many had a pitched roof. Due to the lack of water and the rock structure of the wadi, they had carved out huge cisterns to collect rainwater in. Their survival in this inhospitable area (I could see little sign of vegetation, and no animals) is a lesson to the human race in man's ability to adapt.

"Eventually, we went back to England, but only for a short while."

After the abortive raid in the north, the war in Oman continued, but this time in the south. After the first initial reconnaissances by Colonel Watts and Major de la Billière, it was decided to occupy the southern coastal towns. An SAS HQ was established at Um al Gwarif, on the outskirts of Salalah, the southern capital, and just a short distance from the RAF base. While Salalah and the air base took several long-range attacks, both were defended by an outer ring of fire bases called 'hedgehogs'. These were situated in a defensive arc between the Jebel Dhofar and the air base, and were manned by the RAF Regiment. They were well equipped with mortars and Green Archer (radar which detected and back-tracked was so well hidden that the BAC Strikemaster light attack aircraft of the Sultan of Oman's Air Force could not locate it. The SAS, too, could do little to alleviate the situation. On one occasion, for example, several shells landed in the village, killing one woman and wounding several others. Nevertheless, the *adoo* did not always have matters their own way. Outranged by the gun, the mortar had its range boosted by pouring 5cm (2in) of petrol down the barrel. This increased the distance dramatically. However, it is not a practice to be recommended as, firstly, the extra range is not constant and, secondly, a careful eye needs to be kept on the bottom of the tube and base plate for the moment cracks start to appear. Nevertheless, the boosted mortar gave the *adoo* something to think about!

Most of the attacks came at night, when a stand-off battle of some 2,000m (6,555ft) would be exchanged. These normally lasted for about 10 minutes, initiated by the *adoo* mortars backed up with small arms. During the monsoon season, the *adoo* made several daring close-range attacks, managing to get within spitting distance of the wire perimeter before being repelled. There is some evidence to suggest that these close-in attacks were training for the assault on Mirbat which came later.

*The old fort at Taqa, so typical of the ancient fortifications used to protect the coastal villages. Prior to the war being taken onto the Jebel Massive, this fort would come under enemy fire daily.*

On one occasion at Taqa the men in the mortar pit heard noises inside the wire compound and quickly asked the fort to have a quick look with the night-sight. As the mortar pit was isolated from the fort, the ground to the front and the open side had been festooned with razor wire about a metre above the ground as a means of stopping any sudden rush by the enemy. The fort reported seeing nothing, and things settled down for a few minutes, until a sudden fall of stones could be heard just a few metres away. Two grenades were quickly thrown in that direction and the fort, from its elevated position, laid down several protective bursts of heavy fire across the pit. At this stage the two mortar men, who normally slept in the pit, made a run for the back door of the fort. Nothing else was heard, but next day a hole was found in the wire and a dead donkey lay 20m (66ft) away with boxes of Soviet-made ammunition scattered around its body. The position of the mortar pit was comparable to that of the gun pit at Mirbat – the prime target during that engagement.

The *firqats* were to endure the most of the *adoo* assault when the SAS and Omani forces finally attacked the Jebel. As it turned out, some *firqat* units were better than others. The *firqat* from Taqa, the Kalid bin Walid, was superb. Some members had been *adoo*, but had been

*The 81mm mortar was the mainstay of the SAS defences throughout the war in Oman. This picture illustrates a typical mortar pit which was the first thing to be constructed in any SAS firm base.*

*A typical BATT patrol working in Oman during the early 1970s. Living conditions were little more than a hole in the ground, and conflict with the enemy a daily accordance. The soldier, third from left, suffered terrible injuries from a landmine not more than a mile from where this picture was taken. He never fully recovered from his injuries and died some years later in Hereford.*

alienated by the hard-line ideology of the PFLOAG and had seen the work and determination of the new Sultan, and therefore returned to play a vital part in building their country.

Once the *firqats* were ready, the time came to attack the *adoo* in their own back yard, and plans were accordingly made to assault the Jebel Dhofar. Operation 'Jaguar' was launched to establish a firm base on the Jebel Dhofar, and it began in October 1971. Dispensation had been given by the senior Qadi (religious leader) to all Arabs fighting during the Ramadan period, which is normally a time of fasting.

This was the start of the war proper, with almost two full squadrons of SAS, together with their *firqats*, spearheading the operation. Additionally, several companies of the Sultan of Oman's Armed Forces (SOAF) and various support units also took part. The whole force was led by Johnny Watts, a brilliant commander who above all had the respect of his men. Watts had a quick, decisive mind, yet he would not commit the SAS without committing himself. He was no stranger to the battle front, and often could be seen running forward with one gun group or another carrying boxes of ammunition, shouting orders as he did so.

Getting the men on to the Jebel Dhofar was not easy, even though a diversionary plan had been implemented several weeks earlier (heavy patrolling had been initiated from Taqa and Mirbat in the direction of the Wadi Darbat, which had always been an *adoo* stronghold, with the intention of making it seem that a full-scale attack was imminent). Helicopter hours were limited, and although some could be used in the initial lift on to the Jebel Dhofar, most would be required to ferry ammunition, water and rations in the early days of the operation. The helicopters were needed to sustain the effort until an airstrip could be built and secured on the Jebel Dhofar, so that the helicopter effort could be replaced and expanded as Short Skyvan fixed-wing transports took over the supply and reinforcement effort.

Later that morning Omani aircraft brought in the other SAS squadron. The SAS and *firqats* from Mirbat and Sudh climbed the Jebel Dhofar from the east, scaling a feature known as the Eagle's Nest, and then worked their way westward during the day, thereby helping to divert the attentions of the *adoo*. Meanwhile, a full squadron undertook a gruelling march to occupy an old airstrip at a place nicknamed Lympne, after an airfield in Kent. This march still stands out in the minds of the men involved. The route was over very difficult terrain, and the bergen carried by each man contained enough ammunition and water to last for several days. Nevertheless, so severe was the march that upon their arrival even the SAS men were in no state to fight until rested. Luckily the *adoo* were occupied elsewhere, and later that morning Omani helicopters and Skyvans started bringing in the other SAS squadron and the Firqat Kalid bin Walid. Colonel Watts decided to move to a more defensible position, so on the morning of the second day the SAS and the *firqat* unit which had arrived by helicopter – and were therefore fresher than the units which had marched in – set off for a location known as Jibjat. With the Firqat Kalid bin Walid in the lead, the Mountain Troop of G Squadron topped the small rise around Jibjat and came face-to-face with a large *adoo* group having breakfast. A firefight developed and the surprised *adoo* started to pull back in an effort to disperse, but not before a full-frontal attack was jointly carried out by the *firqat* and SAS, who overran the *adoo*

position and continued to clear the area to the south, whereupon any further advance was stopped by a large wadi.

The firefight was unrelenting until the SAS heavy support teams turned up. Each team consisted of a GPMG and three men: one carried the whole unit (gun plus tripod) while the other two carried ammunition and acted as gun loader and spotter (each man carried up to 1,000 rounds of GPMG link ammunition – a ferociously heavy load). In the early days of the war these gun groups proved decisive in winning firefights, especially as the supporting Omani Strikemaster aircraft were at first not so quick in reaching the scene.

All through the second day of the offensive, small battles could be heard flaring up at one location or the other. By the third day, Colonel Watts had split his force into three battle groups, two of which were dispatched to clear the Wadi Darbat and a ridge line known as the *Gatn*, pronounced 'Cuttin' by everyone.

For several days the *adoo* fought with everything they had, mistakenly thinking this was nothing more than a short operation by the Omani forces and that in a few days they would give up and leave. It was not to be, though. The Firqat Kalid bin Walid, many of its men back in their own territory, fought as well as professional soldiers, bounding forward stride for stride with the SAS men. By October 9 the initiative was clearly on the side of the Omani forces, and the *adoo* broke up into smaller groups and disappeared into the small bush-covered wadis.

Meanwhile the eastern battle group, which had moved to a location called 'Pork Chop Hill', began to have problems with its *firqat*. This was not the first time the Firqat A'asifat had posed problems: from the start its men had been reluctant in many areas, and now they wished to observe Ramadan. Therefore, despite the Sultan's urgings and the Qadi's dispensation, the *firqat* was withdrawn to Jibjat for the month of Ramadan. A few days later, Colonel Watts descended on the *firqat*'s leaders and left them in no doubt as to how he viewed

> *In the early days of the Oman War, re-supply relied entirely on Huey helicopters of SOAF. Without a constant supply of water and ammunition, the SAS would have been unable to operate.*

their unprofessional attitude.

As both sides eased back a little, a main base was established at a place known as White City. By this time, the choppers were quickly running out of flying hours and desperately needed servicing. Likewise, supplies of ammunition (especially mortar bombs) were dwindling, and water was at a premium. It was suggested by Colonel Watts that an airstrip should be constructed in the middle of White City so that the Skyvans could alleviate the supply situation. As troops began arriving at the location, the men of the *firqat* were sent to picquet the high ground while SAS men set to work constructing the runway. They worked all night, several times coming under enemy fire, but by dawn the airstrip was ready to receive the first aircraft. Again the battle flared up. Each time a Skyvan landed the *adoo* were waiting: mortar bombs began to fall and small-arms fire was employed

in an effort to shoot down several of the aircraft. To prevent this, heavily-armed dawn patrols were sent out to engage and occupy the enemy while the aircraft unloaded. This period saw some of the heaviest fighting of the war.

Despite the problems with the other *firqats*, the Firqat Kalid bin Walid in the western group continued to fight hard. When news arrived that a large contingent of *adoo* had been observed in the Wadi Darbat, most of them suffering from the terror of recent battles, the Firqat Kalid bin Walid set about planning a raid. Aerial bombing and artillery bombardment had little effect and ammunition was in short supply, but eventually a strong patrol was sent against the *adoo*-occupied village of Shahait. A fierce gun battle erupted which left two *adoo* dead, but many others escaped before the SAS and *firqat* could arrive.

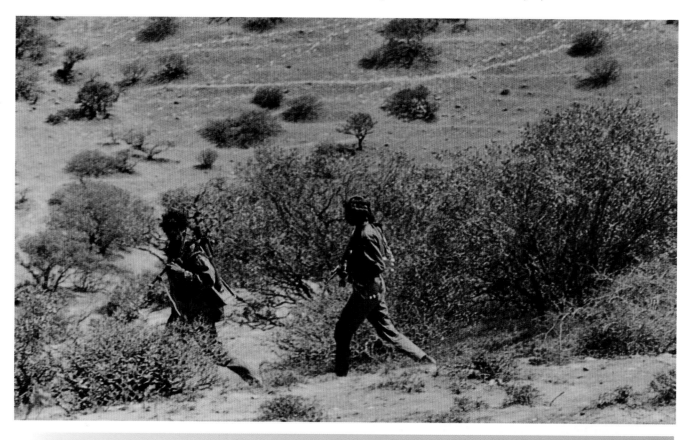

*Firqat from Taqa, who were known as the Kalid bin Walid. They were fearsome fighters with many having served in the Trucial Oman Scouts. Some of the junior NCOs had a sound understanding of British military fighting tactics.*

*Three dead adoo. While their dress may have been unorthodox they were without doubt some of the finest fighters the SAS has ever had to confront.*

From a distance of 5km (three miles), a large group of *adoo* was spotted by an SAS trooper who, pinpointing their position on his map, called in an artillery barrage from gun lines at Taqa. It was an unbelievable sight when the first spotting salvo landed smack in the middle of the *adoo*, and the trooper could be heard screaming into the radio: 'Fire for effect – fire for effect!'

At first the conflict was fluid as the three main battle groups started in the east and pushed their way west. Those first weeks were by far the toughest and, as with all things new, it took time for the systems to fall into place and for effective co-ordination to be established with the supporting arms, such as the Omani artillery, Omani Air Force and, most of all, the *firqats*. It would be remiss not to stress the importance of the bond between the *firqats* and the SAS. The *firqats* had certainly been trained to act as military units but, in reality, were far from being military units in any real sense of the phrase. Yet they possessed a feeling for their own back yard which the SAS did not have. It was not uncommon for their men to wander into battle with their rifles slung over their shoulders and then, quite suddenly, to drop to the ground and start darting forward. It was a movement the SAS soldiers came to recognize: it meant *adoo* were near. In battle, they were courageous, always

dashing into the fight even if sometimes their firing became a little erratic. They were also honest, and if for some reason the SAS unit did not do as they requested they would soon make their point obvious. At the same time, when they were around one was guaranteed a good night's sleep. Studying the *firqat* gave one some idea as to what the *adoo* were like (in fact, as mentioned above, many of the *adoo* who had been captured or surrendered themselves would help swell the ranks of the local *firqat*).

The *adoo* were mostly well equipped. It was not uncommon after the battle to find dead or wounded *adoo* dressed in a better kit than the SAS: khaki shorts and shirt, ammunition belt, water bottle and AK-47 assault rifle, all topped off with a blue beret complete with red star (plus a copy of the Thoughts of Chairman Mao in his pocket). Dead *adoo* were often stripped of their weapons and ammunition before being left by their comrades.

In the first weeks of battle, contacts were very close and in large numbers. Rarely an hour passed without one of the three battle groups coming under fire. It was a matter of advancing to contact, holding the firefight, bringing up gun groups and calling in jets. Winning the

*Evidence that an SAS Pyops team had been in the area. Their aim was to inform the remote villages scattered across Oman of the new Sultan's intentions. In addition to leaflet drops, the SAS would also supply thousands of radios, flags and t-shirts.*

# Theatre of War: Oman

*The defence of the town of Mirbat undoubtedly changed the face of the war. Despite their careful planning, the adoo hadn't counted for two squadrons of SAS to be around. It was one of the hardest-fought battles of a war in which there were few straightforward firefights.*

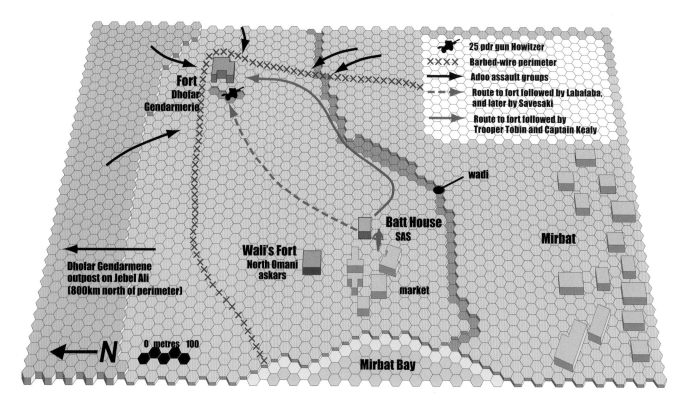

25 pdr gun Howitzer
Barbed-wire perimeter
Adoo assault groups
Route to fort followed by Labalaba, and later by Savesaki
Route to fort followed by Trooper Tobin and Captain Kealy

Fort
Dhofar
Gendarmerie

wadi

Batt House
SAS

Mirbat

Wali's Fort
North Omani
askars

Dhofar Gendarmene
outpost on Jebel Ali
(800km north of perimeter)

market

0 metres 100

**N**

Mirbat Bay

*As the adoo poured unexpectedly into the town, the local firqat were totally oblivious to the fact – they were almost all out on patrol. The element of surprise was great, but with some decent firepower and impressive individual bravery, the SAS and their allies won the day.*

*The battle was over when reinforcements arrived from up the coast. A SOAF jet plane had already played its part and held the attackers back just long enough. The jet was later forced to crash due to a lack of fuel.*

*A problem for troops on both sides was identifying the enemy: early morning mist and gunsmoke made conditions treacherous.*

firefight is the basis of all victories: hit the enemy with a wall of accurate fire and he will stop. For the SAS, this firepower was supplied by two of the best infantry weapons ever: the 81mm (3.2in) mortar and the GPMG.

During a squadron patrol to clear a wadi of *adoo*, the commanding officer thought it prudent to protect his one exposed flank. The problem lay with a smaller wadi running parallel to the one the British and Omani force intended to search, for this offered the *adoo* excellent concealment and an escape route. To solve the problem it was decided that one SAS section, complete with about 10 *firqats*, would patrol the adjacent wadi. This worked out fine until the men reached a dry waterfall in the wadi bed. Fortuitously, for the SAS party, its men happened to be at the top of the falls while a group of five *adoo* were coming up in the opposite direction. The *adoo* were trapped, isolated in what looked like a Roman amphitheatre. The *firqat* called out for them to lay down their arms, as they were surrounded. A burst of automatic fire was the only reply, and so battle was joined. For the SAS men it was a turkey-shoot, as they sat on the top of the falls and poured down fire. M79 grenade launchers, LAW rockets and full-automatic fire from at least 20 other weapons reduced most of the larger rocks in the area of the *adoo* to rubble. When at last the dust settled and a party went forward to investigate, nothing but a few bits of blood-stained cloth remained. Then it dawned on everyone that they had all missed and that the *adoo* had legged it. They gave chase, close enough for the blood on the rocks still to be wet, but on this occasion the *adoo* got away. There are many yet untold stories of the Oman war, the most outstanding being the *adoo* attack at Mirbat (discussed below).

The war progressed into a steady round of stand-off raids by the *adoo*. In reply, strong patrols and ambushes were carried out by Omani forces operating from their established bases. However, it soon became obvious that to stop the enemy two things were needed: to sever the *adoo* line of communications and re-supply, and to win the hearts and minds of the Jebel people. The first was a matter of laying mines and establishing a firm defence line in order to monitor the *adoo*'s movements. The second was a task at which the SAS have become masters.

To win over the locals, small aid stations were set up and manned by SAS medics, while SAS Arabists would regularly talk to village leaders, and their problems became the problems of the SAS. Civil aid teams soon moved into the liberated areas. Water was found and drilling teams brought it to the surface. In a land where water has a priority second only to life itself, the expression on a *jebali*'s face when the cool, clear liquid gushes from the ground is one of pure wonder and delight. In addition, communications open up trade and commerce, and this became clear when at last a metalled road linked the Jebel Dhofar with Salalah.

One special operation known only to the SAS and a few others was Operation 'Taurus'. Thousands of goats and cattle were rounded up and purchased by the government for food, at the same time denying the *adoo* of one of its main sources of food. It was a truly remarkable sight as the animals were rounded up by the *firqat* and, amid skirmishes with the *adoo*, herded down the Jebel Dhofar to Salalah, support being provided by Strikemaster jet aircraft.

With the establishment of the airstrips and a good re-supply system, more adventurous patrols were undertaken. One such task was in the Jebel Aram.

It was cold and dark as the patrol set off from White City at around 20:00. The patrol consisted of some 15 SAS, 30 *firqat* and a platoon of Omani soldiers. The weight carried by each man made movement very slow. The bulky rucksacks contained mostly ammunition and water, but in addition three of the SAS men carried an 81mm (3.2in) mortar between them. This group made up the tail-end of the lead group, and behind them each member of the Omani platoon carried two bombs. This was all the support the party would have until it had reached the Jebel Aram and established a strong base upon it.

At last the men came to a halt, and with it the chance to rest from the merciless weight they carried. The SAS, apart from the mortar crew, and the *firqat* had gone forward for a reconnaissance. It was estimated that they were about 500m (1,635ft) from their objective. The SAS and *firqat* had almost reached the old tree which was to serve as their objective (old trees in the desert are almost always used as landmarks). There was barely anything for them to see, and no obvious cover from where the enemy could spring an ambush. Thus they advanced fairly swiftly towards the objective.

Like all *firqat*, the men were sure-footed in their own

*The loading and unloading of aircraft was highly important to the soldiers – supply is everything to an army. The stony desert ground made thing easier.*

back yard, and presently they halted the patrol. Suddenly one of them dropped down on one knee and pointed, whispering '*adoo*' at the same time. The SAS used night scopes to survey the ground ahead. There, at the edge of their night vision, stood the ancient tree. The SAS commander signalled for the remainder of the group to close up and indicated the direction by pointing into the darkness. Then he quietly relayed the information back to the Omani commander. When he had finished, he gave instructions to set up the mortar. As this was done, the men of the Omani platoon dropped off their bombs at the mortar location, then spread out in defence, covering the rear. Once everyone was ready, the SAS and *firqats* moved to the base of the tree.

The cold, damp atmosphere signalled that the coming day was not far away: even as they approached the tree, the sky to the east showed a thin, grey band. Then it happened. From the silence and the darkness came a crashing orchestra of light and sound, turning the desert into daylight, and the weird tapestry of hell unfolded. Everywhere, men could be seen running or diving for whatever scant cover they could find. Almost instantly, the SAS mortar thundered into action, the ground thumping as the bombs hit the pin at the base of the barrel and the propellant ignited. "The base of the tree," someone yelled, and blindly everyone fired in that general direction. Abruptly, several 'gimpies' (GPMGs) began their steadfast chattering, with reassuring effect.

Suddenly the commanding officer's voice cut in with clear and concise fire orders. Slowly the firefight died, the silence interrupted only by long-distance sniper fire.

By daylight, the patrol had settled down and set up a defensive position overlooking the Jebel Aram. This included the construction of a mortar pit and the clearing of a helipad for the delivery of ammunition, water and defence stores. That evening, short patrols were sent down into the wadi situated at the back of the Jebel Aram. These small patrols could rely on accurate covering fire from the mortars and GPMGs, which all had spectacular views of the immediate area.

An SAS soldier present during the conflict takes up the story: "For a few days we settled in nicely; then it was decided to send out a day-time patrol down into the wadi bed. Things went well until they got 'bumped' by the *adoo* and started to withdraw. The wadi bed was filled with short bushes and trees, making observation difficult for accurate mortar control with our own friendly forces in the area. So it was decided that a reinforced patrol would move farther down the hill to give support. It was a big mistake. The *adoo* had anticipated our move and had cleverly concealed themselves in the long grass. I was part of the reinforcements, and as we rushed forward, they caught us in the open. The first things I remember was seeing the *firqat* next to me stop in mid-air. His feet were off the ground and his rifle dropped from his hand. In that split second I watched a plume of bright red blood explode from his back – he fell dead. I saw the *adoo*. He was lying some 15m (50ft) away, behind a few rocks, his head and weapon the only parts of him exposed. I thought of firing, but running downhill my momentum just seemed to pull me on. I saw the *adoo* fire and knew instantly that I was hit. Luckily, for me, the burst hit the rocky ground just in front, before smashing up into my legs. I remember vaguely going up and turning over in the air; then I slammed back down on to the hard rock. Reality seemed a long way off as I collapsed. At first the pain wasn't so bad; then it registered, and darkness came and blocked it out. Through dulled senses, the noise of gunfire returned and I remember screaming for my partner, Jock Logan. Painfully I rolled my head to one side and saw the dead *firqat* close by. His chest was ripped wide open and bloody bubbles popped and oozed as air escaped from his shattered lungs.

Suddenly Jock dropped down beside me. Quickly he started to pull the small rocks together to improve the protection around our shallow hole. Jock was breathless and panting like an excited dog. Finishing the meagre shield of rocks, he thrust his 'gimpy' over the top and sent a couple of blasts in the general direction of the *adoo*. Then he turned back to examine me. 'It's your knee, but it's not too serious.' He was laughing as he applied the field dressing. 'Medevac choppers are on the way.'

"Some 20 minutes later I was on the operating table at the Field Surgical Hospital in Salalah. Jock had been right; the damage was light. Most of the bullets had hit the rocky ground first and splintered; the one which had stayed intact had lodged itself deep into my left kneecap. Whatever, two weeks later I was hobbling around the bars of Hereford. To this day I still have the AK-47 bullet head the doctors gave me."

Despite the casualties, by the end of 1971 the SAS had established a presence on the Jebel Dhofar, and had saved the Sultan's regime.

The war in Oman continued, and at dawn on July 19, 1972, a large rebel force some 250 strong attacked the port of Mirbat on the southern coast of Oman. Similar to the neighbouring town of Taga, Mirbat was protected by an old fort situated to the north-west. A small SAS unit, stationed a short distance away inside the town, operated both the fort and gun. The official report records that the fate of Mirbat and of its occupants during the battle depended wholly on the resolve of the Civil Action Team. But for the action of these nine men, and particularly the leadership of Captain Mike Kealy, the town would undoubtedly have fallen.

Mirbat was the last great attack by the *adoo*. The rebels of the People's Front for the Liberation of the Occupied Arabian Gulf (PFLOAG) had planned it well: they had been losing ground, and the assault was designed to show the people their continuing power. Only a single stroke of bad luck threw out their calculations, for by coincidence there were two SAS squadrons in Oman at that time due to an end-of-tour handover. This simple fact, combined with the professionalism of the Sultan of Oman's Air Force (SOAF), truly upset the *adoo*'s plans. Had the result been different, the SAS war effort would have suffered a severe setback.

The skill of the *adoo*'s planning and preparation was surpassed only by their security. To mass such a body of men, together with heavy support weapons, and bring them out on to the coastal plain undetected was in itself a major achievement for the *adoo*. They arrived under cover of darkness, almost an hour before the first grey skies would filter through the monsoon mist. It was this seasonal cover of low cloud upon which they relied, not just to protect themselves from SOAF aircraft but also to provide a clandestine approach.

At around 05:00 the picquet at the top of Jebel Ali, a small hill 1,000m (1,095 yards) to the north of Mirbat and halfway towards the Jebel Dhofar, was being manned by a section of Dhofar Gendarmerie (DG). The Jebel Ali is a dominating feature covering the town and the surrounding coastal area. The DG section was the first to be taken out. Surrounding the location to make sure there were no escapees, the *adoo* attacked; stealthily at first, as they cut the throats of those still asleep, and then, as the alarm was raised, opening up with small arms. The exchange of fire was heard by those in the British Army Training Team (BATT) house. It was soon to be followed by 'thump, thump, thump' as the *adoo* mortars kicked in. Inside the BATT house, this chorus of explosions gave little cause for alarm, as the enemy often lobbed in a few mortar rounds each morning. The first rounds had been off-target, but by the third salvo they were shaking off the plaster inside the BATT house. Quickly the boys ran up the makeshift stairs leading to the roof. Here a defensive barricade of sandbags had been erected to form two gun-pits: one for a GPMG in the north-west corner, and one for a 0.5in Browning in the north-east corner. Just in front of the house was an 81mm (3.2in) mortar pit. Captain Kealy, the BATT commander, and his men observed the fire coming from the direction of the Jebel Ali. They also saw several streams of tracer fire lace their way over the house and into the town. Almost at once, several more mortar bombs fell close to the Dhofar Gendarmerie fort situated on the northern side of town. In addition, the *adoo* had opened up with several artillery pieces, and a crushing barrage descended on the town. As the shells exploded, the *adoo* rose in waves and advanced towards the DG fort.

The BATT house took more incoming rounds but the SAS men, although ready to defend, held their fire. Among them were some of the most experienced soldiers the Regiment had; men who had already seen their share of action. To them, this sounded like nothing more than

a stand-off attack, and so the first thing was to assess the situation. From the roof of the BATT house, Captain Kealy could see the firefight raging on top of the Jebel Ali. Turning, he checked to see what damage had been done to the town itself. He then shouted orders for the 81mm (3.2in) mortar to open fire in support of the Jebel Ali, while the rest of the SAS men took up their positions behind the sandbagged emplacements and waited for targets. The amount of incoming fire worried Kealy, and as a safeguard he ordered his signaller to establish communications with SAS headquarters at Um al Gwarif. Additionally, a big Fijian, Trooper Labalaba, left the house and ran the 500m (1,635ft) to the DG fort, where he manned its old World War Two-vintage 25-pounder artillery piece. By 05:30 it was light enough for Kealy to make out the silhouette of the gun position and the DG fort just to its east.

Despite the ferocity of the attack, at this stage there seemed no reason to think that this was anything more than a strong stand-off attack. However, the duty signaller at Um al Gwarif was informed and told to listen out.

The rest of the guys back at base were happily getting showered and making ready for the ranges. Most of them were from G Squadron. Their signals sergeant, 'Ginge' Reese, passed comment over breakfast about the attack: "Mirbat are still taking a hammering; it's a bit long for a stand-off." Five minutes later, 'Duke' Pirie, the B Squadron commander, started to organize a relief force.

At Mirbat most of the *firqat* was out on patrol, leaving the town lightly defended, the houses manned by old men, women and children. Only a few *firqat* members had remained behind and these, together with the group of Dhofar Gendarmerie manning the old fort (the Wali's Fort), were the only help the SAS could call on.

Around Mirbat, *adoo* shellfire continued to increase. Suddenly, a vast amount of small-arms fire started pouring into the town. Through the mist, figures could be seen approaching the perimeter wire from the direction of the Jebel Ali. At first there was some hesitation as to their identity; it was possible that the *firqat* had returned. Then the advancing figures opened fire: they were *adoo*. As battle was joined, both SAS machine gun bunkers opened up, and at the same time the 81mm (3.2in) mortar increased its rate of fire. In the gun-pit by the DG fort, the 25-pounder gun sent

*Most of the pilots serving with SOAF were seconded from other armies. The SAS relied heavily on these pilots, as they were the first line of rescue whenever an SAS soldier was wounded.*

shell after shell into the massing *adoo*. The battle flowed back and forth: then a radio message came through on the Tokki (a small commercial walkie-talkie used by the SAS throughout the Oman war) from Labalaba, saying that he had been hit in the chin while operating the 25-pounder gun. A man of such stature is not given to reporting such trivia, and those at the BATT house suspected he was badly injured. Immediately, Captain Kealy sent Labalaba's Fijian countryman, Savesaki, to his aid. The gunners provided supporting fire from the roof of the BATT house as they watched Savesaki run the gauntlet of tracer and exploding shells. Zigzagging, he ran as if on the rugby field and going for a try. He finally dived headlong into the gun-pit.

Savesaki found Labalaba firing the gun on his own. The big Fijian gave no indication that he was injured. Instead, he pointed to the unopened ammunition boxes, and indicated the desperate need to keep the gun firing. Much of the *adoo* attack was now directed against the gun itself, and its crew needed more help. For a brief moment, Savesaki left the pit to solicit help from the DG fort a few metres away. As the rounds zipped past his head, he banged on the fort door until

at last he was heard. The first man to appear was the Omani gunner, and Savesaki grabbed him. Together, both men raced the few metres back to the gun-pit. Savesaki cleared the sandbags, but the Omani gunner fell forward as a bullet ripped out his guts.

It was now light enough to see groups of men near the outer perimeter fence which protected the three open sides of the town. Behind them, wave after wave of *adoo* could be seen advancing towards Mirbat in support. At that moment several rockets slammed into the DG fort, causing great chunks of masonry to be blown from its ancient walls. The *adoo* looked calm and seemed disciplined, moving forward in sections of about 10 men. From all around, whistles could be heard driving the *adoo* on. Suddenly another mighty blast rang out, and the front of the fort exploded in a cloud of dust, totally obliterating it from sight. As vision returned, the SAS on the BATT house roof focused on a new threat. The *adoo* were at the perimeter wire. Swarms of young men threw themselves headlong on to the barbed, razor-sharp steel: as one died another took his place. Men could be seen all along the wire, but the main breakthrough seemed to be in front of the fort. At this stage, most of the enemy fire was concentrated on the fort in general, and at the gun-pit in particular. Several more heavy explosions were heard, and once more the old fort disappeared in a cloud of dust (it was discovered later that apart from the recoilless guns and mortars, the *adoo* had a Carl Gustav rocket launcher which had been stolen from British forces in Aden some years earlier).

The *adoo* were now inside the perimeter and advancing on the fort and the gun position in large numbers. In support of Labalaba and Savesaki, the men at the BATT house brought all their guns to bear. When the *adoo* still outside the wire started to realize where all the return fire was coming from, they swiftly retaliated.

(There is a corroborated story that as the *adoo* penetrated the wire perimeter in the early stages of the assault, a lone figure could be seen driving them on. He was described as being very tall and extremely well-dressed in full Chinese army uniform, with courage to match. In full view of the horrendous firefight which surrounded him, he stood proudly urging his men on – until a bullet took him down).

The gun, now levelled directly at the wire, boomed as

*During the defence of Mirbat, as the enemy were about to overrun the SAS position, SOAF jets screamed in to the rescue. Cutting below the low cloud they managed to hold the adoo back.*

Labalaba fired point-blank into the charging figures. Both Fijians moved in unison, Savesaki passing the rounds and Labalaba slamming them home, before blasting them into the wall of humanity just a few metres away. Suddenly, Savesaki cried out, 'I'm hit!' and slumped back against the sandbags. Without a loader, the gun fell silent. His shirt soaked with blood, Savesaki propped himself against the sandbags, grabbed his SLR and continued to fire; Labalaba made a quick grab for a small 60mm (2.36in) mortar that lay close by. He almost made it, but then a bullet took him in the neck. The mighty mountain of a man, a true gladiator, fell dead.

Communications with the gun-pit had been lost, and Captain Kealy decided that he and an SAS medic, Trooper Tobin, would risk going forward to give assistance. Before they left, Kealy contacted Um al Gwarif, informing them that things were not going too well and that air cover was desperately needed. He also requested a helicopter to evacuate Labalaba. Additionally, he explained that if the firefight continued at its frenetic pace, more ammunition would be required. It is a little-known fact that if an SAS man gets into serious trouble, he requests 'the Beast'. This call alerts the headquarters unit to the seriousness of the situation, and every SAS soldier who can carry a weapon is pressed into service. In the case of Mirbat, the Beast had been put on standby. Most of those mustered were from the newly-arrived G Squadron. The men were already dressed and equipped for the range; all that was required was a little extra firepower. It was customary for senior troop leaders to go off to the locations which they would be taking over. While they were doing this, the rest of the squadron would unpack stores and test-fire their weapons on the range. Such was the case on the morning in question. As 'Ginge' Reese spread the news throughout the cookhouse, most of the men stopped eating and ran for the armoury. It took about five minutes for 22 of them, under the command of Captain Alistair Morrison, to get together an impressive array of weapons. Eight GPMGs and several grenade launchers were among the group – the enemy was going to know about it when these men entered the fray. The total ammunition count for the reinforcements was in excess of 25,000 rounds.

In Mirbat, Captain Kealy and Trooper Tobin were working their way forward to the gun-pit. As they approached, the firing intensified and both dived for cover. Luckily for them, there was a shallow wadi running in their general direction, and this afforded them a measure of protection. With a final dive, Tobin rolled into the gun-pit. Kealy was about to follow but, realizing there was not enough room, and tripping over the body of a dead gendarme, he threw himself headlong into the sandbagged ammunition bay.

Tobin could not believe the mess. Labalaba lay face down and was very still; Savesaki sat propped against the sandbags, SLR still in hand, and nearby the Omani gunner moaned as he clutched the wound in his stomach. Assessing the priorities, Tobin quickly set up a drip on the severely wounded Omani gunner. Savesaki was badly wounded in the back, but despite the severe loss of blood he continued to fight, covering the left side of the fort. The firefight had reached its height, and the *adoo* made a real effort to overrun the gun. As Kealy concentrated amid the mayhem, he saw *adoo* close by the fort wall. They threw several grenades, which bounced by the lip of the gun-pit before exploding. An

*adoo* appeared at the side of the gun-pit, but Kealy cut him down. In the pit, Tobin reached over the inert body of Labalaba and then, realizing there was little he could do, made to move away. At that moment, a bullet took away half his face. His whole body stiffened, and then he fell by the side of the big Fijian, mortally wounded. The gun-pit seemed done for. Kealy, rapidly running out of full magazines, reloaded quickly, keeping his head below the sandbags. Suddenly there came an almighty explosion – the SOAF jets had arrived. Kealy called into the Tokki, managing to make contact with the BATT house: "Laba's dead. Tak and Tommy both VSI. Get help." Back at the BATT house, they heard the sound of an aircraft and, thinking it was a casevac (casualtly evacuation) helicopter, one of the soldiers went to see it safely landed. Then he realized it was not a chopper but a BAC Strikemaster light attack aircraft. The soldier ran back to the roof and, snatching up his SARBE radio, directed the pilot with precise information regarding enemy forces. Despite the monsoon weather, the pilots had dived out of the cloud just feet above the ground. There before them was the enemy. Their machine guns roared as the first two jets made pass after pass, driving the *adoo* back into a large wadi outside the perimeter wire. As Kealy silently thanked the pilots, he saw a large 227kg (500lb) bomb unhook itself from one of the Strikemasters and fall into the wadi where the *adoo* had taken refuge.

The SOAF pilots did a fantastic job, streaking over the DG fort and keeping the *adoo* from any further penetration through the perimeter. Time after time

*The adoo assault on Mirbat had been well planned, but they had not counted on a second SAS squadron being in theatre for the change over. G Squadron were quickly formed into a relief force which was loaded into three choppers. The choppers covered the 50kms (31 miles) to Mirbat in just under 10 minutes.*

*The desperate defences on the escarpment above the Shirshitti caves. The battle to take the adoo supply caves was not an easy one with both sides suffering heavy losses. This picture was taken the morning after the SAS were forced to retreat back to their firm base.*

they dived from the low cloud to run the gauntlet of ground fire pouring up towards them. Barry Davies was at the airport ready to fly out with an 81mm (3.2in) mortar, and heard the radio traffic from the whole battle broadcast live over the intercom: there was a similar system at Um al Gwarif. He recalls:

"We heard a pilot call: 'I'm hit; I'm hit. No fuel: repeat, no fuel.' Seconds later, as the fire trucks raced across the tarmac, the jet could be seen lining up for the runway, its tailpipe bleeding black smoke. The pilot literally slammed the jet into the ground as fire tenders, which had raced side-by-side with the aircraft, pumped foam to extinguish the fire."

By this time the desperate situation was clearly understood at Um al Gwarif. The G Squadron relief force had already been loaded into three choppers and was rapidly heading down the coast, covering the 50km (31 miles) to Mirbat in about 10 minutes. Because of the cloud, the men of the relief force were dropped off to the south of Mirbat and instantly made contact with an *adoo* patrol which was covering the rear. The *adoo*, consisting of one older soldier and three youths, were held up in a cave and refused to surrender. Several 66mm (2.6in) LAW rockets slammed into the entrance, followed by fire from several GPMGs, and in this fashion the *adoo* picquet was quickly neutralized.

With the jets taking the sting out of the *adoo*, Kealy had time to crawl forward and examine the gun-pit. He could see that the Omani gunner was still alive and so, too, was Tobin, although his wound looked horrendous. Savesaki lay listless against the sandbags; his whole body seemed covered with blood, but he still managed a smile. Slowly, he and Kealy covered the othes up and gave what comfort they could.

The SOAF jets had pushed the *adoo* back, and were now dropping 227kg (500lb) bombs on the Jebel Ali. Kealy and Savesaki tried to shout at the gendarmes in the fort to open the door, but it was to no avail. Then the SAS relief force arrived. Moving through the town had been difficult: as with the SAS in Mirbat, identifying friend from foe in the misty monsoon conditions was not easy. The G Squadron men had to be alert, as *firqat* members had positioned themselves in groups of twos and threes around the town.

As the mess started to clear and the *adoo* withdrew, harassed all the way by the Strikemasters, concern was raised about the main *firqat* patrol which had been lured away before the attack. Obviously, having heard the amount of gunfire coming from the direction of Mirbat, they would immediately return to their base. The problem now was whether they would run headlong into the retreating *adoo*. Although several of the choppers had been hit, they continued to ferry in more reinforcements, extracting the wounded in return. The seriously wounded Tobin and the Omani gunner were 'casevac-ed' on the first available flight. Savesaki, who had suffered wounds from which a normal man would have died, walked calmly to the chopper without assistance. Three young *adoo*, captured and held in the BATT house, were also sent back for interrogation.

Meanwhile, the relieving force commander Alistair Morrison reorganized Mirbat's defences and, with the aid of two Land Rovers, started to collect the dead and wounded *adoo*. The final count of enemy dead was 38. They were stacked neatly in the back of a Skyvan transport and flown to the southern capital, Salalah, where they were laid out for the whole population of the city to see.

The Dhofar war was never the same after the Battle of Mirbat. The *adoo* had given it their best shot and failed, but only just. The chances that a second SAS squadron would be just 50km (31 miles) away at the time of the

attack was something they could not have foreseen. Additionally, they underestimated the expertise and nerve of the SOAF pilots.

Two years later the SAS fought another great battle in Oman: the Shirshitti Caves operation. This took place in 1974, more or less as the war was coming to an end. Major General Creasey, commander of the Sultan of Oman's Armed Forces, ordered the Iranian Battle Group (an Iranian Special Forces battalion had been sent to the support of the Omani forces by the Shah) to advance from the air base at Mansion and secure the coastal town of Rakyut, some 27km (17 miles) to the south. Its mission was to clear the *adoo* stores complex located in the caves of the Shirshitti Wadi. These caves were said to hold tons of weapons, food and combat supplies. Their capture would help end the war.

The attack started in mid-December but did not get very far. The *adoo* had seen the Iranians coming, and in heavy fighting inflicted severe casualties on them. Unable to sustain the losses, the Iranians had called off the attack. At this stage of the war, though, defeat was not an option for the Omani government. Almost immediately, a decision was taken by Creasey to launch another attack, using Omani forces, SAS and *firqat*. There was a problem, however, in the fact that all the Omani regiments in the south were already hard-pressed with prior commitments. So it was that the Jebel Regiment was flown down from northern Oman. After some swift training, it was sent into battle.

By January 4, 1975, the force was ready. The plan was simple: seize an old airstrip called Defa in order to establish a supply point, and then secure the ridge which overlooked the Shirshitti depression, in which the *adoo* cave dumps lay. As always, the SAS and *firqat* led the advance. Defa was quickly taken and the advance rapidly continued. As the lead elements approached a landmark known as the Zakhir Tree, they met serious resistance. For some reason the *firqat* did not perform well, but the SAS men laid down a thick and furious fire. By mid-afternoon they had managed to reach a clearing called Point 985, whereupon a base was established. During the night the *adoo* attacked at very close range, killing four Omani soldiers and severely wounding many more. At times it was difficult to establish the locations from where the *adoo* fire was coming, and as a result the Omani soldiers in the perimeter defences became extremely agitated, and fired more for relief than to hit a specific target.

Next day the force advanced down into the Shirshitti. By mid-morning the Regiment's Red Company had reached the Shirshitti Wadi, but the commander realized that he had moved too far south, navigation in the thick bush being difficult. There also seemed some confusion as to the location of the other two companies. At this stage, most of the SAS men had attached themselves to the various command headquarters. With Red Company was Lance-Corporal Thomas. As the lead platoons broke cover (against Thomas' advice) into an area clear of bush, the *adoo* opened fire. Within seconds, most of the platoon's men were dead, cut down by the ferocious *adoo* firepower.

The company commander and several other men rushed forward to get a better look at the tactical situation. The *adoo* were waiting, and laid down murderous fire. Even to the hardened SAS men, it became clear that the situation was getting out of control. As usual in such circumstances, they quickly grouped together for support. All around them, though, the surviving Omani soldiers dropped their weapons and ran, despite the desperate efforts of their British officers – many of whom were killed – to restore control.

It is not recorded in official sources, but it was only at gunpoint that order could be restored. In order to regain control of the situation, the SAS party with Red Company headquarters called in an air strike. However, such was the confusion on the ground that the first strike mistakenly hit the company headquarters, one of the rounds striking an SAS soldier in the back. Fluorescent air-marker panels were hastily pulled from belt kits and wrapped around the shoulders for recognition. Eventually, with massive firepower from artillery, mortars and Strikemasters, the *adoo* were driven back. Amid all this carnage, there were several individual acts of great courage, as men braved the horrendous fire to rescue friends and comrades.

Although the dead were left behind, all the wounded and weapons were recovered before a tactical withdrawal was ordered. As the shaken troops made their way back to Point 985, shots could be heard coming from the wadi - the *adoo* were confirming their kills. To alleviate this gruesome sound, a full-blown mortar barrage was called down on the battle area.

That day the *adoo* had won a victory, but they were later to pay the price. As the defences at Point 985 were reinforced, it was decided to blast the *adoo* out of their stronghold. So it was that for each minute of the following two days, every weapon which could reach the Shirshitti Wadi was fired. Artillery, armoured cars, mortars and warplanes were involved, and a bombardment was even delivered by an Omani warship lying off the coast. The air thundered with high explosive, and the dust and phosphorus smoke hung over the Shirshitti Wadi like a permanent cloud.

At this stage, both SAS mortar men controlling the baseline at Point 985 had been wounded, and Barry Davies was one of those withdrawn to replace them.

"There were six mortars in two groups of three. Each half-hour it was our turn to fire, each tube firing 10 rounds, a mixture of white phosphorus and high explosive. In the next few hours, the mortars alone consumed 8,000 rounds.

"Even with this massive barrage, the *adoo* still found time to carry out night attacks on our position; additionally, despite the carnage taking place in the wadi, they still found it possible to launch three giant rockets into our camp, with devastating effect. I watched in disbelief as the first one flew over our position, a great flame burning from its tail. When it fell to earth, the whole world seemed to shake. Luckily for us, only one hit the camp; just as unluckily, it hit the ammo bunker."

In the end, the Shirshitti caves were taken, and vast *adoo* stores were captured. And although the Oman War will be known for the Battle of Mirbat, battles such as that for the Shirshitti caves will remain for ever with those who were there.

The SAS returned later in the year. Together with a company of the SOAF, they intended to establish a firm base at Defa, to the north of the famous Zakhir Tree. By September 15, 1975 the base held a company of SAF, a troop of Saladin armoured cars and several 25-pounder guns. The SAS had a whole troop in the location, but due to Ramadan the *firqat* were very thin on the ground. There remained only one problem with Defa. During the Shirshitti operation the enemy had pounded the position with Soviet Katyusha rockets and, despite the caves having been cleared, they now began to rain down again – this time from somewhere near the Zakhir Tree. As the monsoon provided a thick mist, especially in the morning, the SAS decided to silence the rocket fire by sending in a heavy patrol, backed by the SOAF and the armoured cars.

On the early morning of September 19, 13 SAS and two *firqats* under the command of Captain Charles Delius slipped out of Defa, making their way towards the Zakhir Tree. Due to the darkness and mist the patrol found themselves on a small spur to the west of the Zakhir Tree. Delius decided to remain at the position with six men while Sergeant Rover Walker took the other six down the spur for a recce. They dropped lower into the wadi, but as dawn grew stronger and the mist patchy, it became obvious that their tactical position was not good. Walker, a highly experienced SAS soldier, moved his men and dispatched Corporal Bell and one of the *firqat* to proceed across the wadi bed and up the other side in search of the Zakhir Tree, in order to fix their position. Bell moved cautiously until the mist cleared and he was able to observe the landmark and take a bearing. However, as he and the *firqat* moved back to rejoin the patrol, they came across several sets of freshly-made footprints. Moreover, there was a very strong smell of meat hanging in the damp air.

While Walker waited for Bell to return, he observed a man walking through the mist, heading roughly toward Delius's position, and quickly sent a message. Delius was still on the radio when three enemy soldiers appeared directly to their front and a rapid exchange of fire broke out. All three enemy were cut down by the SAS, but one of the enemy had time to fire, and one of the bullets found its mark, hitting Lance-Corporal Geordie Small in the thigh and severing the femoral artery. The patrol medic quickly bandaged the wound and Small was moved to higher ground. Contact was made with the SAF at Defa and an armoured car was sent to pick up the casualty. Sadly, no one realized how bad the internal damage was, and Geordie Small died while the medi-vac helicopter was flying him to the Field Surgical Team (FST).

On hearing the shots, Walker ordered his men to make their way up the wadi, heading north for the high ground. They had just started to climb when a burst of fire signalled an all-out contact. The men dropped and wriggled forward, using the scanty mist as cover; however, the weight of fire was so close that it seemed as if the enemy were right on top of them. Suddenly

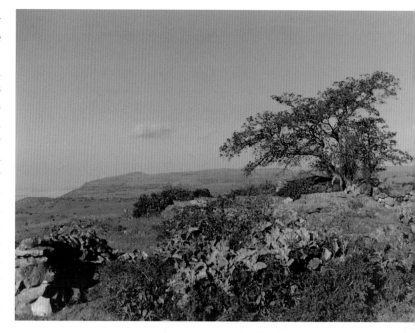

*In order to prevent the adoo firing their larger weapons down on the coastal towns, a series of fortifications under the codename 'Diana' were set up along the escarpment. This picture shows the radio 'sanger' at Diana 5.*

Lance-Corporal Tony Fleming was hit badly in the back; Walker at first thought he was dead, only to see his eyes open. Dragging Fleming between them, the patrol forced itself forward, but such was the enemy fire they eventually decided to stay put and defend as best they could. Walker explained to Delius his only option; they must stand and fight and wait to be relieved. Delius immediately called for mortar fire, but due to the mist and the fact that he did not know Walker's exact position, adjustment control was difficult.

Walker's men huddled together, with those able to shoot firing at anything which moved while the medics attended to the wounded. The mist cleared briefly, and one of the patrol shouted with relief; a line of smartly-uniformed soldiers was advancing towards them in open order. SOAF had arrived. Walker got to his feet and shouted, indicating their position, whereupon the soldiers opened fire. Walker was hit and dropped to his knees. Another round hit him, and he fell to the ground. He tried to rise, and was hit a third time. The enemy advanced to within 20 metres, into grenade-throwing range. Still the SAS held their ground, but were forced to switch to single shots as ammunition ran low. Walker, who by this time had been given morphine, shouted for Bell to take over the patrol, when suddenly an armoured car appeared coming down the slope; the enemy started to disengage.

By 09:00 the battle was over. Captain Delius rejoined his men, only to find that every man in Walker's patrol had been wounded. Fleming and Walker were the worst and Delius ordered that they should be placed on one of the armoured cars and carried to safety.

[Note: As with most battles, word is quickly spread to the SAS base at Hereford and from there to the sub-units operating around the world. What makes this story so good were the comments made by Fleming as they bounced along on the back of the armoured car returning to Defa. Danny had been cradling Fleming's head when the latter whispered, "Danny I'm going off."

"No," replied Bell, "hang on in there – think of those you love!"

Fleming smiled; "No, Danny; I'm falling off the fucking armoured car."

Tony Fleming bravely battled against the disability which resulted from his wounds. He died in 1994.]

# Belize

A couple of months later the SAS was in action once again, this time in Belize in Central America.

Belize was discovered by shipwrecked English seamen in 1638. Over the next 150 years, more English settlements were established. This period was also marked by piracy, indiscriminate logging and sporadic attacks by Indians and the neighbouring Spanish settlements. The area became the Crown Colony of British Honduras in 1862. Several constitutional changes were much later made to expand representative government. Full internal self-government under a ministerial system was granted in January 1964, the official name of the territory was changed to Belize in June 1973 and full independence was granted on September 21, 1981.

Throughout this time, the British Army remained responsible for the protection of Belize, and accordingly a British garrison remained in situ. This force was

*Living conditions in the jungles of Belize were not good. Some of the trees had a sap similar to acid, and the wildlife was vicious.*

designed primarily to deter military advances from neighbouring Guatemala, which is much larger and lays claim to Belize. From time to time, the Guatemalans have rattled their sabres and begun preparations to take Belize by force. Much of their rhetoric was taken with a pinch of salt, but on one occasion they seriously intended to invade. This was in November 1975, and the 1,800-strong garrison was rapidly reinforced. One of the SAS soldiers takes up the story.

"It was one of those quick-move jobs. One minute we were happily doing a spot of training in Hereford, and the next we were winging our way over the Atlantic. The faithful Lockheed C-130 Hercules transport took off from Brize Norton bound for Belize, with a refuelling stop at Nassau in the Bahamas. Here we were given permission to leave the aircraft and stretch our legs while the transport was being serviced. It was at this stage that I noticed the RAF loadmaster beating one of the engines with a broom. About 10 minutes later we were informed that the flight had gone US (unserviceable) and that we would have to spend the night in Nassau – I could have kissed him! If you've ever wondered why the sailors of old never returned from these islands, one breath of the relaxing air would explain everything.

"Forgetting the war, we were taken by a fleet of taxis to a Trust House Forte hotel. Here the whole Squadron was given grand rooms, many right on the beach: 'Eat what you like, gentlemen. For you, Happy Hour has just begun,' said the manager, as a way of saying that it was all free.

"Unfortunately, next morning the Hercules was fixed and we continued our journey to Belize, with most of us nursing a hangover. We arrived about 14:00 in the afternoon, and quickly set about equipping ourselves for the jungle. I was given a seven-man patrol. This was a bit large for the jungle, but it suited our task. We were to penetrate the thick jungle in central Belize and move up to the border with Guatemala. By 16:00 we were ready to get choppered in, and that's when this guy arrived from the government. He had come to tell us about the type of jungle in Belize. To a man, the Squadron sat on the floor as Major Rose introduced him. The first words he said were 'fer de lance' or something like that. We looked at each other in some amusement, wondering what the hell he was going on about. He then proceeded to tell us all about this snake which could fly. It would leap out of the trees and bite your neck, and then you died. Charming; and on top of this, we still had to take care of the Guatemalans.

"We infiltrated at dusk, and after clearing the drop-off found a spot to hole up for the night. To be fair, the boys went into jungle mode straight away: no talking, no cutting, everyone alert. Next day we set off, and as two of the guys were new to the troop I decided to carry out one or two contact drills. This we did, and I'm confident that, had we hit the enemy, the patrol would have held its ground and extracted in good order.

"Three days later, as we neared our objective, I suddenly saw the lead scout, Tony, move to one side and bring up his weapon. I heard two loud bangs, followed by the cry 'fer de lance!' Initially thinking that this was an enemy contact, the boys behind me had gone directly into combat mode, ready to take on the worst. Two seconds later, as the words 'fer de lance' pierced the air; you couldn't see them for dust. Fighting Guatemalans is one thing; flying snakes are another.

"Our task was to observe a main jungle route which led from the Guatemalan side and stretched over the border into Belize. It was thought the Guatemalans might use this to infiltrate troops. In the event of invasion, we were to report all enemy movements and strengths. If we were compromised, the plan

was to bug-out and run north to Mexico (agreement had been reached between the British and Mexican governments for the internment of all UK soldiers until the end of the war; blood money was issued to make this journey possible).

"By Day Five, Harriers of the Royal Air Force had arrived. They flew down the border in teams of four, stopping now and then to hover, like giant angry bees waiting to sting. In full sight of any Guatemalan forces, they flaunted their massive firepower. It was enough, and a day later the Guatemalans called off any thoughts of invasion. Once more British gunboat diplomacy had worked, and Belize had been saved from the threat of war.

*In November 1975, the Guatemalan army began preparations to invade Belize. In response, the British government increased the 1,800-strong garrison by sending in a squadron of SAS. These were immediately sent into the jungle to watch the border for incursions by the Guatemalans.*

"We remained in the jungle for several more days carrying out 'hearts and minds' activities before being extracted to Belize City and thence home. Before I left, I purchased a T-shirt with 'I fought the Guats' printed on the front and 'ALL DAY' on the back."

## Northern Ireland Again

Back in Britain, it was announced that the SAS would be sent to Northern Ireland to curb the increase in IRA violence. True, they had been in the province since 1973, but most of these were just visits, where a SAS man would be attached to a local regiment. In 1976, they were to become a political tool. Results came quickly: on March 12, 1976, Sean McKenna, a known IRA member, was lifted from his home over the border in Eire. He was dragged from his bed and frogmarched into Northern Ireland, whereupon he was handed over to the RUC. Less than a month later another IRA member, Peter Cleary, was lifted from the home of his fiancée, who lived just north of the border. The house had been under observation for some time, as it was known that Cleary was soon to be married, and it was just a matter of waiting. Once the suspect had been taken into custody, the SAS men moved to a pick-up point and waited for their helicopter. However, Cleary tried to escape, and was shot dead as he did so. The incident did not go down well: the IRA claimed that he had been murdered.

Several senior officers in Northern Ireland were aghast at having a bunch of men such as the SAS in their midst, but as the Prime Minister, James Callaghan, had sent them, there was little they could do. However, the situation did serve to send a message to the IRA: 'Border or not, we will come and get you.'

*Helicopter ins and outs became a more frequent feature of the SAS's tactics as they found themselves in Northern Ireland.*

This theory was confirmed when, at 18:00 on May 5, 1976, the Eire police stopped two men in a car at a checkpoint within the Republic, and discovered that it had members of the SAS on its hands. To make matters worse, two back-up vehicles arrived to assist the first, and in total eight SAS men, together with their vehicles and weapons, were taken into custody by the Eire police. As the news emerged all hell broke loose, and the newspapers had a field day. The men were taken to Dundalk and then on to Dublin. All were charged, and in the end it was just as embarrassing for Eire as it was for the SAS soldiers, most of whom were fined £100 each for having unlicensed weapons.

The SAS suffered another blow when an Intelligence officer, Captain Bob Nairac, was killed by the IRA in Northern Ireland in May 1977. Although not a member of the SAS, Bob did live and work out of the same location in Bessbrook, Armagh. He was from a unit known as 14 Intelligence and Security, a covert unit used to gather information on which the SAS could operate. For some reason best known to himself, Bob Nairac had taken to speaking with an Irish accent; it was good, but not good enough. He also had the idea that he could pass himself off as an Irishman, and to some degree he did. Two days prior to his death he had gone to a shop which sold Republican song-sheets, and purchased several of the well-known melodie, going about singing the verses until he was word-perfect.

A highly intelligent man, and certainly enormously courageous, Bob decided to visit a local pub close to the border with the Irish Republic. The problem was that he neglected to tell anyone where he was going. He drove off from Bessbrook Barracks around 19:30, but he did not reach the Three Steps Inn, near the village of Dromintee, until around 22:00. Here, the evening was in full swing, and at first Bob managed to fit in well with the locals, all having a good time. Several people did a turn on the makeshift stage, mostly singing rebel songs. It was at this stage that Bob got up and joined in, putting him in a position where he would be noticed. It was not so much his accent which gave him away; it was more that no one knew him.

As he attempted to make his way back to the car park, he was followed. Casually, several men inquired as to his identity. A fistfight ensued (Bob Nairac was an excellent boxer and could take care of himself) but during the tussle his Browning 9mm pistol fell to the ground. His assailants grabbed it and he was soon overpowered. What happened after this is not clear, but from various people brought into the police barracks for questioning, a rough picture emerged.

While Bob was held, a telephone call was made to members of the IRA just over the border in the Republic. Blindfolded and gagged, he was taken by car to a field on the border where the IRA members took control. He was tortured and interrogated in the corner of a field, the main instrument being a fencepost, with which they beat him repeatedly around the body and head. Despite what has been called a murderous beating by the IRA themselves, Bob Nairac did not talk. In the end, they shot him with his own pistol and his body was disposed of, never to be recovered. However, some years later a suspect under interrogation in

*Two SAS soldiers drinking in the SAS bar at Bessbrook. For security reasons the SAS rarely share military facilities with other units of the British Army. Note the long hair and casual clothes, all done to fit in with the local Irish community.*

Armagh Barracks offered information as to the disposal of Nairac's body. It was so horrifying that it has never been made public. Strangely enough, the IRA man relating the story had nothing but pride for the way in which Bob Nairac had suffered in silence.

During the late 1970s there were other successes and the odd failure, but slowly the Regiment evolved its own strategy, forming stronger links with the RUC's Special Branch. This link provided more accurate information for the SAS to work upon. One such operation came in June 1978, when information was received that an IRA cell was about to bomb the Post Office depot in Belfast. A member of the SAS who served in Ulster at the time takes up the story.

"It was a classic operation. Special Branch had given us the information and we would provide the solution. It was simple: a team of IRA terrorists was to firebomb the Post Office depot in Belfast. We even knew of their approach route, and made our plans accordingly. The only thing we did not know was the exact time of the bombing. In the event several observation posts were set up, the main one being located in a house. This gave us a clear view of the small alley which ran by the side of the Post Office compound where the vehicles were kept. This compound was protected by a high fence. As well as several cut-off groups positioned around the compound a reaction team, sitting in a van, lay in wait. I hate to think how many hours I spent lying in that van – it was bloody uncomfortable. As the operation progressed over several days, it was deemed a better idea to establish two guys in a large bush during the hours of darkness.

"On the night in question, the task fell to Tony and Jim (not their real names). Tony was in my troop, and a better man would be hard to find. He was solidly built, laid-back and very cool. In this incident and many others afterwards, when the chips were down, he was the man to have by your side. Jim was a little younger and not quite so level-headed.

"The SAS guy in the observation house was bored. He had sat at the window for several days and nothing had happened. Special Branch had reassured him several times that the bombing would take place, but as time went on, he had begun to entertain doubts. Then, suddenly, he saw some figures in the alley approaching the wall of the compound. Before he could raise the alarm, one of the figures moved his arm, and the first

*Captain Bob Nairac was killed by the IRA in Northern Ireland in May 1977. Although not a member of the SAS, Bob did live and work out of the same location in Bessbrook. He was from a unit known as 14 Intelligence and Security. A highly intelligent man but one that was prone to taking chances.*

bomb was already arcing its way towards the target.

"Orders were screamed: 'Go, go, go!' The operation was activated. With Tony in the lead, the two men leapt from the bush. The light on top of Tony's MP5 submachine-gun sent out a beam which illuminated three figures in front of him, two of them about to throw satchel bombs. Tony fired two short bursts, and two men fell dead. The third made a run for it, retreating back down the alley in the direction from which he had come. Tony fired another short burst and the third man fell. It was perfect, except that Jim, who on this occasion was armed with an SLR, decided to confirm the kills, pumping a lot of heavy-calibre rounds into the bodies. Almost as Jim finished firing, two more men entered the alley from the bottom end. Tony immediately issued a challenge, unsure as to the identity of the men. One dropped to the ground and placed his hands on his head, but the other made a run for it. He never made it – a short burst from Tony killed him outright.

"As the situation stabilized, it turned out that the two men were just returning from the pub and had accidentally walked straight into the firefight. Had the man, a Protestant by the name of William Hanna, remained still after the challenge, he would be alive today. I can assure you a clear challenge was given. Without going into too much detail, the fun really started when the legal eagles arrived. The weapons were tagged and taken away for forensic examination. Then each man gave his story. It was all clear and simple until the lawyer asked Jim to give his account in his own words. 'Well, I saw Tony move and I backed him up. He slotted two, but the third made a run for it. As Tony fired, I stepped to one side and shouted to the boys in the bottom cut-off, 'Keep your head down, Bobby.' Then I let rip with a 30-round mag.' The legal eagle stared in horror, while the rest of us just rolled around laughing. Subsequently his story was corrected, and no court case followed."

Not long after, Special Branch in Armagh asked the SAS unit in Portadown to undertake a reconnaissance of a small Catholic church in Castleford. The essence of the information was that there was an IRA meeting-place in a small building at the rear of the church grounds. Special Branch requested that the SAS take a look, and photograph any documents of interest that were discovered.

Two men were entrusted with the task, one of them a lock-picking specialist. They were driven to the town by two other SAS personnel, who would stay mobile in the area and act as back-up. At around 01:00 on a wet and windy morning, the two men were dropped off by a gateway at the edge of the town, and quickly made their way to the rear of the church. The whole church was surrounded on three sides by a 3.65m (12ft) wall, with an iron railing fronting the road. Approaching from the rear, the two men quickly climbed the wall and, remaining in the shadow of the church, approached the meeting-house. The small, two-storey building stood in one corner, with a single door providing the entrance. One of the SAS men produced a set of picks and made short work of the padlock. Once inside, they searched the ground floor. There was nothing of interest, as most of the space was taken up with church props and junk. A small

set of stairs led to the second floor, the entrance to which was also barred by a padlock (which was soon picked). This upper floor had two windows, allowing the single room to be illuminated by the street lighting. The room itself contained several lockers filled with paperwork and books, with a large table and several chairs sitting in the middle. The two men carried out a search of the room and the cupboards, but little of interest was found, and certainly nothing referring to the IRA. A small trap door leading to the loft was discovered, and by placing a chair on the table, it could be reached. Checking the hatch for any booby trap, one of the SAS men climbed inside the loft. After he had secured the hatch behind him, he switched on his torch. What confronted him was a whole pile of large plastic bags, most of which contained bomb-making equipment. Several pounds of Semtex plastic explosive were also discovered, as were 20 ready-to-go cassette incendiaries. The information was relayed directly back to control and an observation unit organized for the next day.

Unfortunately, when Special Branch found out about it, the situation changed. For some unexplained reason, MI5 became involved; this meant no SAS allowed anywhere near and the target being electronically tagged. The two SAS men had the pleasure of taking the MI5 operative into the building, but he was so fat that he demolished half the rear wall as he climbed over it! Then he could not pick the lock, and thus became hell-bent on calling in an expert, until the SAS man picked it. For the SAS, that was the end of the story, although only for three weeks. Then a call came from Special Branch to remove the whole explosives find and bury it in a hide. The hide was to look like an IRA job and be at least half a mile from the church. This we did, and next day an SAS soldier stood on the site as the local Ulster Defence Regiment (UDR) unit searched the area. "It's here, mate," said the SAS man. The day after, the newspapers carried headlines of a major explosives find by the UDR. There was a reason for this subterfuge: it told the IRA, which had put the explosives in the church grounds, that it was being watched, and in the eyes of the general public it also made the British Army look good.

Sadly, another SAS soldier died on June 7, 1978, while travelling alone from Portadown to Londonderry, when his car left the road at Shanalongford Bridge. Dave Naden was the SAS liaison officer attached to Special

Branch in Londonderry. Working alone, it was his responsibility to assess work suitable for SAS operation. As a mark of respect, the RUC Special Branch attended the funeral in very large numbers and continued the wake for several days afterwards.

# Lufthansa Hijack, October 1977

On October 13, 1977, two men and two women belonging to the Popular Front for the Liberation of Palestine hijacked a Lufthansa Boeing 737 which was returning from the holiday resort of Palma, Majorca. What was not known was that the hijackers were working in conjunction with the Baader-Meinhof terrorist group, which had kidnapped a top German industrialist, Dr Hans-Martin Schleyer, a month before. It later transpired that both the kidnapping and the hijack were allied to the same demands.

The hijack team spent several days in Palma posing as tourists and selecting a flight which would take them to West Germany. After having visited several travel companies in the holiday resort, they eventually booked several seats on Flight LH181 which was bound for Frankfurt. Later, it is reported, three of the group returned to the airport where they met a German woman who was pushing a child's pushchair. This woman handed over a biscuit tin to them which contained the weapons and grenades for the hijack.

Flight LH181 took off from Palma for Frankfurt at 12:57 on Thursday, October 13. The in-flight meal had just been served when the hijackers struck. Brandishing pistols and hand grenades, they seized control of the flight and started a drama which was to ricochet around the Middle East. Refuelling at Rome and at Larnaca in Cyprus, the airliner then flew on to Bahrain. Here it refuelled yet again before making its way to Dubai in the United Arab Emirates. The terrorists were now demanding the release of Baader-Meinhof gang members being held in a top-security West German prison, as well as two other terrorists held in Turkish prisons. They also demanded US $15 million. The demand note was identical to that issued for the release of the kidnapped industrialist Dr Schleyer a month earlier. During the first 48 hours of negotiation, the German government in Bonn took a firm line, refusing any concessions and holding to a strategy of continuous

dialogue as a means of achieving the hostages' safe release. At the same time, the West Germans looked to Europe for support in its stand, and received assurances from both France and the UK. In response, British Prime Minister James Callaghan sent two members of the SAS to support the Germans. Barry Davies, who with Major Alastair Morrison assisted the German anti-terrorist team throughout the hijack, tells the story.

"During the week preceding the hijack, I was on duty at Heathrow with eight other members of the SAS Anti-Terrorist Team. We were training on various types of aircraft, familiarizing ourselves with their basic internal layouts and the many variations employed by different airlines. Most of our work was done during the periods allowed for cleaning between scheduled flights. On the afternoon of Friday, October 14, I returned with my crew to Hereford through the beginnings of fog which was thickening dramatically across the country. On arrival at Bradbury Lines, we checked in all our equipment and our vehicles. Ensuring that all my men were on call, I released them for the weekend before setting off for my own home. I had only just arrived when the phone rang, ordering me back to camp. Back at the anti-terrorist team office I found the team commander, Captain Holmes, who informed me that the British and West German governments had agreed on the need for a joint anti-terrorist effort, and that the two of us were to leave immediately for London.

"As the fog was so thick we took a chopper, which flew us directly to Battersea Heliport. Unfortunately the heliport had been closed by the fog, so that when we landed we had no option but to climb over the heliport gates to get into the street. Luckily, one of the first vehicles we saw was a police panda car, which we flagged down. We asked the driver to take us to Whitehall. He was, not surprisingly, dubious about such a request from two scruffy individuals, but our manner, backed up by ID cards, persuaded him to check with his control. They played it safe, telling the PC to give us a lift to see if we were genuine – and to bring us in if we weren't!

"When we arrived outside No 10, we were met by senior military personnel who briefed us on the current situation. Major Morrison of SAS HQ in London joined us at this time. We were further briefed regarding the areas of national secrecy concerning the operation and

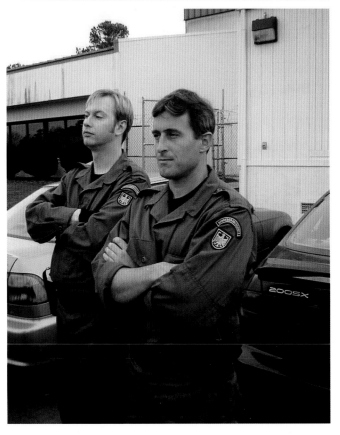

*Two members of the German counter terrorist team the GSG 9 at their barracks in St Augustin. Like their British counterpart they were raised in secret, only becoming public knowledge during the Mogadishu hijacking.*

the equipment employed. It was made clear that we were to give all possible assistance to achieve the release of the hostages, but were instructed not to talk about some of the recent equipment advances we had developed. We got the impression that a couple of politicians from Bonn had arrived, together with two members of a unit barely known to us at the time: GSG 9 (Grenzschutzgruppe 9, a division of the border police trained in anti-terrorism).

"We attended a meeting inside No 10, at which the hijack situation was more fully discussed. Present were various heads of security departments, ministers, Major Morrison, Captain Holmes and myself. It was quickly established that the plane's position was still as reported by the media that afternoon: in Dubai. We in

turn reported that there was an ex-SAS man currently in position in Dubai working under contract for the Palace Guard. We were then introduced to the GSG 9 members, and within minutes realized how much in common the SAS Anti-Terrorist Team had with them, for we had each developed tactics and equipment which would later be of great benefit to both units. I mentioned that we had developed a new type of stun grenade which would detonate almost instantaneously when thrown, effectively stunning anyone in close proximity. The grenade emits a very loud bang and a very bright flash of light in a set sequence, not dissimilar to the effect of strobes in a disco as they flash on and off. The effectiveness of these grenades, together with our expertise and knowledge gathered from the Middle East and our recent training on aircraft interiors, was of such value to the Germans in dealing with the hijack that we were immediately asked to return with them to Germany. They also suggested that once we had talked to the people in Germany, we could, if requested, fly on to Dubai to give further assistance.

"Major Morrison and I were selected to accompany GSG 9, and arrangements were made for eight stun grenades to be sent from Hereford to meet us at Brize Norton. We left shortly afterwards, the intention being to travel by helicopter. However, due to the very thick fog we had to endure a very tedious drive – sometimes at not more than 16–25 kmh (10–15 mph) – arriving at Brize Norton at about 04:00. Here, we met the crew of a C-130 which had been placed at our disposal and was ready for an immediate take-off. Already aboard – and under guard – were the two boxes containing the stun grenades. I checked them at once to make certain that we had operational grenades and not the training variety. The C130 then took off, into weather so bad that we crossed the Channel using low-level radar, and we landed in Bonn at 06:30 on Saturday, October 15. There to meet us were the two GSG 9 officers we had previously met in London, who immediately took us directly to GSG 9 HQ. There we had a very short discussion with the unit's second-in-command (the commander, Ulrich Wegener, was already in Dubai), and it was decided we should demonstrate the British stun grenades to the Germans. The most convenient space, which was similar in size and shape to the interior of a plane, was a long corridor in the cellars of the HQ building. About a dozen

# Theatre of War: Mogadishu

*This plan clearly shows all the details of the Mogadishu hijack. The actual operation itself was played out beforehand in the Rehearsal Area, while the Lufthansa 707 was also used for reference. The assault party clearly took the shortest possible route to the aircraft.*

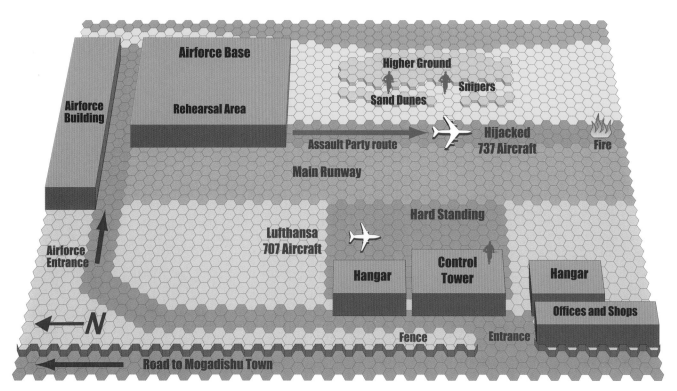

*It didn't take the SAS long to get involved in this major anti-terrorist operation, although it was the German unit GSG 9 that was running the show. It quickly became apparent that the best way to deal with the serious situation was to send in a small number of highly-trained troops. GSG 9 had the men, and the SAS had the plan and extra equipment.*

*Shortly before the eight men were to go ahead, a diversionary fire was set off to the front of the highjacked aircraft. The diversion certainly worked, although the fire was perhaps a bit too much!*

*SAS member Barry Davies, who was deeply involved in the planning and execution, was awarded the British Empire Medal by the Queen for his part in the operation. He also later met the female terrorist who was injured in the operation.*

GSG 9 soldiers took up positions in various recessed doorways. With the lights out, I tossed in a stun grenade. The language was blue, as some very shocked GSG 9 soldiers emerged from the cellar corridor, but nevertheless it proved how effective the grenades were. The second-in-command then made an instant decision to send both Alastair and myself on to Dubai by the speediest means. Unfortunately, this meant getting the 12:12 plane out of Frankfurt for Dubai, and then changing in Kuwait.

"All went smoothly until we arrived in Kuwait. As one can imagine, the entire Middle East was alarmed by the hijack in Dubai. For this reason, Kuwait Airport was on full military alert, and even passengers in transit had their luggage re-checked before being allowed back aboard the plane for Dubai. Although Alastair and I hung farther and farther back in the queue, it was inevitable that we had to put our bag, containing the boxes of stun grenades, through the X-ray machine. I can still envisage the screen clearly showing those grenades, and I still recall, very vividly, the commotion it caused. We were at once slapped under heavy guard and manhandled quite ruthlessly by Kuwaiti soldiers into the main Security Officer's room, followed by our suspicious hand luggage.

"The bag was opened for examination, a procedure which I had to terminate when one of the Arabs tried to remove the pin from a grenade. At this stage, realization dawned on everybody in the room that we were taking the grenades from Germany to Dubai. Luckily for us, at that moment the general manager for Lufthansa in Kuwait came into the security room. After a few moments he left the Security Officer in no doubt that, unless we were released immediately, together with our grenades, to rejoin our original flight to Dubai, no other Lufthansa aircraft would ever again fly into Kuwait Airport. It worked, and we were hustled across the tarmac to the waiting plane before physically being pushed into our seats. Then the bag with the stun grenades was dropped into my lap for me to nurse.

"We arrived in Dubai at around 03:00 on Sunday, October 16 – only to be arrested at the airport for lack of documentation. Our passports were taken from us, and this action allowed one of the Western news reporters covering the hijack to pick up our names. Later he realized our true identities, and that we were SAS.

Alastair made numerous attempts during the early hours of the morning to contact the British Embassy, but got no further than the gate man who was manning the night phone. Then luck came our way in the form of an ex-SAS officer called David Bullig. He had left the SAS and had been seconded to work training the Dubai Palace Guard. When he saw us both, he knew immediately who we were, and events took a completely different turn. Within minutes we were able to roam freely about the airport to assess the situation. David was extremely helpful in many other ways, not least because he had already primed some of the best men of the Palace Guard to be ready to attempt an immediate assault on the aircraft should the terrorists actually start killing the hostages.

"We toured the airport and then spoke to Wischnewski, the German minister who was the acting representative for the West German government. We also met and talked to the defence minister of Dubai, who had taken charge of the situation directly (this was the second hijack he had dealt with). Having fully assessed the situation, we went with David Bullig to talk directly to Colonel Ulrich Wegener, head of GSG 9, who was resting with several other Germans in the airport hotel. We all agreed that there was very little we could do until the morning and we would be better off refreshing ourselves with a little sleep and meeting later that day.

"David Bullig took Alastair and myself to his home, where his charming wife plied us with sandwiches and coffee while we laid out our plan of action. David scribbled notes, listing our demands for kit and equipment. Our most expensive request was for the use of a Boeing 737 for training and practice purposes. At around 05:00 both Alastair and I fell asleep. After a couple of hours' dozing we were awakened by Mrs Bullig with the news that David had managed to fulfil most of our demands. All three of us left for the airport to meet GSG 9 and three other British officers David had found from various units in Dubai. In addition, he had selected eight of the best men from the Dubai Palace Guard.

"We set out a very quick Immediate Action drill to meet the needs of the worst possible scenario: that is, when we would have had no choice but to assault the aircraft with the limited force available. Of course, the more time we had, the more our plan would improve. By now most of the kit and equipment we needed had arrived: shotguns, masking tape, walkie-talkies, various ladders, padding and a host of other items. We had two quartermasters standing by with four jeeps and an apparently endless supply of cash to obtain anything else required. Most importantly, a Gulf Air Boeing 737 had been given on loan and was parked at the far end of the airfield, well out of sight of the hijacked plane. I was about to start a crash course in anti-terrorist techniques.

"On the personnel side, my resources were limited to a hard core of five men who had received at least some professional Close Quarter Battle (CQB) or anti-terrorist training. These included Alastair, David, myself and the two GSG 9 officers. Additionally, I had three other British officers and the eight soldiers from the Palace Guard. I concentrated our first efforts on the Immediate Action drill needed to counter any terrorist deadline.

"The Boeing 737 is a simple little animal where anti-terrorist drills are concerned. There are only three options for entry: tail, wing and front catering area. We thought that if the terrorists began to carry out any threatened shootings, they would naturally take the precaution of covering the main doors. It seemed less likely that they would cover the two emergency exit doors leading on to the wings, so the basic plan which fell into place was to attack through these entry points. The fact that the wing emergency exits were designed to be opened easily from the outside was another strong factor in favour of adopting this mode of attack. In addition, we had also discovered a blind spot where the wing joins the aircraft body. Two men could easily sit beneath the emergency doors and not be visible from any of the plane's windows. By comparison, the entry and exit points at both the front and rear require considerable manhandling and some time to get them open.

"Although our basic plan was quite uncomplicated, we calculated that it would require a great deal of practice to get the timing right, especially the time it would take the assault teams to effect their entry and make their way to the front and rear of the passenger cabin. We reckoned that as soon as we dominated these points, the only people in serious danger would be the crew in the cockpit.

"By 08:00 on October 16 – 67 hours after LH181 had left Palma – the training and practice began. We took a break around 14:00, using the time to iron out every detail, searching for anything which might increase the odds in our favour. One thing which did improve the odds were

the Palace Guards. I was truly amazed at the quality of the soldiers we had with us: they turned out to be extremely tough, very quick and could be relied upon to do exactly as they were told in what was, for them, an entirely new kind of situation. We now felt fairly confident that if the terrorists forced us into immediate action we had a better than average chance of success. We were now sure that we could approach the airliner and establish all our people in their starting positions unobserved. We knew we could put eight men – the four assault pairs – inside the airliner. We knew that the outside assault teams were fully aware of their duties regarding getting the doors open, effecting their own entry and giving assistance where necessary.

"We refined our assault plan as best we could and then started to develop external additions. We worked out a suitable distraction for the terrorists. We considered how best we could locate their positions inside the airliner – extremely valuable information if we could get it. We also gave considerable thought to the possibility of an attack at night, during which, if it came off, we would have an extra man underneath the plane to shut down the APU (Auxiliary Power Unit). This is located at the rear of the wheel housing, and one yank on the red and yellow handle would kill all the lights and power in the airliner at the moment which suited us.

"At about 15:30 the Dubai defence minister left his watch in the control tower and came to check on our progress. We went through our operation on the Gulf Air Boeing 737, and I have to admit that it looked pretty impressive. Then, just as we finished our demonstration, the unexpected happened. LH181's engines came to life and she took off, taking with her any hope that the hijack would end in Dubai.

"Fortunately, the Germans had a Boeing 707 for the use of the negotiators. Everybody from Germany concerned with the hijack, as well as Alastair and myself, went aboard and we took off to follow the hijacked plane. First indications were that it was going to land at Salalah in southern Oman. This sounded like good news, for the SAS had men in the area with anti-hijack skills. Our expectations were dashed, however, when we learned that LH181 had in fact landed at Khormaksar Airport in Aden. Captain Schumann, piloting LH181, had been too low on fuel to fly anywhere else, and he skilfully put the aircraft down on the hard sand alongside the runway.

*The Germans asked the Somali forces to assist in the assault by causing a diversion. Enthusiastically they set fire to a full fuel tanker, resulting in one of the best diversions in the field of counter-terrorism. It did the trick, allowing the GSG 9 and SAS to gain access.*

"Our Boeing 707 had to fly on to the international airport in Saudi Arabia. Here, confined in the aircraft, we sat on the ground awaiting further developments. During this waiting period, the negotiating psychologists attempted to persuade the hijackers to release the hostages in exchange for the $15 million, which we held in a large suitcase on board our plane.

"Then came the shocking news which brought an immediate end to negotiations: Captain Schumann had been shot dead aboard LH181. Now the decision more or less made itself. Wherever LH181 was, wherever she was forced to fly, we would make our rescue attempt. For the first time, I saw the true determination of our German partners concerning their own nationals. The killing of Captain Schumann decided the matter: any further ideas about peaceful negotiation were instantly dismissed.

"Our next news was that LH181 had again taken off from Aden, the first officer at the controls and the dead captain still aboard, and had flown to Mogadishu, capital of the Somali Republic. We got airborne in the Boeing 707 and sought permission to land there as well. Our flight from Saudi Arabia to Mogadishu took us directly across the war zone lying between Ethiopia and Somalia.

"On approach to Mogadishu we were given permission to land, but the situation was complicated by the presence of LH181 sitting in the middle of the main runway. Our pilot was equal to the challenge, however. Using only a short length of runway, he brought off a superb landing, using every metre of concrete available and rolling to within literally metres of buildings and houses on the airfield perimeter. Even the intensity of the overall situation could not obscure this brilliant feat of professional skill, and everyone aboard broke into spontaneous and grateful applause.

"On the ground, two top Somali officials collected all passports – and were surprised to discover two of the British variety among them, though they remained most courteous and friendly. The German minister went off to meet the Somali Prime Minister to discuss the developing political aspects of the hijack. The rest of us were taken to one of Mogadishu's top hotels and given accommodation and a meal. We were kept in constant contact regarding the hijack situation through the Mogadishu security services, who were extremely cordial and helpful.

"The terrorists now announced that their deadline was 15:00 on that same day: Monday, October 17. Negotiators in the control tower at Mogadishu airport asked for an extension, explaining that the Baader-Meinhof terrorists jailed in Germany, together with the two Palestinians held in Turkey, would be released but that they could not, however, be flown to Mogadishu in less than 10 hours.

"After prolonged discussion, the terrorist leader, 'Captain Mahmoud' (Zohair Akache), agreed on a final deadline of 03:00 the next morning, Tuesday, October 18. In the meantime, Minister Wischnewski obtained permission to bring in the German anti-terrorist team, flying to Mogadishu with the option of an assault on LH181. While awaiting its arrival, we all worked together to modify the assault plan to match it to the current situation. Joining us in our planning was a colonel from the Somali Special Forces.

"We stuck to the basic plan to approach the aircraft in single column from the rear, breaking into four sub-sections, each moving to its assigned position with the intention of making simultaneous entries through both wing emergency exits, the port front and starboard rear doors. We modified the choice of ladders for the assault on the doors, using double (side-by-side) instead of single ladders. The advantage of these was that two men could go up together. At the top, the left-hand man could turn the door handle and swing his full weight away from the fuselage, so pulling the door open quickly. This made it possible for the second, right-hand man to penetrate the airliner immediately. We needed outside help for two reasons. First, before the assault began we wanted the negotiators to start talking positively to the terrorists to ascertain as closely as possible their whereabouts inside LH181. We also thought we might encourage them to come to the cockpit by lighting a very large fire at the

'Captain Mahmoud' (Zohair Akache), leader of the hijack team. He was last to die, holding out in the cockpit for several minutes. He was more of an assassin – the PFLP had hired him for the hijack.

far end of the runway. This job was entrusted to the Somali soldiers, who were also responsible for ground defence around the aircraft.

"The GSG 9 men arrived in a second Boeing 707 at 20:05 on the evening of October 17. Their commander briefed them immediately, and they set about preparing their equipment for the assault. We ran through a quick rehearsal, using the GSG 9 Boeing 707, which was parked out of sight of LH181. By 23:30, the whole group was in position about 70m (225 feet) to the rear of the airliner. In single file we approached the plane, and in complete silence the ladders were put in position at each wing root and against the chosen doors. Major Morrison and I were on either side of the fuselage, at the rear of the wing roots. Our initial task was to throw stun grenades over the fuselage just as the doors were opened, to achieve the penetrating effect of noise and light in the cabin. I was also to throw a stun grenade over the front of the cockpit to disorientate the terrorist leader.

"The approach to the aircraft was very slick and smooth. The only problem we had was that the airfield lighting around the control tower created long shadows. Had the window blinds been up, any one of the terrorists looking out could have seen us approach.

"The GSG 9 commander was in direct contact with the tower. Just before the operation began, he transmitted to all his assault teams that the two male terrorists had been heard in the cockpit. At this moment the fire was ignited at the end of the runway. In spite of the tension, this caused some amusement, for it was plain that the Somali soldiers had let their enthusiasm run away with them. It looked as if they had set fire to a complete tanker-load of petrol. The GSG 9 commander counted down and gave the 'Go' signal. Everything happened at once: the quiet African night erupted. The front and rear doors opened as the left-hand ladder-men swung on them; their right-hand partners heaved themselves out of sight into the plane. The wing assault teams stood up, punched the emergency exit panels and vaulted in as the doors fell into the cabin – all these actions orchestrated by the bangs and flashes from the stun grenades. Immediately the rear starboard door swung open the first terrorist was sighted, amazed by this turn of events. She was shot instantly by a GSG 9 soldier, who then threw himself flat into the rear catering area, firing up the aisle where the other female terrorist had been spotted.

"The front assault team was involved in a brief firefight with the two male terrorists. Lasting for about a minute, it ended when they had both been fatally shot. During the firefight we heard two dull explosions inside LH181. These were hand grenades exploding as the terrorists' strength drained away and their grip on the grenades they were holding relaxed voluntarily. Thus, as the first few minutes of Tuesday, October 18, ticked away, the hijacking of Flight LH181 ended.

"As soon as the firing died away, the passengers began to disembark. The GSG 9 men on the ground took swift and firm command of the exits, guiding people down the assault ladders or assisting them through the mid-section emergency exits down to the ground via the wings. The passengers were in a state of sheer bewilderment: they had, after all, spent five long days cooped up in a very confined space, in hot, filthy conditions and with failing sanitary facilities. On top of all this physical discomfort, every hour would have been heavily weighted by the fear feeding on the uncertainty of their future. The climactic few minutes of the assault, involving loud explosions, flashes, smoke, rapid movement, gunfire and raw danger, must have disoriented many of them. As they disembarked they were ushered to the rear, where a fleet of ambulances and other vehicles ferried them to the passenger lounge in the terminal building.

"The casualty list showed three of the terrorists dead – two men and one woman – and the second woman terrorist severely wounded. As she was taken away for medical treatment she gave the V-sign and screamed an assortment of slogans. One member of GSG 9, one member of the aircrew and five of the passengers were slightly wounded. 'After any necessary medical attention, the passengers were soon taken aboard the negotiators' Boeing 707, while the negotiators, the GSG 9 men and we two SAS men boarded the GSG 9 707 to be flown back to Germany.

"Although apparently over, the hijack of LH181 still had a twist in its tail. Questions remained to which no answers have been found. During the flight we heard on the radio that the leading members of the Baader-Meinhof terrorist gang, confined in separate cells in Stammheim Jail in Stuttgart, had committed suicide. Andreas Baader and Jan-Carle Raspe had shot themselves; Gudrun Ensslin hanged herself, while Irmgard Müller had made an unsuccessful attempt to kill herself using a stolen bread knife. How did the terrorists, locked in separate cells in a maximum-security prison, simultaneously learn of the German government's success in Mogadishu, 5,600km (3,500 miles) away, within a few hours of its occurrence? How did the two male terrorists obtain pistols and ammunition in that same jail? These mysteries remain unexplained.

"Upon arrival at Frankfurt, Captain Morrison and I were separated from the GSG 9 people and taken to the VIP lounge. Arriving in London at around 21:00, we were moved off to a secret rendezvous for a full debriefing regarding the operation.

"So came the final end to the hijacking of LH181, together with the SAS/GSG 9 operation to rescue the hostages and crew. The success of our joint operation was marred, for me, only by the death of Captain Jürgen Schumann, shot in Aden. He was a very brave man and, like so many other aircraft captains, upheld his professional responsibilities to the end by seeking to protect all those in his care, passengers and crew alike."

The success was soon worldwide news, and governments all over the Western world applauded West Germany's determination in the face of an international terrorist threat.

# Chapter 5

# From the Jungle to the Desert

*Hot and humid conditions prevailed in the jungles of Borneo. Clothing was kept to a minimum.*

In 1960, 22 SAS was still barracked at Merebrook Camp at Malvern in Worcestershire: it was the Regiment's first permanent camp since the SAS had been reformed. However, later that same year it moved to the old Royal Artillery Barracks in Hereford, known as Bradbury Lines. The buildings, known as 'spiders', were constructed of wood and had been erected during the Second World War. The whole camp was second-rate and in dire need of repair, but it served the Regiment well.

*The 'Pinky' – a cut-down long-range Land Rover that arrived at the SAS base in the early 1960s.*

The change of address also heralded a change in SAS training – the development of a modern method of fighting known as close-quarter battle (CQB). It had two forms; armed and unarmed. Armed CQB covered a wide range of pistol and sub-machine gun techniques, while SAS unarmed combat perfected fast and deadly methods of killing. These include learning about the defensive and offensive parts of the body, and how best to use them or protect against them.

The early 1960s also saw many new recruits enter the SAS, among them several Fijians. The relationship between Fiji's fighting men and the Regiment had started in September 1952 when D Company of the 1st Fijian Infantry took part in a joint operation with two SAS squadrons called Operation Hive. A few years later a number of Fijians joined the British Army, some making their way into the SAS. They achieved great standing with their peers; two in particular, Corporal Labalaba and Trooper Savesaki, are remembered for their outstanding courage during the battle of Mirbat.

In addition to recruiting new blood and evolving new and unique training techniques, the Regiment also took delivery of new equipment. In the early 1960s the first specialist Land Rover aimed at meeting the specific requirements of the SAS was developed. The Regiment decided to paint its new vehicles pink after learning that an old aircraft shot down during the Second World War had been found in the desert and the wind-blown sand had burnished it pink.

The 'Pinky' or 'Pink Panther' was a cab-less, door-less long-wheelbase vehicle which held a crew of three, including the driver, a front-seat passenger and a rear gunner. This latter crewman occupied a small seat fitted between two long-range fuel tanks which were self-sealing if ruptured by enemy fire, and from which a centre-pivoted GPMG could be fired. The drop-down tailgate was used for storing the crew's bergens and other necessary equipment, and the vehicle was fitted with sand channels, which hooked on both sides of the main body, as well as two rifle boots, fixed for easy access over the front wheel arches. Four banks of three smoke dischargers were fitted, two on the front bumper and two on the rear superstructure. Other additional items included spotlights, astro-navigation equipment and vehicle camouflage nets. The original Pink Panthers suffered many problems, not least the under-powered

Malaya, he was transferred to Oman, where he took up a position as second-in-command of the Omani Muscat Regiment. In June 1963 an eight-man party consisting of French and SAS troops and led by Cooper made a rendezvous with royalist forces near Sana. The group included three members of 22 SAS – Sergeant Dorman, Corporal Chigley and Trooper Richardson – who trained the royalist tribesmen, arranged for them to be supplied with weapons by air and gathered intelligence which confirmed Sallal's reliance on Egyptian aid.

After three months the group was ordered to leave the country, but Cooper returned to assimilate more intelligence and to arrange further air-drops to the royalists. He continued to work alone in this way for a further 11 months, although prior to the air-drops he was joined by two SAS men, Cyril Weavers and David Ailey. Cooper spent a total of three years in North Yemen, gathering information on Egyptian forces and training royalist soldiers. The nine air-drops were carried out by the Israeli Air Force – a fact entirely unbeknown to the Arab guerrillas. In 1963, in response to calls for assistance, Britain intervened with military aid. Cooper's solitary mission in the Yemen was finally completed in 1966.

## Borneo

Around the same time, but thousands of miles away, trouble was once more brewing in the Malayan archipelago. Initially, the focus of the problem was the Sultanate of Brunei, a former British Protectorate tucked away in the north-west corner of the island of Borneo and sandwiched between the Malaysian states of Sarawak and Sabah.

Malaysia was seeking to bring together Singapore, Sabah, Sarawak, the Sultanate of Brunei and itself under the banner of the Federation of Malaya – an idea fully supported by Britain. However, the Indonesian

engine and weak half-shafts, which had a tendency to break in the most isolated patch of desert: however, they survived until the mid-1980s, when they were replaced by the new Land Rover 110.

On the political front, Britain faced two areas of possible confrontation: Aden and Borneo. Aden had been under British rule since 1839. By 1963, it had joined the British-governed Federation of South Arabia (FSA), originally set up in 1959 as an amalgamation of several small states, emirates and sultanates. Aden joined the FSA on the stipulation that Britain would maintain a presence there after full independence, scheduled for 1968 or before.

However, the Soviet Union had thrown its weight behind unrest in neighbouring Yemen, leading on September 26, 1962, to the overthrow of the ruling Imam in a military coup instigated by Colonel Abdullah Sallal. Sallal, who also had the backing of President Nasser of Egypt, declared the Yemen an Arab Republic. Yemen claimed territory in the lands held by the FSA and supported two resistance groups in the Aden Protectorate: the National Liberation Front (NLF) and the Front for the Liberation of Occupied South Yemen (FLOSY). The deposed ruler, Imam Mohammed al-Badr, escaped and raised an opposition army, based in the Aden Protectorate and secretly aided by the British and French governments.

As their man on the spot, the British chose an SAS officer called Johnny Cooper, an outstanding soldier who had joined the original SAS as a trooper. In 1959, while commanding A Squadron in Malaya, he had been badly injured 'tree-jumping' into the jungle: withdrawn from

# Theatre of War: Brunei

*There had been trouble brewing on the Malayan archipelago for some time, before it eventually erupted, causing the British Army to become involved. They elected to send in the SAS. A Squadron, numbering some 70 men, was responsible for patrolling a border that stretched for nearly 1,000kms (700 miles).*

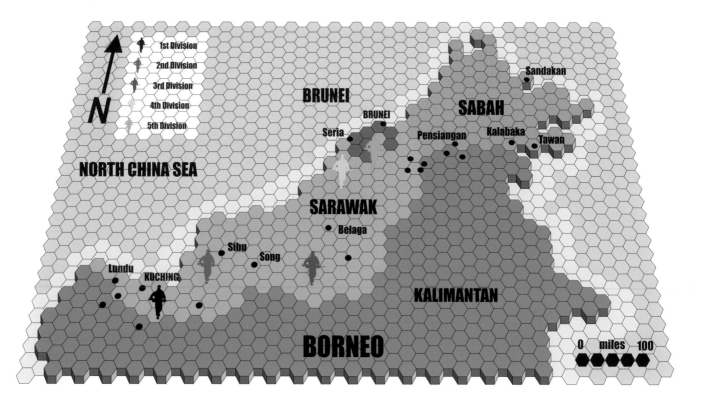

*Quickly, it was realized that the best use for the SAS was in groups of two or three men, with objectives to warn of any Communist or other threats to the country.*

*In some ways, the other task that the Regiment was charged with – waging a 'hearts and minds' campaign – became more important than their primary objective. The troops helped natives with medical aid and education as well. This helped enormously for intelligence gathering purposes.*

*Local recruits from all across the border territory were used to very good effect too. These became the Cross-Border Scouts.*

President, Sukarno, vehemently opposed the move, as it threatened his own designs on the rest of Borneo. In 1962, a small anti-Malaysian element rebelled in Brunei, with the backing of Malaysia. It was led by Sheikh Azahari, who planned to become Prime Minister of Brunei, Sarawak and Sabah, which he wanted to unite in an area called North Kalimantan. The revolt did not last long – crushed within eight days by British troops brought in from Singapore.

However, by the following year the situation in Borneo had deteriorated again, with well-trained Indonesian insurgents infiltrating over the border from the Kalimantan region. In response, Britain raised a force of Malaysian, Commonwealth and British troops, including the SAS, to deal with the situation. Unfortunately, the force was only a small one and the border stretched for 700 miles. Not only did they face a threat from the Indonesians, but also from an internal terrorist element, the Clandestine Communist Organisation (CCO), made up mainly of Chinese settlers from Sarawak.

*'Hearts and minds', a policy originally conceived by General Sir Gerald Templar, the Military High Commissioner in Malaya. Its purpose was to gain local support, thereby obtaining the upper hand in defeating the communist terrorists. It was so successful that the Regiment adopted it in subsequent counter-insurgency campaigns in Borneo and Oman.*

The British commander in Borneo, Major-General Walter Walker, initially wanted the SAS to parachute into the jungle, as they had in Malaya, and recapture any helicopter landing areas which had fallen into rebel hands. The CO of 22 SAS at the time, Lieutenant-Colonel John Woodhouse, remembering the high casualty rate which had resulted from tree-jumping in Malaya, persuaded Walker that the SAS would be better suited to patrolling the border instead.

At the time A Squadron consisted of only 70 men, a small number to patrol such a long stretch of border, especially in such hostile jungle conditions. However, by operating in 21 patrols of two or three men and staying in the jungle for long periods of time, they were able to provide early warning of any Indonesian military or communist incursions. As well as patrolling the border, the SAS took on another very important task – that of winning the 'hearts and minds' of the native people. By gaining an understanding of their lifestyle and language,

by living with them and dispensing medical aid when necessary, the SAS gained important allies in intelligence-gathering. The local people, who still crossed the border freely into Kalimantan to trade their goods, often brought back valuable information on Indonesian troop movements.

The SAS also recruited some of the local people as Border Scouts. Their role was primarily one of gathering intelligence, as they proved unsuited to a conventional combat role. In September 1963, a Scout post at Long Jawi, 28 miles from the border, was all but wiped out by a substantial group of well-equipped Indonesians. As a result, Walker restricted the Scouts to intelligence-gathering only. It was in this capacity that they really proved their worth to the SAS, frequently complementing individual SAS patrols by enabling communication between the forces and the native inhabitants.

From 1964 on, the SAS recruited and trained a number of local people into what was to become the Cross-Border Scouts. This force consisted of 40 specially-selected Iban Dyaks, who took part in raids across the border into Kalimantan. The British believed the Ibans would be highly skilled at moving quietly and efficiently through the jungle and, in the event that a mission was unsuccessful, the Ibans would be the most likely to escape alive. Under the supervision of Major John Edwards of A Squadron, 22 SAS, training began in the summer of 1964. The Scouts' first mission was in August, following which they were employed along the border, especially in western Sarawak and around Bemban.

*Under the supervision of Major John Edwards of A Squadron, training of the Iban Border Scouts began in the summer of 1964. The Scouts' first mission was in August, following which they were employed along the border, especially in western Sarawak and around Bemban.*

## Claret Operations

In mid-1964, the Malaysian and British governments approved a request by the Director of Borneo Operations, Major-General Walker, for permission to conduct cross-border operations into Kalimantan, the Indonesian part of the island of Borneo, in order to pre-empt anticipated or suspected Indonesian attacks. Initially, the maximum distance from the border for these operations was limited to 5,000 yards, but later the same year it was increased to 20,000 yards for a small number of specific operations. Such operations, heavily classified as Top Secret, were codenamed Claret.

The troops involved comprised A and D Squadrons,

22 SAS, and the Guards Independent Parachute Company – the latter assigned due to a manpower crisis in the SAS. It was decided that the Guards Independent Parachute Company would be trained in SAS jungle tactics. Initially used for border surveillance, in September 1965 the Company, under Major L. G. S. Head, was allowed to carry out cross-border operations. They achieved excellent results, in one instance ambushing 40 Indonesian soldiers, killing nine and wounding many others. In 1965, several members who had served with the SAS in Borneo were chosen to form the backbone of G Squadron SAS. Other units used during operation Claret were the Gurkha Independent Parachute Company, 1 and 2 Squadrons of the Australian SAS Regiment and detachments of the 1st Ranger Squadron, NZSAS. In addition, 1 and 2 Special Boat Sections, Royal Marines, carried out small-scale raids on coastal targets on either flank.

The Australian Special Air Service Regiment (SASR) was formed on September 4, 1964, with an establishment of 15 officers and 209 other ranks. Initially it comprised a headquarters, consisting of three officers and 37 other ranks, and two Sabre squadrons (designated 1 and 2 respectively), each of which comprised six officers and 86 other ranks. Each squadron consisted of a headquarters and three troops, each of the latter numbering twenty-one all ranks. In December 1964, a headquarters squadron was added to the Regiment's establishment and the strength of each squadron was increased by one troop. Shortly afterwards, authorization was given for the raising of two further squadrons, to be formed by December 1965 and June 1966 respectively. During the period from February 1965 to July 1966, 1, 2 and 3 Squadrons saw action in Borneo where they came under the command of 22 SAS. SASR also participated in cross-border Claret operations.

Typically, these operations consisted of interdiction of tracks, rivers and other routes being used by Indonesian troops, who were mainly well-trained regulars of the Indonesian National Army, the Tentera Nasional Indonesia (TNI). These included para-commandos of the Resemeu Para Kommando Angaton Daret (RPKAD) and marine commandos of the Korps Kommando Operasi (KKO). More than 22,000 TNI troops were deployed in the border areas, supported by large numbers of volunteer irregular forces.

*Rivers are the main navigation routes through the jungle. The SAS employed the local Iban tribesmen to ferry them and their equipment up to the Indonesian border.*

*The SAS would rarely use tracks other than those made by animals. They preferred to contour through the thick jungle, moving slowly. Sometimes a day's march would cover little more that a 1,000 metres.*

The conduct of Claret operations was governed by a set of regulations laid down by Major-General Walker and known as the 'Golden Rules'. These stipulated that all operations had to be authorized by the Director of Borneo Operations personally and that every operation had to be meticulously planned, rehearsed and carried out with maximum security. Only tried and tested troops were permitted to be used, and under no circumstances were troops to be captured, dead or alive, by the enemy. All operations were to be carried out with the aim of deterring and thwarting aggression by the Indonesians. Furthermore, the depth of penetration from the border was to be strictly controlled and it was emphasized that air support could not be given except in instances of extreme emergency. Artillery and mortar support was, however, available on call with 5.5-inch guns, 105mm pack howitzers or 81mm mortars being lifted forward, singly or in pairs, by helicopter to bases on the border in support of specific operations.

During the winter of 1964-65, patrols by B Squadron were concentrated in the Pueh range of hills of western Sarawak, a favourite route for CCO agents making their way to Lundu, where a number of communist cells were located.

## Captain Robin Letts

Captain Robert Letts was not everyone's idea of an SAS hero: self-effacing, shy, short-sighted and a great lover of books and music, he nevertheless showed great initiative and bravery during the Borneo confrontation. In April 1965, he was put in charge of a patrol detailed with collecting intelligence on Indonesian communication routes across the border. The rest of his patrol consisted of Corporal 'Taff' Springles – the signaller, medic and the soldier with the most experience – Trooper Brown and Trooper Hogg.

The area in question, mostly consisting of swamp, had already been mapped out by members of B Squadron, making navigation easier for Letts and his men. Nevertheless, the going was slow, as they were trying to keep their movements quiet. After six days of living in mud and water, the sound of an outboard motor drew them to a 12-foot-wide stream, one of the main tributaries of the swamp, draining into the River Sentimo. Finding an area of dry land about 40

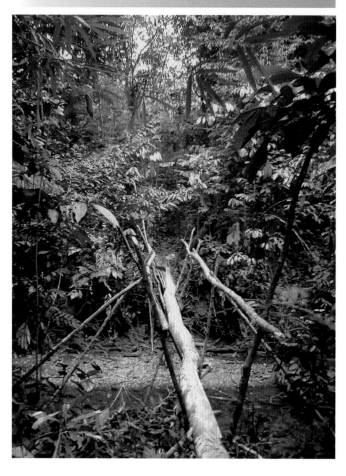

*Man-made objects, such as bridges, provided perfect ambush sites.*

yards back from the stream, Letts and Hogg took off their bergens and left them with the other two men, intending to do a little reconnaissance. To lessen the likelihood of their tracks being spotted by the enemy, they took to the stream, walking and sometimes swimming along it. A short distance downstream they saw a domestic water-buffalo and heard voices, a sign that there was a village not far away. Letts realized that their progress through the river had been just a bit too easy: none of the usual debris of underwater logs or vegetation had blocked their way at any point. This could only mean that the waterway was regularly cleared to allow water traffic through. The realization meant that the men had to get out of the stream – and fast. At any moment a boat could come along and they would be sitting ducks.

Rejoining Springles and Brown, they soon found an

observation point which was ideal for monitoring traffic on the waterway. It was set on a loop in the stream with clear visibility 60 yards to the left and 30 yards to the right. Late that afternoon their patience was rewarded as two boats, both containing two armed soldiers, paddled past them heading downstream.

Leaving Hogg at the observation point, Letts and the others returned to the lying-up point (LUP) to signal base and ask permission to engage the enemy if the chance was repeated. While they were gone, two more boats unexpectedly appeared. Hogg, who was standing up still watching after the first two boats, was caught unawares, his head exposed. He feared for his life, thinking that he had been seen, but luckily the two boats, with their unobservant occupants, passed by without incident.

By morning, there had still been no word back from base giving the patrol approval to attack the enemy. Letts decided the opportunity was too great to pass up and that they would act anyway. The stream was obviously more important than it had previously appeared, and probably served as a main supply route for men and equipment to the enemy's forward base at Achan. The village which Letts and Hogg had discovered earlier possibly served as a staging-point, which meant that any attack would bring swift retaliation.

A plan was drawn up and, at dawn, Letts positioned his men at various positions around the loop. Manoeuvring in the stream at this point seemed to be difficult for the boatmen and required all their concentration, leaving them less alert to the possibility of attack. The layout of the loop also meant that once a boat had passed a certain point it was no longer visible to those following behind, thus creating the perfect conditions for an ambush. With Letts at the apex of the loop, Brown to his left and Springles to his right, the men were ready to take on any boat, no matter from which direction it came. However, as most of the water traffic seemed to be coming from their left, Letts positioned Hogg along that side too, to give warning of any problems. Letts also worked out an escape route; if his assumption about the village was correct, they would need to get out of the area as quickly as possible.

At 20:15 a boat came into view, but this time it carried three armed soldiers instead of two. The extra man sat in the stern, acting as sentry, alert to any dangers ahead. The next boat was the same: two armed men sitting in the front paddling and another, cradling a weapon, in the rear. This new development upped the stakes.

The first boat passed by Brown, as planned, but the second one managed to crash into the bank right next to him. Luckily, the crew was too busy trying to rectify the situation to notice him. As the boat struggled to regain its course, a third boat came into view. As with the others, it also carried three armed soldiers. Eventually the first boat reached Springles' position and Letts gave the signal to attack. He took aim at his first target – the armed sentry in the second boat – but was surprised when one of the paddlers grabbed his gun with amazing speed and lined Letts up in his sights. At this close range and in so little time, Letts really had no chance to get out of the way or to change his aim to the man in the bows. It looked as though he was about to be killed when Springles fired at the Indonesian and killed him.

All the patrol members opened up on the boats in a furious hail of fire. During the firefight, the crews of two of the boats managed to flip them over, throwing themselves into the water. Later, it was surmised that this was part of an anti-ambush drill, as some of them soon re-emerged on the bank with their weapons at the ready.

Seeing the boat go over, Letts fired into the water, hoping to hit some of their occupants. At the same time, the only man remaining alive in the second boat managed to take aim at Letts. The Captain realized his predicament, almost too late, and jumped to one side before turning his weapon on the man and firing. The Indonesian fell forward into the boat. For a split second, Letts looked away to see how Brown was coping with his boat, when the man he had just shot seemingly came back from the dead. Although wounded, he raised himself up and took aim at Letts again. Luckily, Letts saw the action in time and shot him twice. This time the wounds were definitely fatal.

Distracted, Letts had failed to notice that he had become a target for another of the Indonesian soldiers. One of the men from Springles' overturned boat had finally managed to reach the near bank and had immediately taken aim at Letts. Once more his life was saved by Springles, who shot the man dead. Instantly, another soldier emerged from the water and made a grab for the dead man's weapon. Of course, he never had a chance, and was killed alongside his companion.

Brown had dealt with the occupants of his boat

*The Gurkhas were an indispensable force that backed up the SAS on several occasions. Their primary role was to man defensive fortifications close to the Indonesian border. The remnants of these fortifications can still be found to this day.*

relatively easily, and all lay dead. A fourth boat now came into view, but as the occupants realized what was happening, they quickly reached the bank and pulled their boat backwards, out of sight. Hogg fired off a few rounds, but the enemy were already gone. The firefight

was over; the whole thing had taken only four minutes.

Dead Indonesians littered the water, the bank and the boats. Only one managed to escape the ferocity of the patrol's onslaught with their SLRs. Letts gave the order to retreat and the patrol made haste to their LUP, picked up their bergens and headed back in the direction of the border. With the Indonesians now alerted to their presence, they knew they had little time before search parties were sent out. The hunters had now become the hunted, and Letts decided that they would have far more chance if they relied on speed rather than concealment. Their extreme fitness served them well, and they managed to cover a great deal of ground before the enemy mortared the ambush position. Apart from speed, the other advantage Letts and his men had was that the Indonesians had no idea how big a force they were up against and, seeing the damage done, probably over-estimated the numbers they were facing. They would therefore have expected such a large force to be moving more slowly through the jungle, giving Letts' patrol a much-needed head start.

The patrol covered most of the nine kilometres back to the border by the time dusk fell. Springles set up his radio and contacted base to tell them of their success. Before he could do so, he was told that permission had been granted for them to attack the enemy. Luckily for them, the *fait accompli* had worked out well, especially as, in the heat of the moment, they had forgotten that they had still been waiting for that permission to be given.

In the morning they continued, and cautiously made their way back over the border. They called for an extraction and were winched out by helicopter through a break in the forest canopy. The helicopter arrived far quicker than usual, much to their surprise, and they had to forego a tasty dinner cooked by Hogg. Hogg's bad luck didn't end there: while being winched up by the helicopter a jungle vine became tangled around his neck, and he was almost strangled in mid-air and mid-rescue.

Nevertheless, the whole operation had been a complete success, and a few months later Letts was awarded the Military Cross for his part. Shortly afterwards, he joined the Australian SAS so that he could take part in the Vietnam War.

After a short break, D Squadron returned to Borneo in May 1965. This time it was commanded by Major Peter de la Billière, who set up a new regimental headquarters in Kuching, the capital of Sarawak. The fading Colonial house had rusting wrought-iron gates bedecked with barbed wire, and was known as the Pea Green House or PGH. D Squadron continued the cross-border raids with the aid of the Gurkhas, but the enemy often proved elusive. The patrols established likely ambush sites and potential helicopter landing zones. They made notes of all the likely places the Indonesians would try to infiltrate, and charted a previously unexplored region known as 'The Gap'. All intelligence collected was relayed back to SAS headquarters on high-frequency radios, where it could be acted upon immediately.

In July 1965 2 Troop, commanded by Captain Malcolm McGillivray, was given the task of searching Mount Kalimantan for Indonesian units and destroying them. McGillivray had come into the ranks of the SAS via the Black Watch. At first his superiors had not wanted to let him join the SAS, but he managed to persuade them otherwise. First, he completed SAS selection, without permission from his commanding officer to do so. Then, when his regiment persisted in its reluctance, he showed his displeasure by eating nothing but porridge, day after day. Finally, his fellow-officers could stand his obstinate protest no more and agreed to let him go. His qualities soon served him well in the SAS.

His team consisted of 10 SAS soldiers, including Corporal Roberts and Troopers Franks, Henry, Bilbao, Condie, Callan and Shipley, as well as 21 Scouts recruited from local tribes. Air reconnaissance photographs showed that there were a number of huts high up on the mountain, situated in a clearing. Regarding this as a good target, McGillivray had a full-size replica of the huts built and made his team practice an assault on them again and again until he was convinced they had it right.

Preparation complete, McGillivray and his men set out on July 9, 1965, crossing the River Bemban and trekking up through the foothills. This first part of the journey took five days. On the sixth day, McGillivray split the men into six patrols to search the area for any signs of enemy occupation. At first, the intelligence on which they had been working seemed to be right on target, as a patrol of Scouts returned with the news that they had found bootprints and smelled cooking. After a long conversation, made more difficult by the language barrier, McGillivray finally worked out where the enemy force was likely to be found. He gathered his team

*Pea Green House situated in Kuching, the capital of Borneo, served as headquarters for the SAS. It is rumoured that the house backed onto a local brothel. The house still stands today.*

together again and they set off.

Unfortunately, by the time they reached the place where the Scouts had found the camp, there was no sign of it; every evidence of human occupation, if there had been any, had been removed. Either the enemy was very clever, or else all their intelligence had been wrong and the Scouts had imagined what they saw and smelt. McGillivray looked about him at the landmarks he had memorized from the photographs and other intelligence, and found that they matched what he saw in the surrounding landscape. This was definitely the place, but minus the camp.

No matter how hard they searched, the camp could not be found. However, they were near to a track which was obviously used by the CCO as a supply route to Batu Hitam. At least they should be able to mount an ambush on any Indonesian troops who came their way. After a spot of reconnaissance, McGillivray decided the best ambush point was at a gully just north-west of the river, spanned by a large log. On the north side, where they were, the ground levelled out to provide a broad, flat space, good enough to fire across from the safety of cover. Anyone trapped on the log when the shooting began didn't stand much of a chance.

McGillivray's signaller, 'Rover' Slater, usually worked with the Captain. Together, they argued every decision, and although it seemed sometimes that they were always at odds with each other, in fact they managed to work as a team in some strange, antagonistic way: no idea went unchallenged and no possibility was left unexplored.

McGillivray took Slater and two others with him to keep watch on this point. A group of locals appeared, carrying heavy bundles, and crossed over the gully using the log. Convinced now that this was definitely the place for the ambush, McGillivray sent the two other men back to round up the rest of the team while he stayed at the point with Slater. Shortly afterwards, a group of about 11 armed enemy soldiers came in view. However, at such close range and with such odds, it was deemed unwise to take them on.

The rest of McGillivray's men arrived and deployed initially to the LUP, where he and Slater met up with them. He selected 15 men, including Corporal Roberts, to form the first watch. This group was divided into three separate sections, each with a different responsibility during any attack. The men were all then placed individually in one long line between five and 20 yards away from the track. The 'killer' team, consisting of Roberts, Franks, Nibau and three Scouts, was placed alongside the log. The group on the right-hand side, consisting of Condie, Callan, Shipley and three Scouts, was responsible for keeping watch for the enemy's approach and informing the others by pulling a cord which ran down the line. They were also charged with stopping any escapees and warning of the likelihood of a counter-attack. The left-hand group assumed a similar role to the right.

It was the afternoon by now, and no one expected the enemy to return before dusk, so McGillivray carried on with his preparations. Back at the rendezvous area, he decided he was not happy with the position he had picked and so had the men move the bergens to a new place. As usual, Slater pointed out the downside – that the ambush party would not know where to retreat to and, even if they were told, still might not be able to find it in all the confusion after a contact. However, McGillivray was not unduly worried; he felt he had plenty of time to change the watch over and ensure all the men were fully aware of the new rendezvous location.

An hour later it began to rain heavily, the storm creating difficult conditions for the watchers. Then,

halfway through the afternoon, without warning, the soldiers who had passed through before returned. They were obviously wet and uncomfortable, as they travelled at a very quick pace. Nevertheless, they were spotted by Shipley, sitting out on the right flank, who gave five tugs on the cord. The message was passed down the line in the same fashion until it reached Roberts, who alerted his men just as five of the soldiers stepped on to the log. The 'killer' group all took aim and fired, sending the Indonesians tumbling into the gully below. Roberts, thinking that all had been killed, gave the order to stop firing. Bilbao, however, spotted one of them trying to crawl away and let off two more rounds to stop him, as he had been previously instructed.

However, the five soldiers killed on the log were only a part of the group, as the men on the right flank were about to find out. Alerted by the gunfire, a second enemy group disappeared into cover next to the track and let loose with rifle and machine gun fire towards the ambushers. It looked as though they were about to storm the position of the right-flank group. Condie, who was a little farther back, called out to them to fall back to his position. Shipley, Callan and their Scouts needed no second urging and retreated. Realizing that the area of ground to the rear provided good cover from the enemy's fire, they ran to it – but in the process completely missed Condie, who had taken it upon himself to move forward to check that they had got away and not been wounded or killed. Once Shipley and Callan reached the dead ground they continued on to the old rendezvous point – standard procedure after a contact – expecting to find others. Of course, due to McGillivray's move, they were the only ones there – a fact which caused them great frustration.

McGillivray was also feeling frustrated by Standard Operating Procedures. They prohibited him from joining the action, although at such close quarters he could hear it going on. Slater, still at his side, reminded him that the ambush party still knew nothing about the relocation of the rendezvous point. Stirred into action again, McGillivray ordered two of his Scouts to go to the old location and guide anyone they found there to the new one. Guiding them part of the way there himself, the Captain was suddenly confronted by the first of the Scouts coming back from the ambush. Once again, communication proved a bit of problem, but McGillivray was sure they were saying that Roberts was in trouble. Standard Operating Procedures or no, McGillivray decided that he couldn't hang back any longer, and made his way to Roberts' position. In fact, he had understood the Scouts wrongly; the Corporal wasn't hurt at all, and was instead profoundly displeased that his commanding officer had risked going against procedure so recklessly.

The thick jungle cover slowed the battle and, although the gunfire continued from the enemy's position, they did not seem as willing to advance as they had been before. The bodies of two Indonesian soldiers lay under a log close to Roberts' position, but as yet they had not been searched for weapons or papers. McGillivray turned to two Scouts standing nearby and asked them to carry out the task, something which they seemed to be only too glad to do. McGillivray then went to all of his men's positions to check that they had retreated safely before retiring himself.

At the new rendezvous location, the group gathered together to prepare for the journey out. The Scouts whom McGillivray had sent to search the bodies returned with not only weapons and papers from their enemies, but also their heads. The British men stared, shocked that the tribesmen still took heads as trophies: they thought the practice had stopped long ago. Even some of the most hardened soldiers there were taken aback by the grisly

*The humble 'basha' – home to every SAS soldier that has ever served in the jungle. This simple 'A' frame construction allows a comfortable night's sleep while keeping the occupant dry and free from insects.*

sight, and the apparent jubilation of the tribesmen which accompanied it. But, although revolted by the practice, McGillivray and his men made no attempt to stop it or to dampen the tribesmen's celebration in any way. It seemed an important thing to the Iban, a business which appeared to raise their morale. And, as McGillivray and his men readily recognized, if it raised the Iban's morale, such an act was likely to lower the Indonesians' once they found the headless bodies of their comrades in the jungle. Nevertheless, the head-hunting incident would be wonderful news for any hostile propagandists if it got out, so it was decided that the whole event needed to be kept quiet: and throughout his years in the Regiment, despite the rumours, McGillivray always denied having witnessed any head-hunting.

In August of the same year the SAS, working closely with the Gurkhas, launched a series of cross-border raids which met with varying degrees of success. The search for an elusive foe often ended in frustration. In September, for example, 12 four-man patrols from A Squadron conducted a three-week search for a CCO camp in the area between the headwaters of the Sempayang and Bemban rivers, but nothing was found.

## Geordie and Jock

Training for the SAS is rigorous and demanding, but the skills and techniques paid off for two soldiers towards the end of the Borneo campaign. Sergeant Geordie Lillicoe and Trooper Jock Thomson were both members of D Squadron, 22 SAS, and involved in one of the Regiment's cross-border operations.

Geordie Lillicoe, a very experienced jungle soldier, took part in many of these Claret raids, and on February 26, 1966, led his patrol into the area of an old Indonesian camp situated close to the border. The patrol moved very slowly and with caution, conscious that they were in Indonesian territory. The camp had been found the day before and appeared not to have been used for some time. A cursory search that evening had been cut short by the gathering dusk: however, what little information had been gleaned was of great interest. There were bamboo beds, known to the SAS as 'bashas'; these have no roofs, the latter being provided by a soldier's poncho. The

Dropping their heavy packs would give them greater mobility, and in a firefight the SAS soldier is better off with just his belt-kit and rifle.

They made good time, quickly covering the 1,500 yards from the ERV to the camp. Jock Thomson was the first to reach the outskirts of the camp and stopped there, motioning discreetly for the others to do likewise. They waited, listening to the jungle; all seemed quiet, with nothing to raise their suspicions. Thomson turned his head slowly to query Lillicoe; a perceptible nod told him to continue. Ducking under some bamboo which lay across the track, he emerged on the other side. There was a soldier with a light automatic weapon no more than 12 yards away to his right. The patrol had walked directly into a well-prepared Indonesian ambush.

Almost immediately, the Indonesian soldier opened fire, and at this signal several more guns opened up on the SAS patrol. Jock Thomson was hit in the first burst, taking a bullet in his left thigh which shattered the bone. However, the hit knocked him off the track, where he landed in thick bamboo. Here Jock found himself confronting yet another Indonesian soldier, so close that he could see the tiger's-head shoulder-flash of the man's unit. The soldier was very young and extremely scared; he seemed to be having trouble with his rifle. Jock, who had recovered from the initial shock of his wound, found the Armalite rifle he had dropped and shot the young soldier. He then crawled clear of the immediate danger zone. The sight of bright blood pumping from his thigh made him want to stop, but he knew that if he did not clear the ambush area a second and then a third bullet would find him. Therefore, with the life-blood flowing from him, he crawled into the thick bush. Although not out of immediate danger, Jock felt it was safe enough to dress his wound and stop the bleeding. The pieces of his shattered femur jarred together as he did so, causing excruciating pain which he dulled by injecting himself with morphine – in action, every member of the SAS carries two pre-loaded syringes, operated simply by squeezing the flexible container. While he was doing so, the gunfire died down to a few sporadic shots, but even

camp's military nature was confirmed by the labels on some rusted tins which showed they were Indonesian Army rations.

The patrol, eight in number, had withdrawn for the night to the slopes of Gunong Rawan, where they 'bashered up' for the night and Lillicoe reviewed the orders given him by his squadron commander, Major Roger Woodiwiss, in the light of this unexpected discovery. His main task was to watch the River Sekayan, three miles over the border, which was known to be the enemy's main line of communication. The SAS was operating on Indonesian soil, and did not wish its presence to become known. Yet another reason for avoiding contact with the enemy was that this was, in part, a training patrol, planned by Woodiwiss for the benefit of several recruits to D Squadron, whose third tour in Borneo was only just beginning. Lillicoe's problem lay not so much with his orders but in having to visit the same place twice, for that would contravene Standard Operating Procedures (SOPs). However, few had learned to master the jungle like Lillicoe, and his prime directive was to gather information.

Next morning, Lillicoe decided the camp was worth a second look, but chose to split his forces. His reasons for doing so were based on clear military thinking. For one thing, the patrol was large enough to be safely divided; in any case, he planned to leave the four new recruits in the relative safety of the overnight camp, which would also serve as the Emergency Rendezvous (ERV). They would act as a rearguard and protect the patrol's bergens, which Lillicoe decided to leave behind.

so Jock felt it necessary to keep his senses about him by constantly surveying the tactical situation.

A short distance away, he could see Lillicoe, immobile and covered in blood. As patrol commander, he had been immediately behind Thomson, and the initial bursts of fire had hit them both. As Thomson was thrown to the left of the bamboo clump, Lillicoe leapt to the right, firing to his front as he did so. Almost immediately, he was knocked off his feet. Wounded in both legs and unable to get clear, he was forced to return fire while sitting in the middle of the track. Despite their injuries, both men continued to lay down suppressive fire while the remaining patrol members 'bugged out.' Then, as quickly as it had begun, the firing stopped. Both men sat waiting for a few moments before they began the painful struggle to get away from the immediate killing-zone.

Then Thomson saw a figure stand up and move out into the open. It was an Indonesian soldier coming out to check the killing area – a serious error of judgement. Thomson and Lillicoe fired together. Once more, the area fell quiet. This time, the two exchanged words, telling each other of their injuries, and Thomson struggled to his feet and came forward to give Lillicoe covering fire. Seeing Thomson and thinking he could walk, Lillicoe called out to him to fetch the rest of the patrol. Thomson shouted back that he was hit, but would try to make it back up the ridge, where he could RV with the others. After covering several yards, he fired several bursts into the area where the Indonesians had been waiting. This fresh gunfire from an elevated position led the enemy to believe that reinforcements had entered the area, and for

a while they withdrew.

The remainder of the SAS patrol had decided that the best course of action was to move to the nearest infantry post, which was close by, and lead back a stronger party to search the area. This they did, starting back towards the scene of the contact late the same day.

As soon as he felt it safe to do so, Thomson applied a fresh field dressing to his wound and injected himself with his second morphine syringe. Then, very slowly, he continued crawling towards the ridgeline above him. Darkness fell and gave him some protection; to provide camouflage, he settled down in the mud of a pig-hole to wait out the night.

By morning on the second day, Thomson had managed to cover half the distance back to the infantry camp, firing single shots to attract the attention of any search party. He finally reached the RV, where he was discovered by a Gurkha patrol which had been sent to look for the wounded men. Extremely weak from loss of blood, he required immediate medical attention.

Geordie Lillicoe had also managed to extract himself and hide in the nearby bamboo. There, he too dressed his wound and gave himself morphine. The left leg felt numb and detached; there was no sensation in it. His right leg he could feel, although it would not support him. Everywhere, there was too much blood. A bullet had entered his left leg a little below the thigh and exited by blowing a huge hole through his backside. The lack of pain was because a major nerve had been severed and, luckily, the main artery was undamaged. Bandaging the entry point was easy, but trying to stem the bleeding from his buttock proved an ordeal. These wounds to his legs made it almost impossible to move, but he was able to conceal himself for the night beneath the trunk of a fallen tree. He had lost a tremendous amount of blood, and after a while lapsed into unconsciousness. It was daylight when he recovered, and he could hear Indonesian soldiers all around him. One of the enemy had climbed a tree about 40 yards away and remained

*The arrival of helicopters into the jungle theatre provided excellent insertion and re-supply. Nevertheless, it was appreciated most for its hot extraction, especially when an SAS soldier was wounded.*

there for about half an hour, in full view, scanning the jungle. By this time, a helicopter was airborne, searching for Lillicoe: he could hear it, but with the enemy so near, he was reluctant to activate his SARBE rescue beacon. It was only when he was certain he would not be detected that he risked using the survival radio, calling in a helicopter which managed to winch him out.

Both men survived their ordeal, recovered from their wounds and were fit enough to continue serving in the SAS. Geordie Lillicoe, who was awarded the Military Medal, is one of the longest-serving members of 22 SAS and very much respected for his dedication to training, especially in SAS techniques.

Claret operations ceased on March 23, 1966, just 11 days after the overthrow of Indonesia's President Sukarno by General Suharto. In the main, they had achieved their aim of keeping the Indonesians off-balance, although early operations achieved only limited success. Within Indonesia, all publicity about setbacks caused by Claret raids had been suppressed, principally because of the embarrassment of President Sukarno, who had promised his people that Malaysia would be crushed by January 1, 1965.

The campaign in Borneo is an outstanding example of the tenacity, resourcefulness and skill of the individual SAS soldier. It illustrated what a small number of properly-trained and well-motivated men can achieve. General Walker himself stated: "I regard 70 troopers of the SAS as being as valuable to me as 700 infantry in the role of 'hearts and minds', border surveillance, early warning, stay-behind, and eyes and ears with a sting."

# Aden

The Radfan is a highly mountainous area in the northern district of the Republic of Yemen. When Britain became involved in Aden during the 1960s, her forces suffered many attacks by local tribespeople trained and armed by the Egyptians. In response, the British planned an advance into the Radfan Mountains to defuse the tension with these tribes and to try to discourage them from mining the Dhala road, which was then under construction.

The force set up to re-establish British control in the area was codenamed Radforce. The main thrust into the mountains would be made by A Squadron of 22 SAS, which had recently arrived in the region and established a base at Thumier, 50km from the Yemeni border, with the aim of seizing a rocky feature codenamed 'Cap Badge' overlooking the dissidents' main stronghold of Danaba.

The operation was set for April 29–30, 1964. The approach to Danaba was to be made by 45 Commando via the Wadi Boran, while at the same time 3 Troop of A Squadron was to take 'Cap Badge'. Once cleared, it was to be used as a drop-zone for airborne troops from the Parachute Regiment. Commanded by Captain Robin Edwards, 3 Troop was to be taken some of the way by armoured car, continuing the journey on foot.

Edwards and his men were tough, experienced soldiers, used to fighting in the harsh environments of Borneo and Malaya. Even so, they found progress slow in the rough, rocky terrain. To make matters worse, Edward's signaller, Trooper Terry Warburton, was suffering from severe stomach cramps and they had to pause every now and then to allow him to catch up.

At about midnight, Edwards realized that at the rate they were travelling they would not reach their objective before daylight, and made the decision to halt and seek shelter. Nearby were two old rock-built sangars, and Edwards decided that they should spend the rest of the night and the following day holed up there to allow Warburton time to recover. They radioed the SAS squadron commander, informed him of the situation

*A 'Beverly' transport aircraft landing at Habilain, the main airbase which supported the engineers road built from Aden up into the interior.*

*The SAS accommodation at Habilain from where they carried out short 36-hour patrols. Note the L42 sniper rifle, which was standard issue at the time.*

and then settled down for a long wait.

The following morning, their position was discovered by a goatherd. Fearing he would run off and tell the rebels where they were, they killed him. Unfortunately, the shot was heard in the nearby village of Shab Tem and very soon they were surrounded by rebel tribesmen. A long-range sniping battle broke out, with the rebels soon becoming bolder, climbing the slopes and coming ever nearer to the sangars. The position was out of reach of the artillery, but Edwards managed to call in air support in the form of Hunter aircraft of both 43 and 208 Squadrons. The aircraft held the rebels off for some time, but eventually they had to return to base, leaving Edwards and his men unprotected. Rescue plans were put forward and considered at the SAS base in Thumier, but in the end it was considered too risky to send in another patrol.

Edwards and his men were now on their own, facing an enemy who outnumbered them by eight to one. Deciding to make a break for it, Warburton sent a signal to say they were moving off. Then the radio went dead. Edwards rushed to his signaller's position to find that he had been killed by a single shot to the head.

Leaving Warburton's body where it had fallen, the patrol moved off, hoping to outmanoeuvre the gunmen. They had not gone far when a savage barrage of fire swept their position. Edwards was hit several times and died instantly. During the escape, two more men were also hit, both in the legs. The position was now desperate. Corporal Paddy Baker took command and the patrol, moving slowly because of the injured men, managed to clear the immediate danger area.

The tribesmen, now confident of victory, moved forward and found the bodies of Warburton and Edwards. They then set off after the others. Baker, knowing the patrol couldn't hope to outrun its pursuers, set its slowest members, the two wounded soldiers, to wait in ambush. As the first rebels appeared, they ran into the trap and were shot dead. This tactic was repeated a number of times, until the rebels thought it prudent to halt the pursuit. Finally, the remnants of the patrol made it back to the Dhala road, where they were picked up by

armoured cars and taken safely back to base.

The Edwards patrol was soon to become a major news story. Some days later, a report filtered into Aden that the heads of two English soldiers had been displayed impaled on stakes in the main square of Taiz, a rebel stronghold in Yemen. This was confirmed when a British Army patrol reached the area where Edwards and his men had made their stand and found two headless bodies buried in a shallow grave. The bodies were recovered and reburied with full military honours.

Subsequent SAS operations tended to concentrate on establishing covert OPs and gathering intelligence about the enemy. These tasks were carried out by members of A, B and D Squadrons, who were rotated from operations in Borneo. As the date for British withdrawal neared, enemy activity intensified and the SAS became increasingly worried about a possible attack on its base at Thumier.

Meanwhile, a different kind of war was being fought in the port of Aden itself. The terrorists of the National Liberation Front were operating within the town and the SAS found themselves caught up in counter-terrorism activity. From their base at Ballycastle House, an old married quarters building close to Aden's airport, which had been assigned to the SAS and served as an accommodation and operations centre, a group of 20 men who could pass themselves off as Arabs were busy infiltrating the Crater and Sheikh Othman districts. These operations were known as 'Keeni-Meeni', which is a Swahili word meaning 'snake in the grass'. These covert operations were dangerous, but proved well-suited to the men of the Regiment, especially the Fijians, who were able to pass as Arabs more easily. Some of the techniques learned on 'Keeni-Meeni' operations were later applied to other counter-insurgency work.

Despite the manpower, time, hardship and lives invested in Aden, it was a lost cause. On June 26, 1967, Radfan was handed over to the Federal Regular Army and the British Army pulled out, having gained nothing. However, the SAS had at least developed some new and important skills in the art of counter-insurgency.

The British forces preparing to leave consisted not only of the military units scattered around the city of Aden itself, but outlying stations and individuals. Information came in that a large enemy force was about to attack a large and important RAF base used as a refuelling station for aircraft operating throughout the Middle and Far East, where at this time the British military presence was still vast. As the camp's 200 or so inhabitants made ready for the withdrawal, the SAS carried out reconnaissance in the area. Several long-range patrols were done by Mobility Troop of the newly-formed G Squadron, but no sign of an enemy was observed. A trooper from G Squadron Mountain Troop who was sent to evacuate the airbase recounts the story:

"Two weeks into the baby-sitting role, at 4pm one afternoon, a 'Flash' signal was received by the base commander. The camp was to be abandoned. All documents were to be destroyed; only personnel would be extracted; the camp was not to be destroyed. For the SAS, it was a period of planning. They had received separate orders to extract several VIPs from three separate locations. This was a very simple task: two locations would be evacuated by chopper and one by Mobility Troop using Land Rovers. There was to be no move before 10am next morning, so once the tasks had been assigned and kit made ready, most of the men went to the local NAAFI. As everyone tucked into free drink, the NAAFI manager auctioned off all the saleable stock; it was either that or leave it behind. Cameras and expensive hi-fi equipment were being sold to the highest bidder, in most cases for nothing more than a few pounds. There was also a farewell party, where most people dressed up in white sheets pretending to be Arabs."

Next morning the camp was a hive of activity; several

aircraft had already arrived and some RAF personnel were already being loaded. On the main parade-ground, several bins containing military documents were being destroyed with magnesium bombs. By 10am a Wessex helicopter had arrived and an eight-man SAS team took off. A soldier on this extraction takes up the story.

"The two men we were tasked with extracting worked with the Foreign Office. They were stationed in a town 30 miles to the north of the base. Upon arrival, the town seemed fairly quite, but in this remote region a helicopter was a bit of a novelty. We were dropped off on the roof and, leaving two guys to keep an eye on the local crowd, made our way down into the courtyard. The two FO guys must have been there for a long time, and by the amount of gin stored in the cellar had intended to stay there a lot longer. Although they had received a message telling them about the withdrawal, they had done no packing or preparation. They fussed around like two old queens, but getting nowhere. After about an hour, the two SAS guys on the roof reported that the locals were getting restless, and that a crowd was gathering. In the end we just grabbed the two FO guys and dragged them to the roof. They did not seem too worried about leaving the documents behind: they were too depressed about leaving their gin.

"Eventually, all the VIPs were rounded up and taken safely to the base, from where they were airlifted to Aden. By 3pm that afternoon, less than 24 hours after the bug-out order had been received, the camp lay empty – well, the SAS were still there. We had to wait about two hours until an aircraft came back to pick us up. During this time, I explored the deserted camp. The accommodation barracks had been left neat and tidy: rows of metal beds, with the blankets stacked to regulation requirements. The small hospital was the same, the surgery well stocked with pharmaceutical drugs and equipment. The mess-hall tables stood in neat lines, the chairs stacked on top. In the kitchen, the floor was still wet where someone had mopped it for the last time. In the NAAFI yard, pallets of beer sat in the afternoon sun, while the shop looked as if a plague of locusts had been through it. The saddest thing about the whole camp was the fire station. Three red tenders stood side by side: one of them had only been delivered a month prior.

"At last our aircraft arrived and we piled in, leaving the Land Rovers behind. As we rolled down the runway, we passed thousands of 50-gallon fuel drums, all full. We had wanted to destroy them, but the base commander decided against it. Then, as the aircraft made one last circle, we could see several hundred local Arabs racing for the rich pickings the British had abandoned. I often think about the fire tenders and wonder what happened to them.

"The SAS moved back to Aden and prepared to leave along with the rest of the British Army. However, once the withdrawal had been announced things got really bad, and the rebels started attacking any British personnel they could find. One December morning in 1967, the town of Crater (named because it sat in the base of an extinct volcano) went ballistic. The rebellious locals killed almost every white man, woman and child that could be found; rumours of terrible atrocities quickly spread. At the time, I was sitting in Ballycastle House, near Khormaksar airport, which served as the SAS operational headquarters. I was sleeping in my room when the order came to move. Like the rest of the troop, I grabbed my belt-kit, shouldered my rucksack and grabbed the L42 sniper rifle from the corner of the room. A helicopter was waiting outside on the pad, and

**An RAF Hunter flying over the pass which leads down into the Crater district of Aden. This pass was held by the British Army while SAS soldier-inserted fire teams overlooked the town in order to suppress the uprising.**

*A typical mobility troop vehicle from Aden. As the campaign came to an end, similar vehicles were used to extract isolated British officials.*

outside the office a small group had assembled where the OC was making his selection. Taking one look at the L42 sniper rifle in my hand, he said, 'You on the chopper; all Crater is hostile.'

"Minutes later, five others and myself were flying over Jebel Shamsan, a high mountain that looked down over the town of Crater. As the noise of the chopper faded away, Jock Logan, who was senior, put everyone in the picture. It would seem that the rebels really were slaughtering all the whites, and our task was to shoot anyone or anything roaming the streets with a weapon. That included the local town police, who had sided with the rebels. The patrol, which consisted of six members, all troopers, then made its way into a good defensive position overlooking the town. Three of us were armed

with sniper rifles and, as things turned out, this was the ideal weapon for the situation, as most targets ranged between 300 to 600 metres.

"Over the years, most SAS soldiers become used to death, but in those days I was a novice, and totally unprepared for what I saw. The bodies of butchered men, women and children, had been laid out neatly in the street, deliberately allowing any traffic to run over them.

"The patrol settled down and started selecting targets. At one stage several dissidents climbed a short way up the hill and raised a rebel flag. Jock was on his feet, running down the slope, and ripped the flag down. Thereafter the firing started, but some 10 minutes into the exchange of fire, nothing moved on the streets. Next day, Lieutenant-Colonel Mitchell (Mad Mitch), against the advice of the High Commissioner, bravely led the boys of the Argyll and Sutherland Highlanders into Crater and retook the town. Rumour has it that the local police had cleaned up the bodies and placed them all in tea chests before handing them back to the British – but this was never confirmed."

Once the British withdrawal had been completed, in late 1967, Aden came under the control of the communist-backed People's Democratic Republic of Yemen. It was this regime which backed the overthrow of the Sultan of its neighbour Oman, a conflict in which the SAS was also to find itself involved.

There was conflict closer to home, too – in fact, within the SAS's own doors. The formation of G Squadron in 1965 had caused ructions in the Regiment. Members of the Guards Independent Parachute Company were drafted in to form the skeleton framework, but this did not go down well with the older-established squadrons, as these new officers and men did not have to go through the ordeal of SAS selection. To make matters worse, the original G Squadron members had a Brigade of Guards blue-red-blue flash behind their winged dagger badge. From early 1966, all ranks entering G Squadron had to complete SAS selection just like any other volunteers, but the animosity continued until the blue-red-blue flash was removed and soldiers other than those from the Guards Brigade began to fill the ranks of G Squadron.

# Out of Uniform – CRW

After Aden, the SAS moved back to Britain, and for the next few years had no real active role. During this time, much emphasis was put on training and brushing up individual skills. New departments started to spring up within the Regiment: one such cell was CRW (Counter-Revolutionary Warfare). At first it consisted of little more than one officer and a couple of men sitting in an office at the back of the cookhouse. Their brief was to study the growing terrorist threat and come up with ways of combating the problem. However, CRW continued to grow, and soon became the hub of all anti-terrorist training, techniques and methods. All types of surveillance were practised: vehicle, foot and observation methods. Good camera skills were learned by the SAS, as were the means of developing and printing the film; even infrared photography was taught for night work.

BG (bodyguard) courses were organized. Round-the-clock VIP protection drills were learned, and men were sent on police high-speed driving courses. It was a time of change, and the number of SAS men turning up for work in civilian clothes increased dramatically.

The SAS came to prominence again when, on September 17, 1967, a dramatic mid-air rescue made the headlines. Sergeant Michael Reeves was an SAS freefall parachute instructor watching over students at a civilian club to which he belonged – a non-military weekend activity common for SAS free-fallers. The students were still at the stage of jumping using a static line, which clips on to a rail in the aircraft and opens the canopy automatically a few seconds after the jumper's exit. Normally, the static line breaks safely away from the parachute pack: this time, one of the students exited the aircraft but remained attached, dangling at the end of his static line.

Reeves, who was still in the aircraft, ordered the pilot to increase his height (they had previously been at 2,500 feet), and to circle back over the drop-zone. While he did so, Reeves – who had on his own free-fall parachute – climbed out of the aircraft and down the line. When he reached the student, he seized the man in a vice-like grip with his legs before cutting through the static line. As both men fell away free, Reeves activated the student's reserve parachute. Satisfied that the student would land safely, he then fell away, getting to a safe distance before operating his own canopy and floating down to safety.

Another highlight of this quiet period was a visit to Hereford by Prince Charles in 1968. He was succeeded a few days later by his sister Princess Anne, who enjoyed herself tremendously at a reception in the Sergeants' Mess. Meanwhile in 1969 Trooper Tom McLean made his famous single-handed row across the Atlantic. A most amazing character, he took up the challenge for a bet, used only Army rations and simply rowed his heart out. After 72 days at sea, he hit the coast of Ireland near Blacksod in County Mayo. He repeated the feat in 1982, but this time established another record by crossing the ocean in the smallest vessel, the Giltspur, at only three metres long.

For the rest of the SAS, however, the enforced inactivity caused many of its members to leave and search for new excitements elsewhere. It was a trying time; however, the departures soon came to a stop once the Oman War got under way.

# Chapter 6

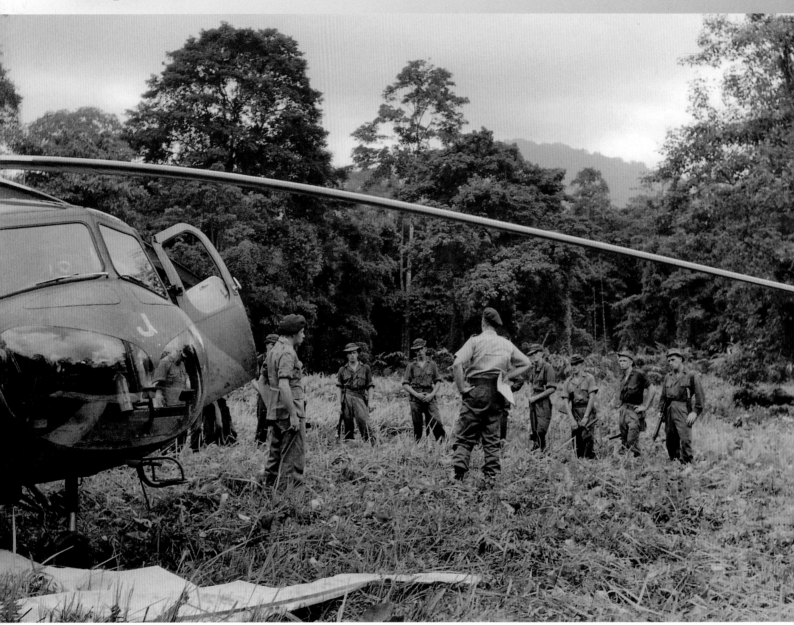

# Jungle Training and Desert Ops

*Troops receive instruction on how to bring in a helicopter at Ulu Langat, near Kuala Lumpur.*

In 1942 with the fall of Singapore to the armies of Imperial Japan, the British suffered their biggest ever military disaster. General Percival's surrender condemned thousands of British and Commonwealth troops to three years of brutal incarceration.

More importantly, the sight of white soldiers from the previously invincible British Empire being brought to their knees by a smaller Asiatic army made many imperial colonies raise an eyebrow. This meant work for the British in general, and the SAS in particular.

Despite their bitter hatred of the Japanese, the British still refused to arm the local Chinese population, preferring to keep the defence of the small island exclusively in the hands of its predominantly white defenders. The British had always had trouble trusting the oriental inhabitants of their Empire. With the help of the local population – mostly members of the Chinese Communist Party of Malaya, who had been in existence since the 1930s – a few diehard officers, like the remarkable Freddie Spencer Chapman, stayed on and began organising resistance against the Japanese. They were supplied with weapons and equipment by Force 136, a department of the Special Operation Executive headed up and run by men like the SAS Regimental Adjutant Major C.E. (Dare) Newell OBE. With the desperation that war brings it wasn't considered what the outcome of arming, training and equipping so many communists might be after the war was won. So blind were the British authorities to the threat, that after the war they not only awarded the communist leader, Chin Peng an OBE in the Victory Honours list, but also invited him to London to take part in the celebrations.

In truth, as soon as the Japanese had been defeated in 1945, the communists greased and then buried their weapons. By now there were at least 4,000 British and captured Japanese weapons at their disposal, together with tons of ammunition and equipment. In three short years they had grown from a small ineffective political party to a well equipped, well trained and highly motivated force. Inspired by Chinese leader Chairman Mao and his defeat of the western backed Nationalist Chinese Army during a protracted guerrilla war, the Malayan Communists returned inspired from the 1948 communist convention in Calcutta. Chin Peng quickly realized that the ongoing campaign of urban disruption through strikes and riots was gaining them little, and probably costing them much popular support. Armed rebellion seemed to be the only answer. Taking advantage of the dissatisfaction felt by the half million or so Chinese squatters, living in squalid conditions close to the jungle edges, the guerrillas changed their name from the Malayan People's Anti-Japanese Army, M.P.A.J.A. to become the self styled, M.P.A.B.A. – Malayan People's Anti-British Army. Following the doctrine of the Chinese master tactician, Sun-Zu, "Kill one, frighten a thousand" they began their campaign. Their plan was a simple one. From

secure bases concealed deep inside the Malayan jungle, they were going to strike out and through a campaign of murder, intimidation and economic disruption instil fear and terror into the local population and – more importantly – their imperial masters. During the Second World War they eliminated in excess of ten thousand so-called informers and collaborators.

With this in mind, thousands of wartime guerrillas dug up their weapons and equipment and returned to the jungle in 10 'regiments', only one of which was not entirely made up of Chinese veterans. The odd one out was made up of Malays as the communists attempted to claim that they were fighting a war of liberation against the British for everyone, not just for the communist cause. In reality, Malays took little part in the fighting. The communist regiments were also supported in the field by the Min Yuen, a clandestine group of Chinese civilians who were used to supply the armed wing with food, intelligence and money. They proved to be very effective.

# Red Menace

Between April and June 1948 the communist offensive began. Using time-honoured methods of terrorism, any individual person of prominence such as Chinese Managers and Officials would be hunted down and murdered in as public and painful way as possible (methods adopted to good effect by the Viet Cong and North Koreans). After invoking terror in the local Chinese and Malay population, it was soon the turn of the Europeans to suffer at the hands of the CT (Communist Terrorists). During the early morning of June 16, 1948, three Chinese youths cycled into the Elphil Estate in Perak and shot dead British planter Arthur Walker. A short distance away Mr Ian Christian and his manager Mr J. Alison were bound to chairs and murdered in front their work force. A State of Emergency was declared the same day.

The war escalated quickly from urban terrorism to full-blown jungle battles. At the beginning of the emergency the 6th Gurkha battalion took on the brunt of the fighting, but they were poorly equipped and several were found to be suffering from TB. They were quickly reinforced by the Devon's, Inniskillings and Seaforths from Singapore as well as two further battalions of Gurkhas. Despite their efforts they

*Troops guiding in a helicopter landing in a jungle clearing at Ula Langat, near Kuala Lumpur, November 1957.*

achieved little except discovering how organized and well equipped the CT were. The guerrillas seemed to be able to attack and murder at will with very little practical retaliation from the British Forces. The regular army were neither equipped nor trained to tackle the kind of campaign they were now being asked to sustain. The Malayan jungle provided a guerrilla's paradise. That had been proven during the Second World War and many of the CT were experienced campaigners.

Malaya was a federation of states ruled by hereditary sultans who governed as constitutional monarchs while their British advisers prepared the country for independence. Made up of a mixed population of aboriginal tribesmen, Chinese, Tamil Indians, Malays and just over twelve thousand Europeans, mostly rubber-planters, civil servants and managers. Five hundred miles long, the Malayan peninsula is four-fifths jungle.

Trees climb to over two hundred feet in height, blocking out the light and turning day into permanent dusk. In parts, visibility is so limited that entire patrols could pass next to each other without knowing. Deep, evil-smelling swamps combined with the extreme heat, humidity, and a score of different insects and reptiles that are able to bite, suck your blood, infect or poison you, turned the jungle into a highly specialised theatre of war.

Initially, the army cobbled together a group of veterans from force 136 together with a few volunteers from the regular army and forty-seven Dyak trackers from the Iban tribes, brought in especially from Borneo. This unlikely combination of fighters became known as the Ferret Force. Although effective in discovering and destroying several CT camps it was a drop in the ocean. After losing several officers to other units, the Force was finally disbanded.

Despite all their efforts, the British seemed powerless to combat the CT or stop their campaign. By March 1950, 863 civilians, 323 police officers and 154 soldiers had been murdered. Despite their advances the CT didn't act with complete impunity suffering 1,138 dead, 645 captured and 359 who surrendered. Despite these losses however, the CT showed no sign of reducing their campaign.

General Sir John Harding, Commander-in-Chief of Far East Land Forces, had to come up with a solution quickly or risk losing the peninsular itself with all the implications that went with it. In 1950 he sent for Brigadier (Mad Mike) Calvert. Calvert was a legend. If Stirling was the founder of the SAS, then Calvert can certainly lay claim to being the modern father of the Regiment. Calvert was a hard, tough, unorthodox man, with a sharp mind and famous for his idealism, chivalry and leadership. Calvert had always taken an active interest in guerrilla warfare. In 1940 he had written a paper on the subjected entitled, 'The Operations of Small Forces behind the Enemy Lines' when a German invasion of England was considered imminent. Calvert also worked with Ian Fleming's brother Peter to organize a guerrilla defence force in Great Britain. A Cambridge double blue (one for boxing) he gave up his commission to see some action, and later became a founder member of the Commandos, serving for three years behind Japanese lines in Burma with Wingate's Chindits and becoming an expert in jungle warfare. Finally, in 1944 he took command of the SAS Brigade from Rod McLeod and led it for the rest of the war. Bored and cooling his heels in Hong Kong, Calvert jumped at the chance of becoming operational once more.

## Events unfold

Harding, together with Lieutenant General Sir Harold Briggs, had several meetings with Calvert. Harding eventually instructed Calvert to prepare a report on the emergency and come up with serious counter-terrorist proposals. Over the next six months Calvert travelled over a thousand miles and interviewed hundreds of people both civilian and military. Calvert even joined military units patrolling the jungles, being ambushed at least twice. Although Calvert's work was important and set the base for all future plans, it was the controversial Briggs plan that was to set the pattern for the eventual

destruction of CT in Malaya. Briggs, also a veteran of the Burma campaign, had been coaxed out of retirement to act as Director of Operations in Malaya.

The essence of the Briggs plan was to deny the CT food by cutting them off from their sources, supplies and intelligence. To achieve this plan Briggs proposed moving the Chinese squatters into protected new villages. This was no mean achievement as it entailed relocating some 600,000 people from 410 'villages' over a period of two years. Calvert's contribution was to establish a force that could attack and disrupt CT lines of communication, attack their bases and curtail their patrols. To achieve this his force, who became known as the Malayan Scouts, would have to remain in the jungle for weeks and sometimes months on end. To do this the patrols would have to live in, and off, the jungle, something never achieved before by British troops. Calvert began to search for likely recruits throughout the Far East. One of his main problems was time. Under pressure from Whitehall for quick results he had no time to spare with involved recruitment techniques or with any prolonged training schedule.

As a result he eventually recruited a mixed bag of some one hundred men to form A squadron. Some were useful former members of SOE, SAS, Force 136 and the Ferret Force. Others, on the other hand, were just bored with their lives and looking for some action. One group surprisingly consisted of 10 deserters from the French Foreign Legion who had jumped ship en-route to Indo-China. Calvert then went in search of high quality officers and NCOs. In this he was more successful recruiting from a group of wartime reservists now forming part of the Territorial Army unit, 21 SAS (part of which had been recruited for operations in Korea which never materialised). Commanded by Major Anthony Greville-Bell and it boasted such luminaries as Alastair McGregor and Bob Bennett – one of David Stirling's 'originals'. These highly experienced men arrived in Malaya in January 1951 and formed B Squadron. After a short trip to Rhodesia, Calvert recruited a further hundred men from over a thousand volunteers. These men formed C Squadron and after a similar visit to Hong Kong he brought back Chinese interpreters and counter-guerrillas, who had also previously served in Burma, to form the core of his Intelligence staff.

Their original camp was established at Kota Tinggi

**Men from the 22nd Special Air Service Regiment.**

near Johore (later Calvert also established an operation HQ at Ipoh) where training was done under the watchful eye of Major John Woodhouse. Woodhouse, who would go on to command the Regiment, was a former Dorset Regimental Officer with little interest in the formalities of army life, but was a stickler where battle discipline was concerned and was undoubtedly one of the best Squadron Commanders the Regiment ever had. Stirling himself agreed that Woodhouse was as important as himself to the founding of the SAS. Prior to Woodhouse's influence, training was at best *ad-hoc*, with no specialist instructors and most of it done on the hoof. It wasn't long before Woodhouse saw the limitations and long term problems this was going to cause, and established a new tough selection course before retuning to Malaya to command 22 SAS. For the time being however, his men had to learn quickly and mainly through patrol experience. The jungle wasn't the easiest landscape to fight a campaign and men not only had to cope with an active enemy, but also the jungle itself. Johnny Cooper, another of Stirling's originals, gives one of the best descriptions of conditions during a patrol in his memoirs:

"Apart from the enemy, leeches were our main adversary. They would fall off leaves and latch onto one's softest areas, around the neck, behind the ears, under the arm-pits, and on a long patrol they would even find their way to one's private parts. You couldn't feel them, but as they slowly sucked blood they enlarged into horrible black swollen lumps. If you were a smoker, it was easy to get rid of them – just a touch with a burning cigarette and they would fall off."

Operationally, Calvert's idea was to send 14-man patrols with a powerful radio and assisted by Chinese interpreters and police officers into the jungle to establish front line bases. From these bases four man patrols were sent out to explore the jungle, plot CT lines of communication and set up effective ambushes. To achieve their objectives these patrols would have to learn to live in the jungle for weeks at a time. Army thinking at the time was based on the concept that a patrol could not survive in jungle conditions for more than seven days. However, with the introduction of helicopters used for the first time during the Malayan campaign and flown by Royal Navy pilots, these periods were being gradually extended. One patrol led by Lieutenant Michael Sinclair Hill remained in the jungle for 103 days, a record and a remarkable achievement.

These patrols also made contact with local tribes. Calvert realised how important having these tribes on his side was to the eventual success of the operation and began a campaign of 'heart and minds.' To this end primitive but effective clinics were established from where drugs such as penicillin were dispensed, curing local tribesmen and their families of a variety of diseases, including the skin disease Yaws. Although there are no official casualty figures for the CT during this period, Calvert's casualties numbered four, one police officer, a Chinese auxiliary, an SAS soldier killed while staying with a local tribe, and a second killed during a fierce firefight with the CT.

In late 1951 Calvert was finally invalided home, suffering from malaria, dysentery, hookworm and 12 years of hard soldiering. Although questions always remained about the behaviour of the Malayan Scouts, especially A Squadron, Calvert was as loyal to his unit as ever. There can be little doubt that many A Squadron men were totally unsuitable for special forces, equally their methods could be unorthodox. However, Calvert considered that most acts of so-called indiscipline, which included drunkenness, fighting and reckless discharging of firearms at base camp, were no more than soldiers letting off steam after long periods in the claustrophobic jungle conditions. He also blamed newly-arrived reservist officers who were, he considered, 'a bit soft.' John Woodhouse, one of

Calvert's most gifted officers, probably summed up the general feeling. He wrote,

"Numerous widely publicised, sensational and mainly true stories circulated for years, and very nearly led to the disbandment of the unit. But if Calvert must accept much of the blame he deserves credit too, for his far-sighted perception of the broad strategy and tactics of counter-insurgency, which I learned mainly from him… Another cause of the bad start in Malaya was the woeful inadequacy of the administrative and 'Q' staff. Malaya Command should have known that a strong staff was essential, but they failed to appoint one, and Mike Calvert did not insist on replacements. Blame us by all means for our failings, but learn from them too. Most of us had our hearts in the job and if we had not made a start perhaps no-one else would have done so."

Whatever was said about Calvert and his techniques later, he had the satisfaction of knowing he had resurrected the SAS into an effective and necessary fighting unit.

# Reorganization

Calvert was replaced by Lieutenant-Colonel John (Tod) Sloane, an orthodox infantryman who had been second-in-command of the Argyll and Sutherland Highlanders in Korea. With no special forces, or jungle warfare background he recruited the help of both John Woodhouse and Dare Newell (who became the Regimental Adjutant) to assist him in reorganizing the Regiment. Sloane was a keen disciplinarian who was insistent in bringing a new order and discipline to the Regiment. Weapons would now have to be clean, all administrative matters affecting soldiers' welfare brought up-to-date and many of the Regiment's 'bad boys' returned to their parent regiments, or any other regiment that would take them. It was estimated half those recruited in Malaya were disposed of in this way. Although it sounds like a drastic measure the men left behind were of the highest calibre, as indeed were the new recruits that began to come through from the UK, having undergone a proper selection process and training. The SAS were also pulled out of deep penetration operations into the jungle until a period of further training could take place. Instead they would spend their time working with the police and regular forces on the edge of the jungle.

By now, largely thanks to Calvert's recruiting campaign, the SAS now had four squadrons in Malaya, A, B, C and D. Sloane immediately removed the Regiment from the jungle insisting that it required specialist training if the Regiment were going to be effective. In essence this involved not seeing the jungle as your enemy, but like desert during WW2, seeing this inhospitable landscape as your friend. To this end, the training had to be hard and effective if the SAS were going to be able to achieve their objectives.

In February 1952, all three squadrons of the SAS took part in Operation Helsby. Thanks largely to the success of Gibb's plan in keeping food from the CT they were forced to start growing their own. In order to do this large areas of jungle had to be cleared. These areas were easily and quickly spotted from the air, giving the government forces an opportunity to attack the communist camps. One such location was situated in the Balum Valley, close to the Thai border. Here just over a hundred communist guerrillas were subsisting off the land, while using the base to strike out at a variety of targets. Operation Helsby was designed to destroy the base and flush the CT into the open, where they could be destroyed. A and C Squadrons, together with a detachment of Royal Marine Commandos, a few Gurkhas, and local police approached the valley on foot, while just over 50 members of B Squadron were dropped in by parachute (first time the SAS had parachuted into an operation since 1945). Although later the Regiment perfected the art of jungle stealth, on this occasion the operation was a total failure. The sound of hundreds of men pushing their way through the jungle warned the CT in plenty of time and they had long gone.

To get to your target quickly and silently, parachuting seemed to be the answer. Dropping into Europe is one thing but dropping into the dense foliage of the Malayan jungle is another. That, combined with the fact that most of B Squadron hadn't dropped since the Second World War, there were no training facilities, and no instructors (although all this was later sorted out). Safe jumping zones are rare in the jungle and even these are fraught with danger. High trees, sharp bamboo that shattered easily causing serious injury to descending and vulnerable troops. To try and make parachuting in jungle conditions safer 'Tree Jumping' was introduced. The idea was simple enough, each trooper was issued with a hundred foot coil of rope. After their parachutes snagged on a tree, they first lowered their pack and then lowered themselves onto the ground safely using the rope. Although it proved effective and there were few injuries on Operation Helsby, future experiments proved less successful. Major John Salmon, second-in-command of 22 SAS, who admitted to feeling terrified during his parachute jumps, explains the feelings and experiences he had when jumping.

"Next thing you know, you are floating through the air and it's one of the most wonderful feelings in the world; then you see the trees coming. You are coming down beautifully, steering for the middle of the trees. The hot air makes you swing violently, as if a giant had caught hold of you. You let the air spill out of the chute and look for a good, healthy tree. Sometimes you make that spot; often you don't. It's hard to tell until you're a few feet away. When you hit a tree you don't know whether you'll stay there or not. Often the branch snaps, you hurtle down, smashing into branches on the way, until you finally come to a halt. If it holds you, then you know you're safe."

*Troops carrying a casualty to a waiting helicopter for removal to hospital during training in a jungle clearing.*

and highly resourceful Military High Commissioner, General Sir Gerald Templar. In answer to a question about the number of men he had on the ground to fight the communists, Templar replied "The answer lies not in pouring more soldiers into the jungle, but rests in the hearts and minds of the Malayan people." With these few well chosen words Templar summed up the SAS philosophy that has remained with them to this day. It was never SAS numbers that made a difference, but the originality of their ideas. It had also been Calvert's dream when he established the Malayan Scouts.

## Major operations

Between 1952 and 1958 the SAS were involved in numerous operations, two of the most noted being Operation Hive and Operation Termite. The first of these operations, Hive, was in essence a continuation of the Gibbs denial policy and was carried out in late 1952, in the state of Negri Sembilan. During the eight week operation, together with the Gurkhas and Fijian units, they patrolled large areas of Serembon and disrupted the CT's lines of communication, denied them food, and kept them away from the local population and forced them to fall back on their own supply dumps. Working deep inside the Malayan jungle the hope was to kill upwards of a hundred guerrillas known to be operating in the area. Their eventually tally was only 16 killed, not many it would seem, but in the context of the overall campaign, where the SAS killed just over a 100 Communists in nine years, it wasn't a bad tally.

The problem with Hive, like in so many other operations the SAS were involved in, was their strategic misuse. It was quickly understood that the Regiment were better employed in gathering Intelligence, and in shaping the opinions of the local population. Although they weren't 'medal chasers' and won few awards, their role was significant and largely due to their presence, casualties amongst British soldiers fell dramatically. The

Later, with several deaths and numerous injuries during training (including the new C/O Lieutenant-Colonel Oliver Brooke, who had just taken over from Slone), and the introduction of the helicopter for dropping troops and equipment into specific areas (which was used by the army for the first time in Malaya) the method was eventually abandoned.

With the effects of the Briggs plan now being keenly felt by the CT they moved deeper into the jungle, and the SAS went after them. Armed now with the new Patchett carbine and shotguns, they led jungle operations in both Pahang and Kelanton, parachuting or being dropped in by helicopter. While the regular units continued to attack the CTs, the SAS began to contact local aboriginal tribes. Landing in groups of 15 and staying with the local tribesman for up to 13 weeks they turned the villages into armed camps as well as building landing strips and medical centres to treat local tribes. It was also often the job of a single trooper to convince local tribes to assist the government forces, and adopt a policy of self-defence.

The policy of 'hearts and minds' came from the new

*Troops receiving instruction on how to bring in a helicopter in a jungle clearing at Ulu Langat, near Kuala Lumpur.*

SAS hearts and minds campaigns were proving more successful than anyone could have hoped for. However, although Operation Hive wasn't all they had hoped it would be, the SAS once again learnt valuable lessons.

During Operation Sword in January 1954, the SAS suffered three dead as a result of parachuting into the jungle in Kedah. However, during their next major operation, Operation Termite which was to last from July to November 1954 and was designed to wrest control of a large area of country, including the central mountain spine from the CT as well as establish relations with the local tribes, all three operational squadrons dropped into Perak. Despite continuing to try and perfect tree jumping, they succeeded with only four injuries, largely due to unstable thermals throwing

troopers all over the sky. The operation had begun with heavy jungle bombing to clear areas for the later airborne assault. Jungle bombing, like tree jumping however, was a controversial tactic. The bombing was indiscriminate and killed and injured as many friendly aborigines as it did CTs. It was considered, especially by the Regiment, counter-productive and a 'damn nuisance'. Again, like tree jumping, it was a mistake that wasn't to be repeated in Borneo. Despite using two squadrons of the SAS plus an additional four infantry battalions, total casualties amongst the CT were only 15. A small return for such a large and dangerous operation. It was estimated at the time that it took 1,800 man-hours of patrolling to kill one CT. The SAS quickly discovered that the CT weren't their biggest enemy, the jungle was. They had to learn to live within this hostile environment quickly making the jungle their friend not their enemy. Interestingly, despite all the problems, the historian Gregory Blaxland points out that 'Termite' was a success not so much for the number of the CTs killed and captured, but in the conversion of the aborigines to the SAS cause. It was a classic example of the power of the 'hearts and minds' campaign.

The years 1955 to 1956 were highly significant to both the campaign in Malaya, and to the long term development of the Regiment. John Woodhouse returned to the regiment after years heading up training in the UK as a squadron commander, under the command of the new C/O, Lieutenant-Colonel George Lea. A large man in every sense, Lea was another in a long line of tough commanding officers. He quickly disposed of any officer that he considered was not up to the mark and returned them to their parent regiment. He also recruited a number of top quality officers, including Captain Peter de la Billière (who later went on to command the Regiment) as well as promoting many of those he inherited. C, Rhodesian squadron, commanded by another hard man, Peter Walls (who went on to command all Rhodesian force after UDI) were returned to Africa (although retained their SAS identity). Although effective they were susceptible for some strange reason to the various jungle diseases, as well as having problems relating to the dark skinned aborigines which wasn't good for the 'heart and minds' campaigns. To replace them, D Squadron was raised locally and commanded by the legendary Johnny Cooper (one of Stirling's originals) who established his own training programme. During this period the Regiment's time was largely taken up building jungle forts and building relationships with local aboriginal tribes. Once the fort was finished it was handed over to the Malayan police and regular army detachments. This fort building really marked the start of the SAS involvement with Templer's 'hearts and minds' initiative. The men of the Regiment learnt the native language and ate their food.

Typical of operations at this time was D Squadron's first patrol in October 1953. Accompanied by a number of Iban trackers, the patrol set off to establish Fort Brooke. Cooper, followed by his patrol, pushed into the jungle in Pahang. Following the Sungei Brok River, they slashed their way through the dense foliage until they reached their destination. Establishing a small clearing they radioed in for a location check. This was followed by clearing an area of jungle big enough for a helicopter to land and building a bridge across the river. Once all this had been established they began to patrol, seeking out the local aborigines and searching for CT camps. One CT gang was successfully broken up, but in another contact two squadron troopers were killed in an ambush. The patrol stayed out for 122 days, during which time fifty per cent of the original complement had to be evacuated due to disease, fatigue and jungle fever. Finally, on February 7, 1954 the remaining 40 men of D Squadron, exhausted, emaciated and with their uniforms in tatters emerged from the jungle to be replaced by a police detachment. It was a remarkable achievement.

## Change of command

John Woodhouse, returning from England, took over command of D Squadron and Johnny Cooper was promoted to Major and took over command of B (Big Time Bravo) Squadron. During the summer of 1955, a squadron was raised in New Zealand. Commanded by Major Frank Rennie, the squadron was put through a tough recruitment and training programme before being sent to Malaya during the latter half of the year. Their total strength was about 140 men, a third of whom were Maoris. They worked well with the local tribes and were first class trackers. Their presence in the Regiment also encouraged a number of the equally tough Fijian soldiers serving in Malaya to apply for selection, and several were recruited. During the same period the SAS were further reinforced by a squadron recruited from the Parachute Regiment (Parachute Regiment Squadron) and commanded by Major Dudley Coventry. By the latter half of 1956, 560 soldiers comprising five squadrons each with four troops of 16 men, plus headquarters personnel and attached specialists, were operating within the jungles of Malaya. As a result the number of people murdered by the CT fell further to about six a month. An impressive result by anybody's standards. The campaign now moved more strongly to one of search and destroy. It was estimated that approximately 2,000 CT were still operating from their increasingly remote bases, deep inside the jungle from where they launched a number of attacks. To deal with

*These Kelabit tribesmen of the Borneo interior have never seen a car or even a bicycle. For some tribes their last contact with the British was in the last century, during the regime of the 'White Rajah' of Sarawak. No wonder the Kelabits refer to the helicopters – this one a Wessex – of 848 Naval Air Squadron as 'Queen Victoria's Iron Birds'.*

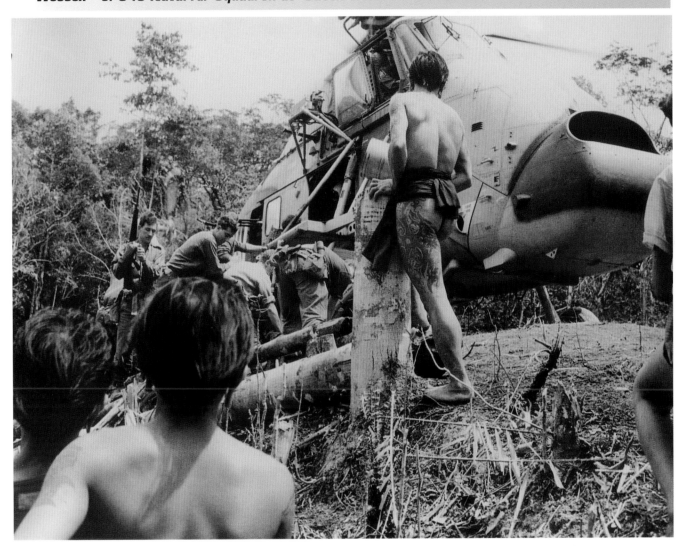

this final phase of the campaign 22 SAS were to gain considerable prominence.

Not that the Regiment was in the jungle all the time. After a lengthy tour of duty patrolling in the jungle the troopers would find themselves with three months pay in their pockets and two weeks to spend it. Life followed a pattern. Two months in the jungle, two wild weeks spending and enjoying life with all the things that Malaya had to offer a tired, stressed and frustrated soldier, followed by two weeks of retraining and then

back out into the jungle. During training, new skills were being continually practiced: parachute jumping, small boat training, demolitions, attacks on RAF stations, jungle knowledge. Training was continual and vital and formed the basis for the modern-day SAS.

By the end of 1955 the CT were in retreat. Its leadership had fled. The reward policy made many surrender. The army and police were taking a steady toll of those that refused to surrender, and with the success of the 'hearts and minds' campaign the aborigines were no

*In and out by helicopter was possible only when clearings were large enough. This one is natural, but others were created by the unpopular 'bombing' method.*

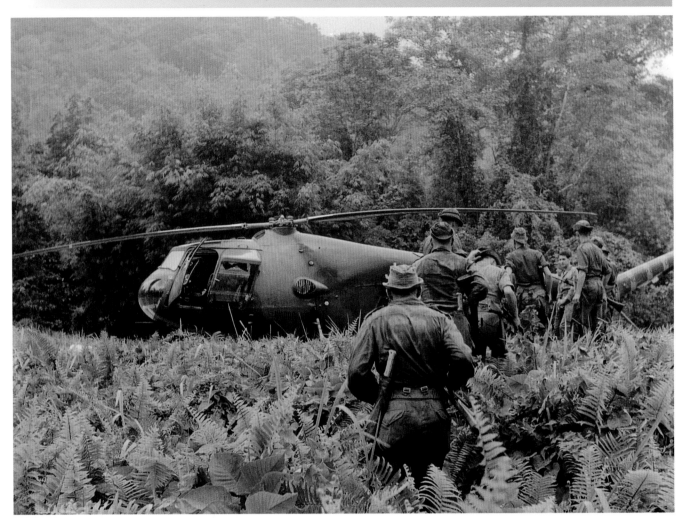

longer scared of the CT and stopped supplying them with food and shelter. It was now that Lea had a radical re-think about the role of the SAS in Malaya. Lea started to put individual squadrons into a jungle base and leave them there for several months so they could thoroughly familiarize themselves with the terrain, the local tribes, and, using the skills they had learnt as trackers, ambush and pick off CTs in ones and twos as they moved through what use to be safe routes. These tactics began to play on the morale of the CTs. There were no large-scale battles, no set-piece actions, just slow, deliberate and patient picking-off of the enemy. There was great inter-squadron rivalry over how many CTs each could kill. This rivalry

became know as the 'kill to contract' ratio. A good example of this involved the legendary Johnny Cooper, this time as commander of B Squadron.

An intelligence report had been received that the communists were running a radio station from the jungle a little south of the Thai border. It was causing problems and Cooper was ordered to destroy it. It wasn't a short or easy trip. First his team had to travel by canoe from Kota Bahru – famous for the Japanese landings in 1941. The squadron then had to cross the Akik Ring range of mountains on foot before descending into the oddly named 'Valley of no Return.' Which was where it was believed the transmitter was being operated. It took

Cooper and his troop eight hard days marching before they reached the crest of the mountain. Here, Cooper split his company into four troops before descending. It was 'Punchy' McNeil's troop that discovered the transmitter, as is often the case in the jungle, quite by accident. Punchy discovered what appeared to be a water wheel suspended over a fast flowing stream. This makeshift but effective contraption was turning a dynamo powering the radio. Launching an attack the CTs were forced into the jungle and the transmitter destroyed. The CT were chased but escaped over the Thai border. Cooper wanted to follow and finish the job, but permission was refused. During the same patrol they managed to track down and kill two further terrorists as well as discover a previously unheard of aboriginal tribe. Often when meeting these tribes for the first time the troopers would be subject to incidents they could not have imagined in their wildest dreams. Pete Scholey remembers coming across one such tribe in Borneo. One of the women was breast-feeding a monkey, when Pete enquired why he was told quite matter of factly, that it was being fattened up for the kill. It was to be their meal that night.

While Johnny Cooper was making history in the jungle, the Parachute Regiment Squadron was busy making its own headlines. After shooting dead a woman terrorist in the Ipoh region, it was discovered that she was carrying a six-month old child. The squadron 'captured' the child and started to bring it up as one of their own.

Without doubt one of the greatest characters to serve with SAS in any capacity was Sergeant Bob Turnbull of D Squadron a former gunner from Middlesbrough. He became close to an Iban tracker called Anak Kayan and achieved an eye for spoor as accurate as Kayan himself. He became one of the finest trackers in the Regiment and as good as any of the Iban that had taught him their skills. On one occasion he led a three man patrol in pursuit of a CT unit whose tracks he had picked up. His patrol followed these tracks for several days through some of the toughest regions in Malaya. Finally, Turnbull heard voices behind a clump of bushes. He moved forward slowly locating the enemy sentry and then sat down to wait. After a short while and due to the heavy rain, the sentry moved back into camp. Turnbull followed, silently. When the rest of the patrol was in position they opened fire and killed all four of the CT inside the camp. Turnbull's weapon of choice was the pump action

shotgun, with which he killed the infamous bandit Ah Tuck – a senior member of the communist leadership. The two men discovered each other by accident. Ah Tuck was reputed to always carry a cocked and ready to fire Sten gun. Despite this Turnbull was too quick for him and fired three times. People who witnessed the incident said the shots were fired so quickly that it sounded like one long shot rather than three individual ones.

By 1956-57 the campaign in Malaya was all but won and the campaign began to wind down. The Regiment had played a significant part in the battle for the jungle and it had not gone unnoticed. In April 1956, the Regiment was visited by Brigadier Fitzroy Maclean who was then serving as Under-Secretary of State for War. One of the first men recruited by David Stirling in 1941, Maclean had taken part in several of the Regiment's early raids and parachuted into the former Yugoslavia as head of a mission sent by Churchill to organize Tito's resistance. He was the ideal choice to congratulate the Regiment on its efforts.

In 1957 the Parachute Regiment Squadron was returned to England where it was needed by its parent regiment. The Regiment was sorry to see them go, they had done a good job, made many friends and were seen as an important part of the Regiment. The next to go were the New Zealanders. They had accounted for 15 of the enemy during their two-year stint. The C/O George Lea was sent home at about the same time. He was awarded a well eared DSO, the first such decoration the Regiment had been awarded since WW2. His citation read as follows:

'He personally directed the operations of his men, was parachuted with them into thick jungle, descended by rope from a helicopter aircraft and shared every hazard, danger and discomfort inherent in jungle operations against a ruthless and fanatical enemy.'

## More Change

He was replaced by Lieutenant-Colonel Anthony Deane-Drummond. A first class officer and excellent choice. The Regiment's last action during the Malayan campaign was Operation Sweep which commenced in February 1958. The plan was to surround and destroy a band of CTs led by a terrorist leader called Ah Hoi, who was nick-named the 'baby-killer.' He had once slit open the belly of a pregnant woman because her husband was a suspected police informer. Hoi was known to be holed

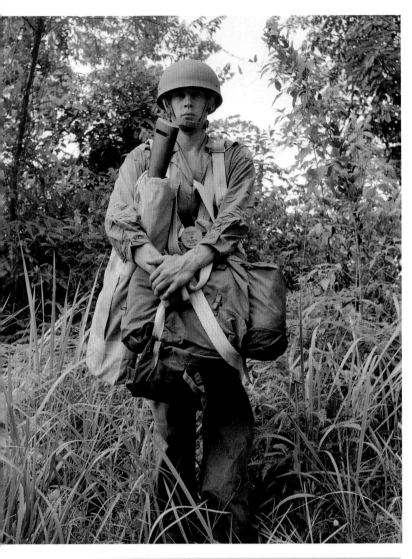

*An SAS soldier fully kitted for jungle operation. The record for a jungle stay was 103 days straight.*

up in the Telok Anson swamp, a miserable insect-infested place 18 miles by 10 on the Tengi River to the north-west of Kuala Lumpur. D Squadron, under the command of the larger-than-life Major Harry Thompson, a Royal Highland Fusilier, had been selected for the task. He decided to parachute into the area, a risky business in the jungle, but wanted the element of surprise. Unfortunately Trooper Jerry Mulcahy, one of the 37 Troopers that dropped from the RAF Blackburn Beverley, got caught in a tree, before dropping to the ground and

breaking his back. A helicopter had to be sent in to evacuate him. The patrol's first job was therefore to make a clearing so the helicopter could land. Unfortunately, due to the swampy nature of the ground, that was impossible and the helicopter had to hover just above the ground while the stretcher was forced on board. Although helicopters were versatile and effective – especially in the jungle – they were also noisy. Harry Thompson's element of surprise had gone.

Thompson knew he had to move quickly. Following the course of the river he divided his force into two groups to track the terrorist passage through the swamps. In doing so the SAS found itself coping with some of the worst conditions ever experienced in Malaya. The weather was appalling and it rained almost continually. The troopers were up to their necks in brown, leech-infested swamp water, and had to cut their way through acres of sword grass. They were continually attacked by mosquitoes which bit their way through their clothes, and their boots rotted off, so several men had to walk barefoot. Peter de la Billière's troop followed the CTs trail for ten days keeping in touch by radio. They came across several CT camps littered with turtle shells which had been eaten by the terrorists. The other troop, led by Sergeant Sandilands, moved to try and cut them off. Several rubber dinghies were dropped in by air and Sandilands used these to move his troop by night along the river, desperately trying to sniff out the communists' camp fires. Later, one of these patrols made first contact with the enemy. Several CTs were cooking a meal close to the river bank. Unfortunately, before they came into range, the terrorists spotted the patrol and deserted their position leaving their equipment behind. Later, an aborigine reported seeing a man and a women standing by the river. Suspecting an ambush, Sandilands took Corporal Finn with him when he went in search of the couple. The aborigine hadn't been lying and Sandilands quickly located the couple. Creeping up behind them Sandilands killed the man, but Finn missed the women, who disappeared back into the jungle. The patrol set of in hot pursuit. The woman's trail was easy to follow and the patrol found what was left of two CT camps. While Thompson was pushing on into the interior and calling up his reserves, the army and police were surrounding the swamp. After nine weeks the net began to tighten around the terrorists. Although working in two distinct groups, they were difficult to pin down. The big breakthrough came when one of the group, a women named, Ah Niet walked out of the swamp and told the authorities that her group were almost out of food and needed help. At first she tried to impose conditions for their surrender. She wanted £3,500 for each of her group and amnesty for those already in prison. The British knew she was in no position to negotiate and refused her demands. Finally she agreed to bring the terrorists out that night. True to her word five terrorists walked out of the jungle and surrendered to Harry Thompson, including Ah Hoi the infamous 'baby-killer'. The surrender was witnessed by Brian Connell: "He was still arrogant, still ranting that the reds would win in the end." He was eventually given the choice of prison or exile to China. He finally choose prison, but was packed off to China anyway. After the initial surrender, Ah Niet walked back into the jungle to persuade several more of her former comrades to surrender, which they did 48 hours later. Although a few diehard CTs kept up the fight and the SAS kept patrolling in Johore in co-operation with the security forces, that was the end of any serious campaigning.

By the time the Malayan campaign ended, the SAS was a different animal to that which had been established in 1941. It had also justified its existence in a post-war world. Several outstanding officers had already served with the Regiment, including men like John Woodhouse, Peter de la Billière, Tony Jeapes, John Watts and Mike Wingate-Gray. The Regiment had also produced first class NCOs who were the backbone of any regiment. By the end of the Malayan campaign the only man left serving with the Regiment who had also been with them during WW2 was Johnny Cooper. Many new lessons had been learnt, new tactics practiced, some found to be excellent, like the 'hearts and minds' campaign, and some disastrous, like tree jumping. A number of officers and men wondered what would become of the Regiment after the campaign in Malaya finished. Training continued apace while they waited. The campaign had lasted longer than the Second World War. It had seen the re-establishment of the SAS as a far different animal to that of the 1939–45 conflict. The worth of the Regiment however had been established and as Britain withdrew from the British Empire, and a dozen small campaigns threatened, the SAS would be needed more than ever.

# Oman and the Jebel Akhdar

In 1950, Sultan, Said bin Taimur, ruled Oman. The country was desperately poor. Those that disagreed with his policies or angered him would find their wells filled and their families banished. His one staunch ally was Britain, who had signed a treaty with the Sultan of Muscat back in 1789. This extended commercial rights to the East India Company in exchange for protection from the Royal Navy. The latter's presence in the area did much to stabilize the coastal trade, from which the seafaring Omanis prospered. The agreement held and passed down the years from Sultan to Sultan, then in 1950, oil was discovered. This was turning this huge desert peninsula into one of the richest regions in the world. In particular, most of this oil would have to pass through the Straits of Hormuz, in northern Oman, thus making it of particular interest to the British.

However, in 1952, neighboring Saudi Arabia invaded parts of Abu Dhabi and Muscat, both of which were rich in oilfields. The Sultan of Oman turned to the British who, at first, negotiated with the Saudis. Nevertheless, it soon became apparent that a Saudi-backed rebellion had started in Oman. By 1957, the situation had developed into open rebellion. The Imam of Oman, Ghalib bin Ali, and his brother, Talib, established a theocratic state and sought to overthrow the Sultan of Oman, Said bin Taimur. The rebels were well entrenched in the mountainous plateau of Jebel Akhdar in the north of the country. The Imam and his brother mustered little more than 100 followers, but they had the backing of Sheikh Suleiman bin Himyar, a powerful tribal chief who had disagreed with the Sultan. The area controlled by Sheikh Suleiman bin Himyar and his tribe was a huge mountainous plateau in northern Oman known as Jebel Akhdar.

There were no roads around the mountain, and access to the scattered mountain villages is only possible on foot. Donkeys made up the local transportation, and even these were restricted to a few pathways. This made the area easy to defend, especially against assault. No foreigner had conquered the Jebel since the Persians in the tenth century. While the British had sent a detachment of Life Guards, equipped with Ferret armoured cars they were little use other than to surround the Jebel. In turn, they soon became a target themselves as the rebels' mined the tracks along which

## Theatre of War: Oman

*Although Jebel Akhdar means Green Mountain in Arabic, save for the monsoon season, the whole area was a barren place for the SAS to be posted. It measured some 30 kms by 15, and formed a unique natural fortress, protected all around by steep sides.*

*A much-depleted D Squadron was ordered from Malaya to Oman in mid-November 1957. Although these were experienced soldiers, they were used to fighting in the close confines of the jungle, and now they would be exposed to the harshness of the desert. By day, they were open to extremely high temperatures, while at night it was cold enough to freeze the water in their canteens.*

*Added to that was the hardship of climbing while carrying rucksacks laden down with water and ammunition. The soldiers also know that any assault would have to be done while constantly under fire from rebel sharpshooters.*

*22 SAS Regiment in the Oman desert.*

the armoured cars would travel. Equally, the Sultan's local army was no match for the rebels and after several attempts to gain access to the Jebel they withdrew to a safe distance. In desperation the Sultan requested more assistance from Britain, to which they responded by ordering units of the SAS to be sent from Malaya to Oman.

The first mission of D Squadron, on November 24, was to establish a base on a mountain that overlooked the stronghold of Aquabat al Dhafar in the north-west. It was to be done in two parts, with 16 and 17 Troops attempting an assault from the north while 18 and

19 Troops made their way up from the south. On the afternoon of the November 25, 18 and 19 Troop went to ground as an exchange of fire took place, it was still daylight and they were trapped by the rebels near the bottom of the Jebel. Sadly, during the firefight, Corporal Duke Swindells, was hit in the chest by a sniper and killed. Swindells was from the Middlesex Regiment and holder of the Military Medal. He was buried in a secret location in a landlocked bay close to the shoreline. His death served to highlight the exposure of moving in daylight and thereafter most patrols were carried out in darkness to avoid the danger of rebel snipers.

The northern SAS units, comprising 16 and 17 Troops, made better headway and managed to reach the top of the plateau unopposed. This in part was due to a local guide who had shown them a route known as the Persian Steps. This ancient route to the summit was well protected by sangers, (stone circular defenses) but the SAS had found them unmanned by the rebels. They had stashed most of their hive equipment at a small village and made the climb in darkness.

Once at the top, the officer in command, Captain Roderic 'Red Rory' Walker, decided to consolidate his position. He ordered 17 Troop to descend the 2,000m track to where they had left their equipment, while 16 Troop held the plateau. It took 17 Troop a full 24 hours to descend to the village where their stores had been dumped, and then remake their way up the Persian Steps. While no rebels were encountered by 16 Troop, they did intercept a small groups of tribesmen who were moving by night. So grateful were the tribesmen at not being shot by the SAS that they offered to work for them, transporting water, supplies and ammunition. Once 17 Troop had returned they reversed roles and 16 Troop descended to collect their equipment, however this time they had four donkeys to help them. Firmly established on the Jebel, the SAS sent out patrols to locate the enemy, although they tried to avoid contact where possible.

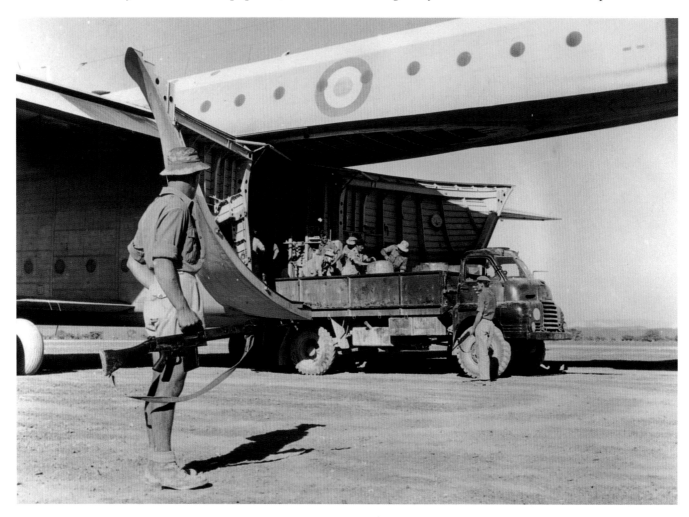

*Standing guard as a Beverley aircraft is unloaded at the desert airstrip of Ibri, Oman.*

From there on the SAS would either send out night patrols or man strategic OP's. The latter normally consisted of six SAS soldiers all heavily armed and capable of defending themselves even against much greater odds. For their part, the rebels resorted to ineffectual long-range sniping with the odd machine gun or mortar attacks on the SAS positions. For the present, the situation was allowed to settle down, but it was plain to see that one under-strength squadron was not enough to shake the rebels from their stronghold.

On the January 1, 1959, progress was made when the Commanding Officer of 22 SAS Regiment, Lieutenant-Colonel Tony Deane-Drummond, arrived in Muscat. On the January 10, A Squadron, commanded by Major Johnny Cooper, also arrived in Muscat having flown from Malaya. Upon arrival at the SAS headquarters in Tanuf, A Squadron set about climbing the Persian Steps in order to relieve D Squadron. Captain de la Billière, who guided them to the sangars on Cassino and briefed Cooper on the current situation, met them at the top. Once this was done D Squadron then redeployed to the Tanuf Slab area and mounted operations in the area to the south of Sabrina.

Two weeks later the combined squadrons mounted a full attack on the Jebel. The SAS devised a deception plan in order to draw most of the rebels away from the commanding postions. Part one was to create an elaborate deception by planning an attack on a plateau stronghold know as Sabrina. Part two was to casually let the donkey handlers know of their plans. The SAS had known from the start that the local donkey handlers were passing vital information to the rebels. The handlers got their briefing from Deane-Drummond, he told them that a diversion was to be made up the Wadi Kamah, but the real assault was to be launched from Tanuf, and the donkey-trains would be going up that way.

On the evening of January 25, A Squadron moved forward for an assault on the northern slopes of Sabrina. At 03:00 hours they received the order to commence their assault. Three troops climbed, all using different routes, while the fourth provided covering fire with machine guns. They reached the summit just before dawn at which time a fierce firefight developed. The fighting was hard with many accounts of hand-to-hand combat, but in the end, the SAS were victorious. Then to continue the deception, three of the troops descended to waiting trucks leaving only 4 Troop to defend Sabrina.

*The travels of a troop on a patrol in the Oman desert are traced on the Operations Room map at the Headquarters, A Squadron, 22 Special Air Service Regiment, at Ibri, by Lance Sergeant Ian Smith and Sergeant Peter Harding.*

D Squadron, in order to convince the rebels that the main attack would come from the west, also launched a diversionary attack. Once the fighting was over, they too left 1 Troop in position while the rest made their way back to SAS headquarters in Tanuf. By evening on the second day six SAS Troops were making their way by road to the village of Kamah ready to begin the real attack.

Hauling ammunition and water in laden rucksacks weighing in excess of 100lbs, A and D Squadrons made their final push to the summit of Jebel Akhdar. The route the SAS had chosen was one the rebels would not expect. Climbing was difficult at best, but the heavy loads made it almost impossible. Nevertheless, the SAS did the impossible. It cost the SAS three lives but they had taken the impregnable Jebel Akhdar.

Colonel Deane-Drummond was awarded a DSO for his planning of the operation, while Military Crosses went to Rory Walker, Tony Jeapes (then a Lieutenant with A Squadron), Johnny Watts and Peter de la Billière.

# Chapter 7

# The Early History of the Regiment

*Looking down the wrong end of the barrel in 1942. The SAS were born in the desert.*

The Allied campaign in North Africa during World War Two was fought to restrict German access to the Suez Canal and prevent them from capturing the Arabian oilfields. For the first part of the conflict, a small British and Commonwealth army faced the Italians and, while superior in numbers, Italy's forces were poorly equipped. However, it was not long before Hitler sent the famous Afrika Korps under the command of General Erwin Rommel, the 'Desert Fox'. As both armies grew in size, the pace of battle slowed to a virtual stalemate.

For the British, the most crucial aspect of the war in the North African desert in 1940 was the maintenance of its military supply lines, most of which terminated along the coast at a network of depots, airfields and ports. This network supplied its vast desert army, which included a unit called Layforce. Named after and commanded by Brigadier Robert Laycock, Layforce was a Commando brigade attached to General

*Lieutenant-Colonel 'Paddy' Mayne, a founding father of the SAS. He was a distinguished sportsman and a professional soldier. After the capture of David Stirling, Mayne took over the running of SAS operations in North Africa and Europe.*

Wavell's Middle Eastern Army. On paper, it was an impressive force, comprising some 2,000 men of 7, 8 and 11 Commandos. One of the 8 Commando officers, a young Scots Guards Lieutenant by the name of David Stirling, had been involved in a number of unsuccessful large-scale raids on enemy targets along the coast around Cyrenaica. Stirling understood the benefits of attacking targets from behind enemy lines, but felt sure the raids would have a greater chance of success if executed by small groups of men, thus using the element of surprise to its best advantage. Stirling had been lying in a hospital bed, having suffered a severe injury during a parachute drop, when he first conceived the idea of the SAS.

In the belief that a small band of dedicated men could operate successfully behind the enemy's lines, he managed to present his plan to Major-General Neil Ritchie, who at the time was Deputy Chief of the General Staff. His idea, set out in a memorandum, finally reached the desk of the Commander-in-Chief in the Middle East, General Sir Claude Auchinleck, and the SAS was born.

David Stirling was determined to build a unit of dedicated men, men capable of self-discipline and ability. He is quoted as saying: "We believe, as did the ancient Greeks who originated the word 'aristocracy', that every man with the right attitude and talents, regardless of birth and riches, has a capacity in his own lifetime of reaching that status in its true sense. In fact, in our SAS context, an individual soldier might prefer to go on serving as an NCO rather than leave the Regiment in order to obtain an officer's commission. All ranks in the SAS are of 'one company' in which a sense of class is both alien and ludicrous." This ethos remains within the SAS family to the present day.

As the founder of the SAS, Stirling's main strength came from his ability to select and enlist men who had both daring and vision. One such man was 'Paddy' Mayne, one of Stirling's first recruits into the SAS. The nickname 'Paddy' came with his Irish ancestry, and before the war he was well known for his accomplishments in the world of sport. In battle, he possessed qualities of leadership which set him apart from most men, and gained a reputation for personal bravery which some, at times, characterized as wild recklessness.

In July 1941, L Detachment of the SAS Brigade, as it was precisely know, came into being. HQ Middle East dreamed up the name in an effort to convince the

*The SAS used LRDG trucks for transport from late 1941 until early 1942. However, Stirling believed that the SAS should have its own form of transportation, and in July 1941 this materialized in the form of the Willys jeep.*

Germans that they had formed a whole new airborne brigade. Whether the ploy worked or not is unknown, but the reality was that L Detachment comprised just 67 men, most of whom had been recruited from Layforce. This 'Brigade' had no weapons, no tents and no supplies. As there was no parent unit, Stirling reported directly to General Auchinleck; it was the first move in securing the independence of the SAS.

The men of the unit begged, borrowed or stole whatever they needed, while Stirling and Mayne got on with planning a tough training programme. Initially, much of this training involved jumping backwards off moving trucks to simulate parachute landings. However, this activity was quickly curtailed following several accidents which severely reduced the unit's ability and numbers. The other aspect of SAS training was an introduction to the Lewes bomb,

a device designed by Lieutenant 'Jock' Lewes with the express purpose of destroying parked aircraft. The bomb, basically a mixture of plastic explosive (TNT 808), thermite and diesel oil, was attached to the aircraft on or near the engine and initiated by a time pencil and detonator.

It was around this time that the famous insignia of the SAS materialized. There has been many a discussion on what the emblem depicts: some say it's the flaming sword Excalibur, while others refer to it as a winged dagger. Whatever it symbolized, it was attached to the unit's equally famous beige berets – adopted after a white beret was first tried, with disastrous results. Introducing an entirely new insignia in the British Army is not easy, but Stirling met General Auchinleck in person at Shepheard's Hotel in Cairo and the emblem was approved.

# Into Action

By November 1941, L Detachment of the SAS was ready to carry out its first operation. On the night of November 17–18, a force of 55 men boarded five Bristol Bombay transport aircraft provided by 216 Squadron. The five sections of this force were commanded by David Stirling, 'Paddy' Mayne, Eoin McGonigal, 'Jock' Lewes and Lieutenant Bonnington. The targets of the raid were German airfields in the area of Tmimi and Gazala. It was widely believed that the Luftwaffe had received reinforcements in the form of the latest type of Messerschmitt 109 fighter aircraft. The raids were designed to destroy these aircraft prior to General Auchinleck's planned offensive, due to commence two days later. Entry was by parachute, dropping some 12 miles from the target.

The five aircraft took off from Bagoush airfield on schedule. Although conditions on take-off were clear and still, as the aircraft proceeded towards their drop zones the weather changed. Thick cloud, heavy rain and high winds hampered navigation. In order to pinpoint their position, the aircraft were forced to drop down to 200 feet, where they encountered heavy flak from the German defences. The drop was disastrous, with the men being scattered over a wide area on landing and several injuries sustained – Stirling himself was knocked unconscious. As a result, the operation was abandoned, and the soldiers had to make their way individually to a pre-arranged rendezvous with the Long Range Desert Group (LRDG).

The problems encountered on this first operation prompted a radical rethink about transporting troops to the target in future SAS operations. Stirling resolved never to use parachute drops again, and instead decided to use vehicles, starting with those of the LRDG.

Like so many *ad hoc* British units, the LRDG came into existence during World War Two and, like the SAS, was the product of a group of eccentric individuals. During the 1920 and 1930s, Major Ralph Bagnold, Royal Corps of Signals, and a group of friends had undertaken a series of journeys with the aim of resolving the not inconsiderable problems of living in and travelling through the desert. His studies resulted in a paper advocating the formation of a military desert reconnaissance force. The provisional war establishment of the LRDG was authorized in July 1940, originally for 11 officers and 76 men. This number

was increased to 21 officers and 271 men in November of that year, and by March 1942 the LRDG numbered 25 officers and 324 men. Operating in open-topped Chevrolet trucks, the LRDG carried out reconnaissance, intelligence-gathering and courier duties. These tasks involved long drives across the featureless desert terrain, followed by observation of enemy posts and convoys. There were also behind-the-lines raiding activities, which forced the Italians to divert troops from the front to safeguard their rear areas.

The SAS used LRDG trucks for transport from late 1941 until early 1942, though Stirling's men caused problems for the LRDG because their aggressive activities provoked greater enemy reaction. Despite this, co-operation between the SAS and LRDG remained excellent. However, Stirling believed that the SAS should have its own form of transport, and in July 1941 this materialized in the form of the Willys jeep. In a much-modified form, the jeep was used by the SAS throughout the war. Light, agile and robust, the jeep was ideally suited to the desert terrain because of its four-wheel drive. The jeep had a top speed of 60 mph and a range of 300 miles, although this could be greatly extended by carrying additional fuel in separate containers. During the North Africa campaign the SAS jeeps were normally overloaded with extra water, fuel and ammunition. They were also burdened with considerable firepower in the form of 0.5-inch Browning heavy machine guns and rifle-calibre Vickers 'K' guns, originally intended for use in aircraft, of which a supply was found sitting in a disused hanger. So equipped, the jeeps were not used simply as a means of transport but also as a weapon. On many occasions they were driven, guns blazing, directly on to the enemy airfields to wreak havoc on the rows of parked aircraft.

# Success at Last

Despite the shaky start, Stirling continued with his planning, and a month later several parties raided the airfields at Sirte, Nofilia, El Agheila, Agedabia, Tamit and Marble Arch (the later gained its name from a large arch erected in the desert by Mussolini to mark the border of the Italian colony of Tripolitania). In all, 97 enemy aircraft were destroyed. The raid on the airfield at Agedabia, a small town situated on the Libyan coast south of

*A much-modified American Willys jeep was used by the SAS throughout World War II. They were light, agile and robust – and ideally suited to desert conditions because of their four-wheel drive. The jeep had a top speed of 60 mph and a range of 300 miles, although this could be greatly extended by carrying additional fuel.*

Benghazi, went particularly well. It was launched on December 21 by a force of five members of L Detachment SAS, comprising Sergeant Bob Tait, Sergeant DuVivier and Privates Byrne and Phillips, under the command of Lieutenant Bill Fraser. Having been dropped off by an LRDG patrol 10 miles south of their objective, they marched throughout the night and reached a lying-up place from which they were able to observe the airfield throughout the following day. Each man carried a water bottle, a compass, a revolver, eight Lewes bombs and a tin of chocolate, plus other rations consisting of raisins, cheese and broken biscuits. After nightfall on the following day, Fraser and his men succeeded in penetrating the defences of the airfield, which was heavily wired and well guarded, placing Lewes bombs on 37 Fiat CR42 fighter-bombers. The raid was a great success: all the bombs went off and all the aircraft were destroyed. In the confusion caused by the explosions the patrol withdrew without any losses and made its way to a rendezvous with an LRDG patrol which was already waiting for them. However, though no casualties were suffered during the raid itself, two members of the unit were killed when two RAF Blenheims strafed their

vehicles, despite the fact that the correct air recognition signals had been displayed. The rest, worn-out and bedraggled, managed to reach the LRDG and SAS base at Jab Oasis on December 23.

In early January 1942, L Detachment of the SAS absorbed the 1st Company of Free French Paratroopers under the command of Commandant Bergé. In March of the same year, the Special Interrogation Group (SIG) also came under L Detachment's control. SIG was a small unit made up of German-speaking Jews, formed and commanded by Captain Herbert Buck MC. They operated in the guise of German soldiers – including wearing German uniforms. Their fate, if captured, was certain death.

Stirling's concept of small raiding parties proved to be a great success when, on the night of January 23, 1942, the SAS struck at a German oil supply depot in Buerat, west of Sirte. They destroyed 18 enormous fuel transporters, each loaded with 4,000 gallons of fuel. At the same time they attacked the dock facilities and accompanying warehouses, filled with everything from foodstuffs to heavy machinery – all just prior to a major offensive by Rommel.

The Berka main and satellite airfields were the targets of L Detachment SAS on more than one occasion. In March 1942, Captain 'Paddy' Mayne mounted an operation involving a number of attacks on Benghazi and the airfields in the area, with the Berka satellite being the objective of a four-man patrol led by Mayne himself. The other members were Corporals Bennett and Rose and Private Byrne. Travelling with an LRDG patrol via the Siwa Oasis, Mayne and his men reached a mountain called (like another mountain, this time in Oman, where the SAS was to win further battle honours in the 1950s) the Djebel Akhdar. From here, they could observe the area of coastal plain on which Benghazi and the airfields were located. Under cover of darkness on the following night, they left the wadi in which they had been lying up and made their way down the escarpment to their target. Moving on to the airfield, they placed Lewes bombs on 15 aircraft, a number of fuel dumps and 12 large aerial bombs before withdrawing and making their way during the rest of the night to a rendezvous, where they were collected by the LRDG.

Another raid on the Berka airfields took place on June 13, 1942. This coincided with a raid on Berka Satellite by the RAF, whose bombers arrived overhead as Mayne,

Corporals Lilley and Warburton and Private Storey were moving across the airfield towards some aircraft. There was little they could do but seek what cover there was on the airfield until the raid was over. With the enemy on full alert, Mayne planted some bombs on a fuel dump and withdrew, avoiding enemy patrols which were already scouring the area, and led his men to the rendezvous with the LRDG. There, he also met Major Stirling, who had attacked a nearby aircraft repair base at Benina, and Lieutenant André Zirnheld with a patrol of L Detachment's Free French troops who had attacked Berka Main, destroying 11 aircraft. The Benina aircraft repair base had been targeted twice before, on each occasion by Stirling, accompanied by Sergeants Johnny Cooper and Reg Seekings. On the first two occasions they found the base deserted, but this time they achieved success. During an RAF bombing raid on Benghazi, they made their way past the sentries and succeeded in placing Lewes bombs on a number of aircraft, some new aircraft engines still in their crates and some machinery. As a *coup de grace*, Stirling attacked the enemy guardroom with grenades as he and his men withdrew.

Not content with the results achieved that night, however, Stirling decided to mount a further raid on the area. On the following night, accompanied by Captain Mayne's patrol, plus a number of other individuals, they drove down the escarpment in a borrowed LRDG vehicle. Having bluffed their way through a German checkpoint, Stirling and his party encountered a number of Italian troops, and although the Italians opened fire they were unsuccessful in halting the SAS vehicle as it sped past. Shortly afterwards, a number of enemy vehicles were spotted by a petrol filling station and these soon had Lewes bombs planted on them. By now the entire area was alive with enemy troops, and Stirling decided to withdraw. Heading across the desert, successfully avoiding enemy patrols dispatched to intercept them, the SAS succeeded in reaching the Djebel Akhdar. As they reached the top of the wadi, which led up the escarpment, Corporal Bob Lilley spotted a time pencil fuse attached to one of the remaining Lewes bombs was burning. Thanks to his split-second warning, all the occupants of the vehicle succeeded in baling out just prior to it exploding. Deprived of transport, Stirling and his men had to complete the journey to the rendezvous with the LRDG on foot.

The SAS continued to raid airfields, shipping and

German supply stations, including Tobruk, throughout the summer of 1942. But with General Rommel in command, the Germans were gaining the upper hand. German airfields around Cyrenaica were able to attack British convoys as they attempted to reach Malta. Stirling planned a number of raids against these airfields for the night of June 13, in order to support the Malta convoys. Most of the targets were in the Benghazi sector, the Derna area, Barce and Heraklion airfield in Crete. Each raiding party consisted of five men; and for the attack on Derna, which was by far the hardest target, Stirling enlisted the help of SIG. The idea was to use the SIG personnel to transport the SAS directly into the Derna airstrips using German vehicles. Unfortunately, one of the anti-German sympathizers attached to SIG betrayed them, and all three teams were lost. Things went better at Benghazi, where the SAS team destroyed 16 aircraft and an additional 30 brand-new aircraft engines. Most of the repair shops and ammunition dumps were also severely damaged.

The raid on Crete comprised a mixed bag of Free French paratroopers who had joined L Detachment SAS at the beginning of 1942, under the command of Bergé. He was accompanied by a newcomer to the SAS, Captain the Earl Jellicoe, and a Greek guide named Lieutenant Costi. After landing at night by inflatable boat from the Greek Navy submarine Triton, the party marched for two nights over the mountains to the enemy airfield at Heraklion, where some 60 Junkers 88s and a number of Stuka dive-bombers were assembled. The party had some difficulty moving on to the airfield due to the quantity of barbed-wire defences and numerous guards. However, Bergé and his men succeeded in placing Lewes bombs on 21 aircraft, a number of vehicles and a fuel dump before withdrawing. They were unwittingly assisted by an RAF aircraft which happened to bomb the airfield at the same time, thereby causing confusion which the raiders used to good effect

After successfully completing their task, the groups spent the next two nights travelling, having been forced to lie up during the day. Bergé's group was within a few miles of the beach and was due to rendezvous with the submarine on the following night. While Bergé and the three other Frenchmen hid in a cave, Captain Jellicoe and Lieutenant Costi went off to a nearby village to make contact with a Cretan who would signal the submarine to confirm the pick-up. Unfortunately, during their absence Bergé and his companions were accidentally discovered by some local people who betrayed them to the Germans. As a result, the four Frenchmen found themselves facing three enemy patrols which heavily outnumbered them. Bergé decided to stand and fight, intending to hold out until he and his men could slip away under cover of darkness. Sadly, however, the Frenchmen ran out of ammunition and had no option other than to surrender. He and his men were taken to Heraklion, where they were tortured before being executed. When Captain Jellicoe and Lieutenant Costi returned to the cave, they discovered their companions' fate. Three days later,

accompanied by 20 Cretan refugees, they were taken off the island by the submarine.

Despite the loss of men, overall the raids had been a great accomplishment. In total, 50 aircraft were destroyed by the SAS before Rommel attacked and advanced towards Egypt. As the Germans pushed forward, the SAS continued to mount attacks behind enemy lines. One such raid, on the night of July 7, 1942, led by Major Stirling and Captain Mayne, was a great success. After an overland approach in

*Lieutenant-Colonel David Stirling talking to Patrol Commander Lieutenant McDonald prior to leaving for a raid.*

vehicles, the initial attack on the airfield was carried out by a group of four men under Captain Mayne, while Major Stirling established a roadblock nearby to attack any enemy vehicles. Lewes bombs were placed on a total of 40 aircraft, but because of faulty primers only 20 exploded. A further 14 aircraft were then attacked and destroyed as Stirling's force raced down the runway in three jeeps, guns blazing. Major Stirling and his men then withdrew without loss. There is no doubt that these raids and the destruction

of German aircraft severely hampered Rommel's advance, allowing Montgomery to prepare his counter-offensive.

During the battle of El Alamein the following November ,Stirling, although not officially required to contribute, was determined to assist in General Montgomery's advance to Tripoli. He devised a plan which meant his men would launch a minimum of two raids a week on the stretch of land between El Agheila and Tripoli, in particular concentrating on the roads being used by the retreating Germans and

*The great jeep raid in July 1942 succeeded in destroying some 40 German aircraft. Scenes such as this were to be resurrected during the Gulf War of 1991.*

*A picture of the south-west of Colditz Castle taken in 1945. After his capture in January 1943 David Stirling remained in Colditz until the end of the war.*

Italians. At the same time the Allied landings in the French North African colonies (Operation Torch) resulted in the retreat of Axis forces into Tunisia. Although the SAS had been quite successful during the Eighth Army's advance, the Tunisian countryside of scrub-covered hills and cultivated valleys was far less suitable for their operations than Libya's deserts. The population was also more sympathetic to the Axis and, as a result, the SAS operations did not achieve the success which was expected.

On September 28, 1942, L Detachment was formally renamed the 1st Special Air Service Regiment. At the same time the SBS came under SAS control, as did the 114 men of the Greek Sacred Squadron. Although Stirling was promoted to Lieutenant Colonel, his independence was diminished as 1 SAS now came under the control of the Director of Military Operations.

Shortly afterwards, in January 1943, the success of 1 SAS was temporarily interrupted when Stirling was captured. He and his team had been en route to raid Sousse, and during a brief break had taken shelter in a cave. German troops appeared and started searching the area; as a result, Sterling and one of his men were captured. Stirling managed to escape two days later, but was betrayed by Arabs and recaptured by Italian troops. He spent the rest of the war languishing in Colditz. However, 1 SAS continued to evolve, and at the time of Stirling's capture it totalled 47 officers and 532 other ranks. By this time David Stirling's brother, Lieutenant Colonel William Stirling, with the British First Army, had also formed 2 SAS.

# Theatre of War: North Africa

*North Africa was where the SAS was formed and the Regiment's first raids were carried out behind enemy lines as the war in the desert was raging. The raids caused no end of problems for the enemy, and the new method of waging war was very successful – the legend of the SAS was born.*

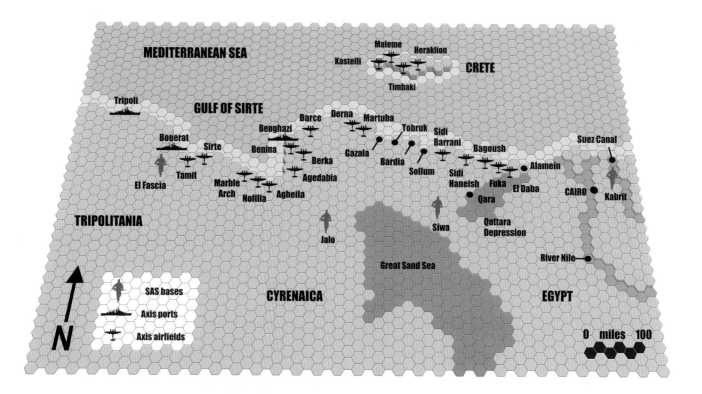

The first recorded raid by the SAS was on the Agheila Airfield (centre, above). It took place on December 14, 1941. This was followed by a further 11 raids, all of them on enemy airfields: Agedabai, Barce, Berka, Benina, Berka, Bagoush, El Daba, Fuka (twice), and Sidi Haneish.

For eight months the Regiment caused mayhem with their carefully-planned attacks all across the North Coast of Africa.

In 1943 they turned their attention to Sicily and then to Europe as the war drew to a close and North Africa ceased to be a battlefield.

## Mayne Takes Over

When the North African campaign came to an end in May 1943, there followed a brief period when the SAS's future was in question. However, the invasion of Sicily meant its skills were in demand once more. With Stirling in Colditz, it fell to 'Paddy' Mayne to take over command. By this time the SAS had acquired considerable waterborne skills, and at the end of the North African campaign 1 SAS was renamed Special Raiding Squadron (SRS), while the Special Boat Section (SBS) came under the command of Jellicoe, now promoted to Major. The SBS was assigned to the Aegean and the Adriatic, while the SRS moved into Sicily and Italy.

## The Aegean Sea

The Dodecanese Islands in the Aegean Sea were the scene of operations by the Special Boat Squadron, commanded by Jellicoe. German forces occupied a number of islands including Crete, Karpathos, Leros, Kos, Simi, Tilos, Astipalaia and several of the smaller ones. Together, these formed part of a defensive perimeter against Allied operations in the Mediterranean.

The SBS established 40 heavily-camouflaged anchorages, which served as bases for operations among the Dodecanese Islands. A schooner, the *Tewfik*, acted as a forward headquarters for the SBS while a fleet of armed caiques, motor launches and other small craft served to put the men ashore. This small flotilla came under the command of Lieutenant Commander Adrian Seligmann RN, who was employed to ferry the SBS squadrons around the islands. Overall control of raiding operations in the Aegean became the responsibility of Headquarters Raiding Forces, based in Cairo, which was formed in late October 1943 under the command of Colonel (later Brigadier) Douglas Turnbull.

However, the SBS had already seen action in the area. Operation Albumen was carried out on June 22, 1943, when the SBS landed on the south coast of Crete near Cape Kochinoxos. The mission was to destroy enemy aircraft on airfields at Heraklion, Timbaki and Kastelli. These were targeted by patrols led by Lieutenants Kenneth Lamonby, Ronnie Rowe and Anders Lassen respectively. Lamonby found no aircraft but destroyed a large fuel dump, while Rose found his objective deserted.

Lassen's patrol, despite engaging in a firefight with alert sentries, succeeded in destroying four Stuka aircraft, an armoured vehicle and a fuel dump. Despite being betrayed by a Cretan villager, Lassen and one of his men succeeded in evading capture and returned safely to the squadron's base, where he met the rest of his patrol.

## Anders Lassen VC

Major Anders Lassen is worthy of a special mention as he is the only SAS soldier ever to win the Victoria Cross. One of the most famous members of the SAS, Lassen, a Dane, joined the British Army at the beginning of World War Two and participated in commando training before joining the specialist Small-Scale Raiding Force. In May 1943 he was in the Middle East as part of D Squadron, 1 SAS, which became part of the Special Boat Squadron. His fighting qualities soon came to the fore, and Lassen was recognized as being an exceptional soldier and ideally suited to elite forces operations where quick decisions, raw courage and ice-cool nerves are often called for. He took part in a number of SBS missions, such as the raids against Crete and Sirni in June 1943, while in 1944 he fought in Italy, the Adriatic and Greece. It was in 1945, however, that he entered SAS legend. In fighting around Lake Comacchio, he was killed attempting to destroy a number of German pill-boxes. Before he died, he had captured or killed a large number of Germans, and his individual presence had even affected enemy strategy in the area. It was for these actions that he was awarded a posthumous VC.

## Attack on Simi

On October 7, 1943, the Germans attacked the island of Simi, which was at that time occupied by a force of 40 members of M Squadron SBS under Major Ian Lapraik. The German attempt to capture it failed, but on the following day Luftwaffe bombers carried out raids during which 20 Greek civilians and two SBS soldiers were killed. One of the bombs landed on Major Lapraik's headquarters and two men, Guardsman Thomas Bishop and Corporal Sidney Greaves MM, were buried under the rubble. As others fought to rescue them, it became apparent that Private Bishop could not be freed without further debris and rubble falling on Corporal Greaves. The

*Major Anders Lassen, the only SAS soldier to win the Victoria Cross. Lassen, a Dane, joined the British Army at the beginning of World War II and participated in commando training before joining the specialist Small Scale Raiding Force. He was killed in 1945, during fighting around Lake Comacchio.*

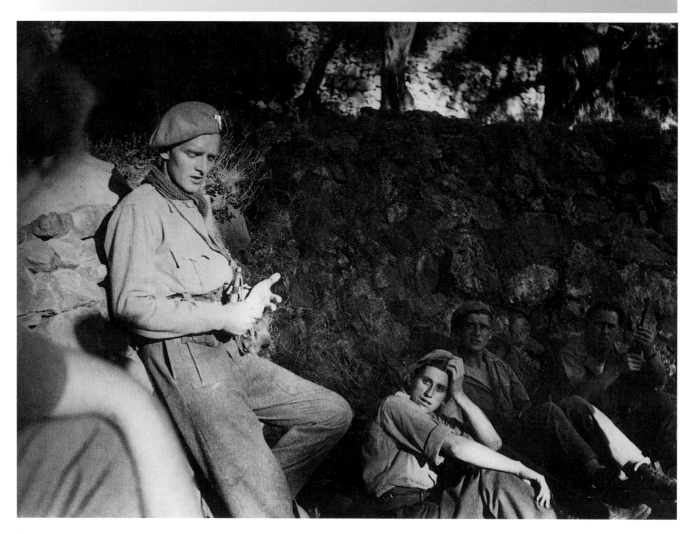

only solution was for Bishop's foot to be amputated, and to this he very bravely and selflessly agreed.

By the light of a candle, lying on his back and working with only the minimum of instruments an SBS medic, Sergeant Porter Darrell, carried out the operation under the guidance of an RAF medical officer, Flight Lieutenant Leslie Ferris, who could not perform the operation himself as he was suffering from an injured wrist. It took 27 hours, as air raids continued, to free Guardsman Bishop. Unfortunately, however, he died soon afterwards from pain and shock, and sadly his death was in vain, as on being pulled clear

Corporal Greaves was found to be dead too.

Simi fell to the Axis, but on November 20, 1943, the SBS returned to the island in the form of a raiding party led by another outstanding officer, Lieutenant Bob Bury. He and his troops faced a German and Italian garrison totalling some 100 men. Having landed, the SBS advanced into the town of Castello and reached the Governor's house. Entering the building, Bury came upon the quarters of a light machine gun detachment whose members were swiftly dispatched when he threw a grenade into their room. Immediately afterwards Sergeant 'Tanky' Geary, who had been covering the main entrance to the house, killed eight Germans who appeared outside on the quayside by the building, and Bury shot another before detonating a 25-pound explosive charge in the building next door which demolished it and also part of the Governor's house. Having planted a booby-trap in the street, which was set off soon afterwards by the enemy, Bury and his men withdrew.

Lieutenant Bury returned to Simi on the night of July 13, 1944, as a member of a combined force of some 220 men of M Squadron SBS together with the Greek Sacred Squadron. The force landed on the island unobserved by the enemy. At dawn on the following day the castle on Simi was subjected to heavy fire by machine guns and mortars. Bury's patrol was part of a force which attacked enemy positions in a monastery, eventually forcing their occupants along a promontory at one end of the island, where they were subsequently persuaded to surrender.

In late October that year, Bury was given the task of carrying out a boat reconnaissance along the coastline of the island of Spetsia. Approaching a bay occupied by royalist partisans who were expecting an attack by communist ELAS guerrillas, his boat was fired on. The partisans had mistaken Bury's boat for the ELAS unit and their fire hit the helmsman. Recognizing that the vessel was not under fire from German weapons, Lieutenant Bury leaped up to take over the tiller and steered the vessel nearer to the shore in an attempt to land, while at the same time trying to make his identity known to the partisans. In doing so, however, he was fatally wounded and died shortly afterwards. His men and the partisans buried him on Spetsia the following day.

# The SRS in Italy

While the SBS was in action in the Aegean, the SRS involved itself in the Italian campaign, starting with an assault on a coastal battery at Cape Murro di Porco, south of Syracuse in Sicily, on July 12, 1943. This was taken easily, and the SRS was immediately given the job of seizing the town of Augusta, which was achieved with minimal casualties. In September the SRS was ordered to capture the port of Bagnara in order to cut German communications and ease the advance of Montgomery's ground forces from Reggio, and its next job was to capture Termoli, which was achieved on October 3. The

Germans launched a heavy counter-attack two days later. The SRS took heavy casualties, but with reinforcements from 2 SAS (the first time the two regiments had fought side by side) together they succeeded in holding the town. Termoli was to be the last operation carried out by the SRS: in December, the unit was shipped to Scotland for re-organization.

Commanded by Bill Stirling, 2 SAS had been more involved in the Italian campaign. The unit had taken part in a series of submarine-delivered reconnaissances of Mediterranean islands in May 1943, and during the invasion of Sicily took part in two operations, Narcissus and Chestnut.

Narcissus was carried out by 40 men from A Squadron on July 10, 1943. They landed from the vessel *Royal Scotsman* on the south-east coast of Sicily to assault a lighthouse where it was suspected enemy artillery pieces were being stored. On reaching the lighthouse they found it to be deserted and so returned to the ship, which was lying offshore, having achieved their objective without any loss of life.

Operation Chestnut was designed to support Operation Husky (July 9, 1943), the Allied invasion of Sicily. The mission became a memorable example of good planning and logistical support, emphasising how essential these are for successful military operations. The original plan was to land two parties of 2 SAS by submarine in northern Sicily to destroy enemy communications. 'Pink' Party was led by Captain Pinckney, and had the task of severing roads and telephone lines along the north-east coast of the island. In addition, it was ordered to destroy the Catania-Messina railway line. By contrast, 'Brig' Party, under the leadership of Captain Bridgeman-Evans, was detailed to attack hostile convoys and the enemy headquarters near Enna.

However, on June 17 the operation was postponed by 15th Army Group until the day before the main Allied invasion of Sicily, which was expected to take place on July 11. On June 20 the SAS operation was cancelled altogether, but was then resurrected on July 6, and on the night of July 12 the two parties were inserted by parachute.

Almost immediately, both encountered serious difficulties. The majority of 'Pink' Party's equipment and radios were damaged on landing, and the men scattered over a wide area. 'Brig' Party was dropped too close to urban areas, which unintentionally alerted the enemy.

*Members of 2 SAS supporting partisans in the Alba area. Note the old 3 inch mortar which is not 'bedded in' due to the weapon being fired on a hard road surface.*

Bridgeman-Evans was captured but later managed to escape. On July 13 a night-time reinforcement drop was planned, but the damaged radios meant that the aircraft were unable to contact either party, and consequently no men were dropped. No further forces were committed to the operation. On the ground, neither party achieved anything worthwhile. The only positive result of Operation Chestnut was that most of the SAS soldiers successfully returned to Allied lines. This was 2 SAS's first parachute drop and the poor preparation resulted in a badly-executed drop with many of the troops being widely dispersed. The official report on the operation stated: 'The value of damage and disorganization inflicted on the enemy was not proportionate to the number of men, amount of equipment and planes used. It provided valuable experience for future

operations and pointed out the pitfalls which are inevitable in any operation which is the first of its kind.'

On September 7, 1943, two seven-man teams from 2 SAS were dropped into the Spezia/Genoa area of north-west Italy, led by Captain Pinckney and Captain Dudgeon respectively. Their task was to sever the railway lines transporting German reinforcements and supplies to the front. Splitting into two smaller groups, the SAS succeeded in derailing several trains and blowing up large sections of track. Nevertheless, they did encounter some misfortune. The poor weather conditions and unhealthy diet caused several of the men to fall ill: in addition, the teams lost one of their commanding officers, Captain Dudgeon, who was captured and shot by the Germans. Due to their ill health, the return to Allied lines

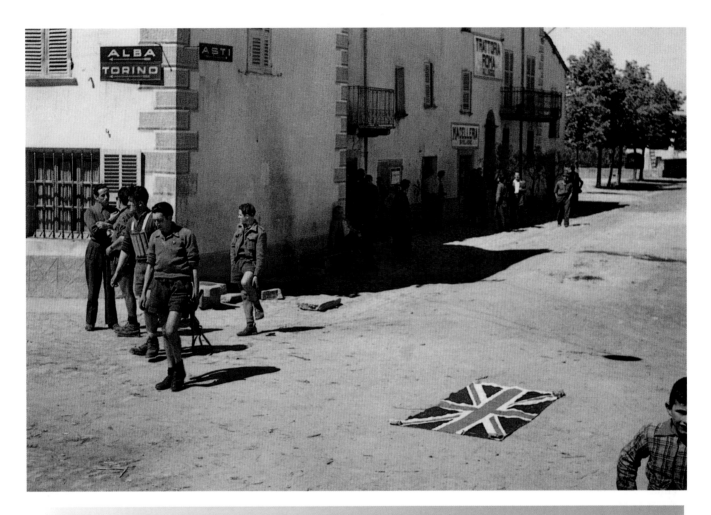

**Allied aircraft were always looking for targets behind the German lines and it was difficult to distinguish between partisans and Germans. The SAS used a Union Jack Flag in order to identify their location; the same system is still used today.**

was extremely fragmented: some men returned after operating for 54 days, others after 73 days, while Sergeant 'Tanky' Challen, spent seven months behind enemy lines, including a stay in an enemy hospital.

Despite these problems, this operation is classic example of a WW2 SAS mission, demonstrating how small groups of men could inflict severe damage on the enemy while remaining at large behind the lines for long periods.

## Disaster – Operation Jonquil

Operation Jonquil, the next raid, proved to be one of the most disastrous SAS missions in World War

Two. The idea was sound enough: the rounding-up of large numbers of Allied prisoners of war who were wandering around the Italian countryside after Italy's surrender. Beginning in October 1943, the plan involved four seaborne parties from B Squadron, 2 SAS, landing between Ancona and Pescara on Italy's Adriatic coast to act as guides for the POWs. Fishing vessels were assembled as transport, but a German attack at Termoli on October 5 meant they had to be moved back to Barn (the Germans had also impounded a number of fishing vessels). For their part, the POWs made it to the beaches, but due to lack of communication they arrived to find no boats, or else the boats arrived and there were no prisoners. The whole mission was a

*An SAS road watch patrol during the North Africa campaign. The modern-day SAS were sent to carry out similar missions during the 1991 Gulf War.*

fiasco, and all those involved were very disappointed.

The SAS returned to the area, this time to attack the railway line between Ancona and Giulianova. In November, led by Major Roy Farran, a small force of 16 men split into four patrols embarked in an Italian motor torpedo boat commanded by a Royal Navy officer. Despite the presence of an enemy U-boat charging its batteries on the surface, Farran and his men disembarked from the MTB in pitch darkness at the mouth of the River Tronto, some 35 miles north of Pescara, and paddled ashore in rubber boats. The four-man patrols, commanded respectively by Major Farran, Captain Grant Hibbert, Sergeant Rawes and Sergeant Seddon, marched until dawn before lying up for the rest of the day. On the following evening a reconnaissance of the railway line, which lay about 500 yards away, was carried out. During the night three of the patrols reached a pre-determined rendezvous, but there was no sign of Sergeant Rawes and his men. Major Farran decided to postpone the attack because of the appalling weather and the three patrols dispersed once more.

On the following night, Sergeant Rawes and his men succeeded in making the rendezvous and Major Farran went ahead with the attack. Three of the patrols laid charges on the line, blowing it in at least 16 places. Meanwhile, Sergeant Seddon's patrol laid Hawkins mines on roads, destroying seven telegraph poles. Sergeant Rawes' patrol also destroyed three enemy trucks which were unlucky enough to arrive on the scene.

*The first SAS incursions into Italy were not too fruitful, but as the war progressed they achieved much better results. Many of the raids were commanded by Major Roy Farran.*

Having completed their tasks, the patrols set out on a long exfiltration, walking some 70 miles towards the coast where they would be picked up by the MTB. The poor weather and difficult terrain hindered their progress and, furthermore, one of the members of Major Farran's patrol was suffering from a severe attack of malaria. They were forced to hide up during the day and could move only by night. A lack of food also obliged them to seek food and shelter from the local people. The slow going meant Farran's patrol had to march during daylight hours if it was to make the rendezvous with the MTB. On arriving at the appointed beach Farran signalled out to sea with his torch, but there was no sign of the torpedo boat. By dawn, he had no choice but to disperse and move inland once more. Fortunately, on the following night the MTB appeared and Farran and his men were taken off. Two of their number, Sergeant Seddon and a member of his patrol, were missing, however, and it is assumed they were captured and executed. Nevertheless, as all tasks had been completed, the operation had been successful.

Three more missions were mounted during November and December 1943, once again to cut the railway lines. Operation Maple, on January 7, 1944, involved an attack on the railway lines radiating from Terni and Orvieto. Most of the targets were destroyed, but all the parties were captured while making for the pick-up.

Railway bridges between Pesaro and Fano were attacked in Operation Baobab, which took place on January 30, 1944. All the men returned safely. Operation Pomegranate was to be 2 SAS's final mission in Italy. Six men were dropped by Dakota to raid San Egidio airfield to aid the Anzio landings. The party split when it was challenged by a German sentry, leaving two officers to carry out the attack. Only seven aircraft were destroyed, and the surviving officer, Lieutenant Hughes, was captured. Hughes was treated for his injuries in a German military hospital. Befriended by two German officers, Hughes managed to have his status changed from political prisoner to

prisoner-of-war; they advised him to escape rather than be shot as a saboteur. Hughes' escape confirmed rumours that the Germans were executing captured Allied parachutists and raiding parties under Hitler's infamous 'Commando Order'.

By March 1944, most of the SAS units had returned to Britain. From its small beginnings only a few short years previously, the Regiment now totalled some 2,500 men. Not everyone was happy with this growth, and many of the original desert veterans saw the SAS turning into a regular army unit. Bill Stirling, commanding 2 SAS, pushed the point hard, claiming that the SAS were better used in their original role of small party raiders. This conviction led to his resignation, and he was replaced by Lieutenant-Colonel Brian Franks.

The SRS was re-formed into the SAS Brigade under the command of Brigadier R. W. McLeod. The brigade comprised 1 SAS under 'Paddy' Mayne, now also a Lieutenant-Colonel, 2 SAS under Franks, 3 and 4 SAS (French) and 5 SAS (Belgian); F Squadron of the 'Phantoms' (GHQ Reconnaissance Regiment) also came under McLeod's command.

## The Phantoms

The Phantoms were a remarkable unit. Founded by Major-General Gerald Hopkinson – later killed while commanding the 1st Airborne Division in Italy – they began secret operations in France as early as 1940; however, their existence was not revealed until the end of hostilities in Europe in May 1945.

Made up of 150 officers and 1,250 other ranks, their job throughout the war was to gather and swiftly pass back vital information. Known officially as GHQ Liaison Regiment, they adopted the nickname of 'The Phantoms' and achieved excellent results by working directly with the front-line troops, keeping Army Group and Base HQ informed almost minute-by-minute of all that was happening and of the positions of troops

*Three members of the 2 SAS who were parachuted into the Castino area move up heavy weapons in order to assist the partisans.*

actually on the ground. Messages were sent from under the noses of the enemy by means of very small wireless sets invented specially for the purpose by Captain Peter Astbury. During the fighting on the Western Front prior to the fall of France, the Phantoms, then commanded by Lieutenant-Colonel McIntosh, sent more than 70,000 of these messages from the battle areas to the headquarters of the 12th and 21st Army Groups.

When France fell, the Phantoms were among those evacuated back to England via Dunkirk and other Channel ports, and sections were deployed around the coast at locations where a German invasion was thought most likely, so news of any attempted German landing could be speedily passed on. Their headquarters were in very innocent-looking surroundings in St. James's Park, London. Here were the base wireless sets on which the Phantoms worked, passing information to GHQ. The headquarters in St. James's Park also contained several lofts for the carrier-pigeons which supplemented the Regiment's wireless.

Towards the end of 1940 a squadron of the Regiment left Britain for the battle front in Greece; and, while almost all were captured, they continued to transmit messages to the end. The Phantoms suffered yet more casualties when they adopted a commando role, sending a squadron to join the raid on Dieppe. In November 1942 two squadrons went with the 1st Army to North Africa and operated throughout the campaign, finally joining up with the 8th Army. There, they listened in to the wireless talk of the German tanks, gleaning every scrap of information which was of interest and from the chaos of battle formulating a clear picture, reporting positions, casualties and strengths. In early 1944, F Squadron of the Phantoms, commanded by Major the Hon. J. J. 'Jakie' Astor, was assigned the role of providing rear link radio communications for the squadrons of 1st and 2nd SAS Regiments (1 & 2 SAS) deployed in France from D-Day onwards, its patrol operators communicating with the squadron base located at the headquarters of the SAS Brigade.

With a strength of six officers and 102 other ranks, F Squadron was organized as a headquarters and four patrols. Two patrols, under Captains Moore and Sadoine, were attached to 1 SAS and two, under Captains Hislop and Johnsen, to 2 SAS. Each patrol comprised an officer and four other ranks. The two French units in the SAS Brigade, 3rd and 4th French

*Pigeon lofts in St James Park London circa 1943. Pigeons were used to supplement GHQ (Phantoms) radio system.*

Parachute Battalions, and the Belgian Independent Parachute Company possessed their own signals units, but F Squadron provided training for them in the use of the newly-developed lightweight radio sets. All F Squadron personnel were parachute-trained and during the first half of 1944 underwent training with the rest of the SAS Brigade in Scotland prior to deployment on operations with 1 and 2 SAS in June.

Some Phantom members were parachuted into France before D-Day, while others went in with the assault troops (it was they who sent back the first news of the Normandy landings). By July the entire Regiment was in France, deployed with the British, Canadian and American armies. This was the result of an inquiry by General Eisenhower who, in the early stages of the assault on Normandy, visited the British 2nd Army HQ, then located near Portsmouth, and was considerably impressed by the complete intelligence picture of operations. He asked how it was done. The answer was: 'Phantom patrol.' It was explained to him how the organization flashed back to England the positions of brigades and battalions in the beach-head battles. General Eisenhower immediately ordered Phantom units to work with the American formations. Likewise, General Crerar's 1st Canadian Army secured a substantial proportion of its intelligence from the Phantoms, and General Patton, commanding the US 3rd Army, acknowledged the value of their assistance. Hour by hour during the attempted German break-out in the Ardennes that winter, the Panzers' every move was reported by Phantoms, distinguished only by a small letter 'P' on the right shoulder.

Towards the end of the war, it was they who made known the first details of the German concentration camps and prisoner-of-war camps and, in one last, spectacular coup, they co-ordinated the link-up between the Russians and the American 1st Army, as always transmitting the news faithfully back to GHQ.

## The SAS and D-Day

Though he had gone, Bill Stirling's pleading eventually bore fruit in the planning for Operation Overlord. The SAS Brigade had originally been assigned to drop behind enemy lines and prevent any German reinforcements reaching the Normandy beach-head. This was later changed, and instead the SAS was used to consolidate the various resistance groups scattered around French, Belgium, Holland and Italy. Acting on their own initiative, they were to organize the resistance movements into fighting forces which would attack the Germans at each and every opportunity.

Many of the SAS were parachuted in prior to D-Day, but reinforcements continued to be infiltrated up until November 1944. Much of this work was done using the American-made Douglas DC3, known in RAF service as the Dakota, a twin-engined transport aircraft with a maximum speed of nearly 200mph and an 800-mile operational range. The Dakota had a crew of three and could carry 46 seated troops or 20 parachutists. A total of 780 sorties were flown, dropping men, jeeps and equipment, and only six aircraft were lost.

## Operation Houndsworth

Operation Houndsworth was the first of some 40 operations the SAS would undertake before the end of the war. The operation involved A Squadron, 1 SAS, under the command of Major Bill Fraser. His orders were to establish a base in the densely-wooded country to the west of Dijon, disrupt German communications, cut railway lines and assist local resistance (Maquis) units. The advance party, including Johnny Cooper and Reg Seekings, was dropped by parachute on the night of June 5, D-Day minus one. The weather was foul and the drop took place in zero visibility, as a result of which

Cooper hit a stone wall on landing and knocked himself unconscious, but the party managed to assemble and release carrier pigeons carrying intelligence reports (though they never reached England).

After making contact with the local Maquis, a landing strip was made ready to receive more supplies and reinforcements. Bill Fraser was the first to arrive, along with two 'sticks' of parachutists led by Captains Wiseman and Alec Muirhead. The Houndsworth unit eventually numbered 18 officers and 126 other ranks, with nine jeeps. Over the next three months, the SAS force repeatedly cut the railway lines around Dijon. Of course, such a force, combined with varying numbers of Maquis, did not go unnoticed, and enemy forces soon moved into the area to deal with them. The opposition consisted of Russians in the service of the Germans, together with the despised *Milice*, a Vichy-supported French national police force which was armed by the Germans and acted in concert with the Gestapo.

The major enemy garrison was at Château Chinon, and in early July the German-officered Russians began a campaign of intimidation in the local villages, taking hostages and burning property. In one incident, they took a number of Maquis sympathizers from Montsauche and set off towards Château Chinon, where their prisoners would face almost certain torture and execution. Alec Muirhead's troop and members of the Maquis set an ambush for them; however, the site was far from perfect, having forest on one side and open country on the other.

Johnny Cooper, one of those who took part in the ambush, recalls: "The first three-tonner, crammed with enemy soldiers, drew level with a wood-pile and over came two plastic bombs. One hit the bonnet and the other the rear of the vehicle, causing pandemonium among the occupants. Many were killed by fire from the Maquis as they fled across the road towards the open fields. Our Brens opened up with devastating effect and many of the Russians retreated back to the ditch, which was in Reg's sights. It was a massacre. Three trucks were set on fire, the hostages were released unharmed from two civilian cars, but the German light vehicle bringing up the rear managed to turn round and make off. In retaliation for this attack the Germans executed 13 hostages from the village of Montsauche, after which they burned the place to the ground."

## Theatre of War : Europe

As the Second World War dragged on, the SAS moved from North Africa to the closer front of Europe. By the mid-1940s there were hundreds of Resistance cells operating throughout Northern Europe particularly, and the SAS were active.

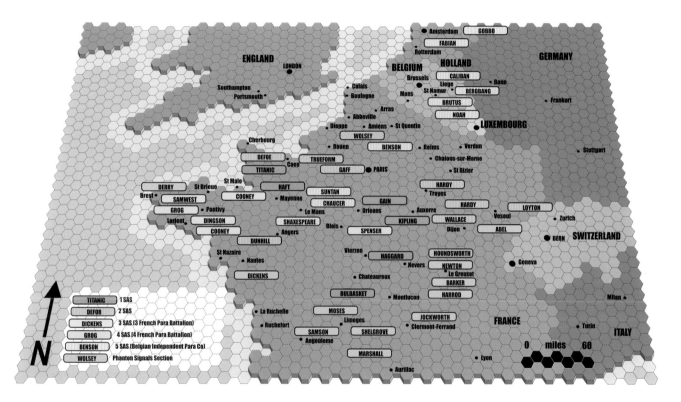

| | |
|---|---|
| TITANIC | 1 SAS |
| DEFOR | 2 SAS |
| DICKENS | 3 SAS (3 French Para Battalion) |
| GROG | 4 SAS (4 French Para Battalion) |
| BENSON | 5 SAS (Belgian Independent Para Co) |
| WOLSEY | Phantom Signals Section |

As early as 1943 the SAS were operating in Sicily. They moved on to Italy and then France, Belgium, Holland, Germany and Norway. Known operations included:
Raids in Normandy and Brittany;
Raids on enemy railway communications;
Landing support;
Arming the Resistance;
Reconaissance;
Intelligence gathering;
Assassination attempts;
Engaging and harassing the enemy;
Supporting the US advance.

Major Ian Fenwick, commanding D Squadron, 1 SAS, had decided to disperse his force for added security. He sent Lieutenant Leslie Bateman with a patrol to link up with a large group of several hundred Maquis at Thimory. These were under the command of a colourful Frenchman called 'Captain Albert', who was preparing for an attack on Orleans. Shortly after Bateman's patrol arrived at the Maquis base, the camp was attacked by a large enemy force equipped with armoured vehicles and flamethrowers. The resistance fighters scattered and the SAS patrol, which was travelling in civilian cars, came under heavy fire as it made its escape. The vehicle carrying Lieutenant Bateman, Corporal Wilson, Lance Corporal Essex and a shot-down US Army Air Force officer, who had been sheltering with the Maquis, was hit. Bateman was wounded but succeeded in leaving the vehicle and gaining the cover of the woods, though the American was killed as he attempted to crawl under the vehicle. Corporal Wilson received a head wound and was initially knocked unconscious. On coming round inside the vehicle, however, he drew his Colt .45 pistol and opened fire on four Germans as they approached, killing or wounding three of them. He was subsequently taken prisoner and, after interrogation, was sent to a hospital in Orleans – from which he was released by American forces which arrived in the city two days later.

Lieutenant Bateman, meanwhile, had met two of his patrol who had also been wounded in the ambush. The three men remained in hiding until they linked up with the Maquis and eventually made their way to an area in the forest where their commanding officer, Lieutenant Colonel Mayne, was waiting. Bateman remained with the Maquis, while his men accompanied Mayne to meet C Squadron at Le Mans.

Undeterred, the SAS decided to attack a German synthetic petrol plant using a mortar section of A Squadron, 1 SAS. The target was well-guarded and protected against air attack by strong anti-aircraft defences. Led by Muirhead, the SAS approached their target without incident and set up their three-inch mortars in dead ground. At 01:30 hours, in bright moonlight, they opened fire on the plant, discharging a total of 40 high-explosive and incendiary bombs in rapid succession. Within seconds, the fuel storage tanks and plant buildings were ablaze and continued to burn for three days. The mortar section was able to withdraw unhindered as the enemy, mistakenly thinking it was an air raid, had retreated to underground shelters.

Houndsworth continued its operations. In one spectacular incident, another plant manufacturing synthetic petrol, near Autun, was destroyed by a mortar attack in early August. By the beginning of September, A Squadron, having continued to hit the enemy at every opportunity in conjunction with Maquis units, was exhausted and the decision was taken to replace it with C Squadron: the latter arrived on September 6. Houndsworth had been a great success: 22 railway lines had been cut, 200 Germans killed or wounded and 30 bombing targets reported.

## Operation Bulbasket

Operation Bulbasket was carried out during the period from June 6 to August 7, 1944, by a troop of B Squadron, 1 SAS, commanded by Captain John Tonkin and 3 Patrol of F Squadron, the Phantoms, under Captain R. J. Sadoine. At 01:37 hours on D-Day Tonkin and one of his officers, Lieutenant Crisp, were dropped blind into the area ahead of the rest of the troop and shortly afterwards made contact with 'Samuel,' a local SOE agent who advised them that the area was too dangerous and that they should move to a safer location. Tonkin's primary mission was to reconnoitre the area of the Vienne and determine whether it was suitable for use as an SAS base. In addition, he was also to gauge the strength of enemy forces and investigate the organization and strength of the Maquis in the area.

On the following night an advance party of nine men, led by Lieutenant Tom Stephens, was dropped successfully to link up with Tonkin and Crisp. The rest of the troop and the Phantom patrol were dropped on the night of June 11. One aircraft succeeded in locating the dropping zone (DZ), dropping 12 men and a number of equipment containers. A second aircraft, having spotted the lights of an enemy division on a main road close to the DZ, turned away and dropped eight members of the troop and the Phantom patrol some 30 miles away.

The rest of the troop had been dropped in four small groups tasked with attacking railway targets in the area before making their way to rendezvous with the rest of the troop. Lieutenant Morris and his patrol dropped near the main railway linking Poitiers and Tours and successfully cut the line, as did Sergeant Holmes and his men. Similarly, Lieutenant Weaver's patrol succeeded in derailing a train on the line between Bordeaux and Saumur. However, the fourth patrol under Corporal Kinnevane suffered misfortune when it was dropped well away from its intended DZ, landing instead in the small town of Airvault. One man was captured and two others lost their weapons and equipment while making good their escape. Despite the loss of one of their number, all four patrols succeeded in rejoining the rest of the troop.

Meanwhile, the rest of the troop was active. The railway line between Limoges and Poitiers was cut on 12 occasions, a train destroyed, another derailed and roads in the area mined. In addition, information on rail targets for air attack was transmitted back to England, and this resulted in 11 fuel trains and 35 locomotives being destroyed. All this activity inevitably generated considerable activity by enemy forces in the area and Tonkin was forced to move his base on a number of occasions, which was difficult due to his force's lack of mobility. Furthermore, the Phantom patrol had still not joined him, and thus his rear link communications with the SAS base in England were hampered. Nevertheless,

*Standing is captain Tonkin, sitting on the right is Lieutenant Morris. The four other men were captured by the Germans on July 7, 1944 and executed.*

he succeeded in submitting a request that four armed jeeps be dropped to him, and this was done on the night of June 17.

During the following weeks Tonkin's troop mounted repeated raids on the local rail network, despite increased enemy activity in the area. On June 25 he moved his force to a new base in the forest near the small town of Verrières. A week later, on the morning of July 3, the base was attacked by a large enemy force which, because of lax security and other lapses on the part of the SAS, achieved almost total surprise. During the ensuing action 30 members of the troop, together with a shot-down American airman, were captured and subsequently taken to Poitiers. On the night of July 6 they were transported in trucks to the forest near Saint Sauvan where they were executed by firing squad, once again under the terms of Hitler's Commando Order of October 1942, and buried nearby.

Captain Tonkin and some 14 of his men, three of whom had been away from the base in a jeep at the time of the attack, escaped and linked up with Captain Sadoine's Phantom patrol. They subsequently carried out a small number of attacks on rail targets but having lost three of the jeeps (destroyed by Captain Tonkin before he escaped) they were limited in their mobility. During the first week of August, Tonkin and his men were relieved by elements of 3rd French Parachute Battalion and together with the Phantom patrol were subsequently evacuated by air to England.

Free French soldiers had served and fought in the SAS since January 1942. By 1944, although under British command, it should not be forgotten that almost half of the SAS Brigade consisted of French soldiers. Their actions, especially in Europe, were among the most daring in SAS history. On June 6, 1944, 160 men of 4 French Parachute Battalion (4 SAS), with four jeeps, landed by parachute in the Vannes area of Brittany. Here they established the 'Dingson' base, contacting and organising the local resistance in order to interrupt the movements of enemy forces. By June 18 the leader of the SAS party, Commandant Bourgoin, had three fully-equipped battalions, made up of resistance fighters and a company of gendarmes. Unfortunately however, these men had little or no military training and were quickly dispersed when the base was attacked by the Germans later that day. Around 40 SAS men managed to escape with no loss of life and a new base was quickly established near Pontivy, codenamed Grog.

The French had better success during Operation Dickens when, between July 16 and October 7, 1944, 65 members of 3 French Parachute Battalion (3 SAS) parachuted into the Nantes/Saumur area of western France. Their mission was to organize the local resistance, disrupt rail communications and gather intelligence about German activity. The mission was a total success, costing the Germans 500 troops and 200 vehicles, with the complete destruction of the railway network.

Operation Derry was another successful mission, conducted between August 5 and 18, 1944, by 89 men of 3 French Parachute Battalion (3 SAS) led by Commandant Conan. The group was dropped by parachute into the Finistère area of Brittany. The plan was to suppress the German advance on Brest and prevent the destruction of the viaducts at Morlaix and Plougastel. The mission was successful on both counts and enormous damage and injury was inflicted on the enemy.

*Some of the SAS men who were captured while on Operation Bulbasket. Their fate was preordained.*

Towards the middle of August, Operation Kipling was undertaken. This mission was designed to aid the Allied airborne landings which were due to take place in the so-called Orleans Gap. The SAS party – 107 men of C Squadron, 1 SAS, with 46 jeeps – began its work on August 13, when an advance party under Captain Derrick Harrison dropped into the area west of Auxerre. Landing successfully and establishing a base, the SAS was then informed that the airborne landings had been cancelled: a change in tactics was therefore required. At this time the situation was very fluid, with the Allies making deep penetrations into German areas. Patton's US 3rd Army was nearing Reims, while other Allied units were pushing north following the Anvil landings. The Kipling party therefore took advantage of the confusion among the Germans to launch a series of daring attacks. Harrison himself attacked the village of Les Ormes, and ran straight into Waffen-SS troops who were in the process of executing suspected Maquis. In a savage firefight, Harrison's two jeeps set the Germans' vehicles on fire, though they were then forced to retire and Harrison was obliged to leave his own damaged jeep behind. For this exploit, he won the Military Cross.

Because of erratic supply drops, the Kipling party suffered fuel shortages, but nevertheless still managed to mount a number of successful patrols. Some of the latter joined the French First Army and took part in the surrender of Autun's 3,000-strong German garrison. By September 26 Kipling was over, and the SAS soldiers were at Cosne enjoying a well-earned rest.

The Germans became highly frustrated at having the enemy snapping at their heels, and reprisals were swift and savage. The first of many such incidents of revenge happened during Operation Loyton. Lieutenant-Colonel Franks was to lead some 91 men of 2 SAS; their mission, to strike at enemy installations and co-operate with the local Maquis (which was problematic at the best of times). They would be situated in the mountainous Vosges area of eastern France. The advance party, together with a Phantom patrol and a Jedburgh team, was dropped on the evening of August 12, 1944, with subsequent drops due to take place over the following days. Jedburgh teams were three-man units set up to train French resistance fighters and were, at least nominally, composed of a British, a French and an American member, though this ideal composition was often not possible. Unfortunately the Germans had placed large numbers of troops on the crests of the Vosges and the east bank of the River Moselle: the SAS party thus parachuted into an ambush. To make matters worse, the Gestapo was also in the area, at Nancy and Strasbourg, and both locations had anti-partisan units. The SAS men had to contend with large numbers of enemy troops and traitors within the Maquis. There were also a number of reprisals against local villages in response to SAS successes. The entire male population of Moussey, for example, was rounded up and packed off to concentration camps: of the 210 men between the ages of 16 and 60 who were taken, only 70 returned. Bedevilled by a lack of supplies and erratic resupply drops, Franks brought the operation to an end on October 9, by which time two SAS soldiers had been killed and 31 captured (all of whom were shot by the Gestapo).

Another SAS operation was undertaken around Doubs in eastern France, between August 27 and September 22, 1944. Operation Abel, under the command of Captain Sicand, comprised 82 soldiers of 3 French Parachute Battalion (3 SAS). One company successfully carried out several blocking actions and hit-and-run raids in a combined effort with Maquis units, troops of the advancing French First Army and the US Seventh Army. The aim was to capture a strategic pass between the Vosges and Jura mountains known as the Belfort Gap. In this and other operations carried out by 3 SAS between July 16 and October 7, the battalion lost 96 men killed, wounded or captured: however, it accounted for 2,340 Germans killed, a further 2,976 wounded and 1,090 taken prisoner, in addition to causing the enemy enormous material damage.

Meanwhile, men of 5 SAS, the Belgians, were dropped in the areas of Le Mans and Chartres to commence Operations Chaucer, Shakespeare and Bunyan. Operation Chaucer was conducted between July 28 and August 15, 1944, by two patrols operating north-west of Le Mans, and was aimed at harassing the retreating Germans. The first party was commanded by Lieutenant Ghys and landed on July 28: the second, commanded by Captain Hazel, on August 9. Unfortunately, however, the drop was executed too late and the groups were forced to pursue the enemy on foot, managing only to meet the rear of the retreating German forces.

On August 16, Major Blondeel and 40 men, together with some jeeps, were parachuted into the Ardennes in Operation Noah. Shortly thereafter Operation Benson began, on August 28, when a second Belgian patrol was dropped north-east of Paris with the task of reporting on enemy dispositions and movements. The operation was highly successful, not least because, as well as sending back a large amount of other information, the patrol captured a copy of the German Order of Battle for formations deployed along the River Seine. The speed of the Allied advance north to the Seine, however, meant this operation was somewhat short-lived.

On September 2, patrols of the Independent Parachute Company were dropped into Belgium in Operation Brutus, their task being to link up with the Belgian Resistance. Three days later, on September 5, a small force of men from the company was inadvertently dropped into Germany as reinforcements for Operation Berbang, thus becoming the first SAS troops to enter the country.

## Bucket Force

The SBS were also busy during September 1944. The Germans were withdrawing from southern Greece and the Peloponnese in order to meet the threat from the Red Army as it advanced through Bulgaria, Rumania and Poland. At the same time, the decision was taken by the British War Cabinet that every effort was to be made to liberate Greece at the earliest opportunity and prevent the communists there taking power. It was recognized that any liberating force would need air support, which would in turn require airfields from which to operate.

An *ad hoc* force, codenamed Bucket Force and commanded by Lieutenant Colonel the Earl Jellicoe, was rapidly assembled for the task. Bucket Force comprised L Squadron SBS under Major Ian Patterson; two companies of the 2nd Battalion, Highland Light Infantry; 2908 Squadron Royal Air Force Regiment; a patrol of the LRDG; a section of 40 Commando, Royal Marines; a Royal Navy Combined Operations Pilotage Party; and a number of RAF ground staff.

The first element of Bucket Force to land in Greece was an SBS patrol, led by Captain Charles Bimrose and dropped in the hills to the south of Araxos airfield. Bimrose reported that the airfield was clear of the enemy but that the port of Patras to the east was still held by the Germans. On the morning of September 23, the rest of L Squadron was dropped on the airfield and shortly afterwards Major Patterson dispatched patrols to the port of Katakolon to the south to reconnoitre it for use by the sea-borne element of Bucket Force. On the following day, Lieutenant-Colonel Jellicoe and his headquarters staff flew in by Dakota and landed at Araxos.

Advancing eastwards towards Corinth, resistance was first encountered at the town of Patras, occupied by a German garrison and a battalion of Greek fascists. After negotiations with Major Patterson, the Greeks decided that discretion was the better part of valour and disappeared. A combination of the SBS armed jeeps and the RAF Regiment squadron's armoured cars produced sufficiently heavy firepower to influence the German garrison to withdraw by ferry.

During the following week Bucket Force succeeded in reaching Corinth. Heading north thereafter, SBS patrols encountered a force of some 700 Germans who were fighting a determined rearguard action. Shortly afterwards they reached Megara, 40 miles west of Athens, where they secured an airfield to be used for the arrival of reinforcements in the form of the 2nd Independent Parachute Brigade Group. On October 12 the SBS were relieved by C Company, 4th Parachute Battalion, plus supporting elements, who were dropped in very high winds on the airfield. On October 14, the 5th Parachute Battalion was also dropped on Megara, and three days later the SBS and 2nd Independent Parachute Brigade entered Athens, shortly after the withdrawal of the last German troops from the city.

In early 1945 the SAS Brigade, commanded by Brigadier Mike Calvert, was given the task by the 1st Canadian Army of undertaking Operation Amherst, which involved landing SAS units behind enemy lines in north-east Holland. Their tob was to harass German forces and prevent them from forming a defensive line against the advance of 2nd Canadian Corps. This action prevented the demolition of 18 bridges over the canals; where bridges had already been blown, the Brigade reconnoitred alternative routes for 2nd Canadian Corps, secured Steejnwijk airfield for the RAF, reported back on enemy movements and dispositions, provided guides for leading ground force units and lent support to Dutch Resistance operations in the area.

The operation was carried out by a total of 700 of all ranks from 3rd and 4th French Parachute Battalions, which had by then been re-designated the 2ème and 3ème Regiments de Chasseurs Parachutists (2 RCP & 3 RCP). On the night of April 7-8, 1945, a total of 50 patrols were dropped in bad weather by Stirling bombers of 38 Group RAF on to 19 dropping zones in the area of Groningen, Emmen and Meppel. A subsequent drop of armed jeeps an hour later had to be cancelled because cloud was obscuring the lights marking the dropping zone.

The French parachutists carried out all their tasks with skill and aggression, on several occasions attacking enemy-held villages with only small-arms. During the following seven days, assisted by the Dutch Resistance, they succeeded in tying down enemy units, intercepting their movements and preventing them from forming any cohesive defence until the arrival of the forward elements of 2nd Canadian Corps, which thereafter continued its advance to the North Sea. Casualties suffered by both French battalions were 29 killed, 35 wounded and 29 missing. Enemy losses totalled 270 killed, 220 wounded, 187 captured and 29 vehicles destroyed.

Operation Cold Comfort (later to be renamed Zombie) was aimed at blocking the railway line leading to the Brenner Pass in northern Italy with a landslide. A successful attack would mean the Germans would be unable to send their troops south through the Alps. A 13-strong party from 3 Squadron, 2 SAS, was dropped by parachute on February 17, 1945, just to the north of Verona. Unfortunately, the party was widely dispersed on landing and resupply was an impossibility on account of the abysmal weather. An additional complication was the hostility of the local inhabitants, who had Germanic origins. As a result, the SAS party was forced into hiding, and the group's two commanding officers, Captain Littlejohn and Corporal Crowley, were captured and subsequently executed under Hitler's Commando Order. By the end of March, the mission was declared a failure and the remainder of the party evacuated from Italy.

# Operation Archway

Operation Archway was carried out by a composite force comprising elements of A and D Squadrons, 1 SAS, under the command of Major Harry Poat, and A

Squadron, 2 SAS, commanded by Major Peter Power. The latter would be joined later in the operation by another two SAS Squadrons under Major Grant Hibbert. The entire force, commanded by Lieutenant-Colonel Brian Franks, the CO of 2 SAS, was christened 'Frankforce' and numbered 430 of all ranks. It was mounted in 75 armed jeeps, some carrying three-inch mortars, and a number of 15-cwt and three-ton trucks which transported the administrative 'tail'. The 1 SAS element was divided into three large troops commanded respectively by Majors Bill Fraser, Alec Muirhead and John Tonkin. A

Squadron, 2 SAS, was organized in two troops under the command of Captains Mackie and Miller.

'Frankforce' departed from England on March 18, 1945, and having landed at Ostend, made its way to a concentration area west of the Rhine to prepare for operations after the main assault crossing of the river, codenamed Varsity, which would be carried out by the 2nd British and 9th US armies. On March 25 its two squadrons crossed the Rhine in Buffalo tracked amphibious vehicles and thereafter pushed forward through the area held by 6th Airborne Division to take

*Many people believe the SAS was entirely British, but this is not so. Here Major General Surtees inspects members of the Belgian SAS.*

up its main role of reconnaissance. Thereafter it operated under the command of 6th Airborne Division, 11th Armoured Division and 15th (Scottish) Division.

Confronted by a variety of enemy units, including Fallschirmjäger of the German 1st Parachute Army, Hitler Youth and Volkssturm home defence units, 'Frankforce' experienced hard fighting during the advance into Germany. On April 8, a section of one of the 1 SAS troops commanded by Captain Johnny Cooper, while reconnoitering an area of woodland in advance of an armoured car squadron of the Inns of Court Regiment, was ambushed by enemy troops, supported by three armoured vehicles. Three men were killed and five wounded, the latter including Lieutenant Ian Wellsted.

A week later, on April 14-15, 1 SAS elements of 'Frankforce' reportedly arrived at Belsen concentration camp where they found some 50,000 to 60,000 inmates living in conditions so appalling as to be beyond description: 'reportedly', because the official documentation on the operation makes no mention of the visit. Four days later, several patrols were deployed in support of the Field Security Police, who were hunting down known Nazi war criminals, and carried out a number of arrests.

## Occupation

Subsequently, 'Frankforce' rejoined the advance through Germany. At the crossing of the River Elbe at the end of April, it was joined by Major Grant Hibbert's squadron of 2 SAS, which had earlier been deployed on Operation Keystone, involving the capture of bridges north of Arnhem, and which had subsequently been cancelled. Thereafter, it continued its advance through Germany, heading through Schleswig-Holstein and eventually reaching Kiel on the Baltic coast. Shortly afterwards, it was withdrawn to Belgium and on May 10 departed for England. Its losses during Operation Archway had been light: seven killed and 22 wounded.

Back in Italy, 2 SAS was harassing the Germans. The village of Albinea in Italy's Po Valley was the location of the headquarters of the German 51st Corps, which was quartered in two houses, called the Villa Calvi and Villa Rossi, and whose staff numbered some 300 personnel. After an overnight approach march down from the Appennine mountains on March 24, an attack

was carried out on the following night by elements of 3 Squadron, 2 SAS, under the command of Major Roy Farran, supported by a force of 170 Italian and Russian partisans, the latter being escapees from German prison camps. Two groups, each of SAS and 20 partisans, attacked the villas, while the remainder of the partisans formed a screen to the south of the objective to block any enemy reinforcements approaching the area. There was fierce fighting at both houses and enemy casualties were heavy, including a number of staff officers killed; among their number was the headquarters' Chief of Staff, Oberst Lemelson. It later transpired that the Corps commander, General-Leutnant Hauk, was away from his headquarters at the time. The SAS suffered three men killed, Lieutenant Riccomini, Sergeant Guscott and Corporal Bolden, and two wounded, Corporal Layburn and Parachutist Mulvey. The partisans suffered five wounded and six captured. Also wounded was Major Michael Lees, an SOE liaison officer working with the partisans who had attached himself to the SAS. Nevertheless, Farrans' force succeeded in withdrawing and, having avoided German forces searching the valley plain, made its way back to its base in the mountains.

## War is over

As the war began to wind down, the SAS Brigade began to disintegrate. The French contingent, 2 and 3 RCP, were reabsorbed into the French Army in July. The Belgian company had been expanded early in 1945 and re-designated the Belgian SAS Regiment, subsequently serving in Denmark and Germany in a counter-intelligence role, but later in the year was handed over to the Belgian Army and re-designated the 1st Regiment Parachutist-SAS. It was based initially at Westmalle but subsequently, from April 1946 onwards, at Poulseur, with a training school located at Schaffen. Members of the regiment saw service during the Korean War as part of the Corps Volontaires Corea (CVC) which saw a considerable amount of action until its withdrawal in 1954.

The British element found they were doing the oddest of jobs, such as Operation Apostle, a mission to disarm the 300,000 German soldiers remaining in Norway at the end of the war. This task was undertaken by HQ SAS Brigade, 1 and 2 SAS, all under the command of

Brigadier Mike Calvert. The two regiments were shipped from Ostend to Tilbury, and in England they were issued with new jeeps, new clothing and equipment.

An advance party made up of representatives from both regiments and a detachment from brigade staff arrived at Stavanger on May 12, 1945, and by the end of the month a total of 760 troops, 17 motorcycles, 68 trailers and 150 jeeps were in the country. The SAS Brigade was based at Bergen to administer the operation. The four months the SAS soldiers spent in Norway were hardly taxing, and most of the men regarded the time as a sort of holiday. The Germans gave no trouble, the locals were largely friendly (although there were clashes with Quislings – Norwegian collaborators) and the weather was warm. The SAS returned to England at the end of August. An amusing footnote to the operation is the so-called 'Battle of Bergen'. The young ladies of the town were quite fond of the daring British soldiers in their midst, a fact resented by many young Norwegian males in the town and members of the local police force. This culminated in a large-scale brawl in the town's centre, which the SAS won hands-down. The 'victory' resulted in British diplomats in Norway urgently requesting the War Office to evacuate the SAS to England.

Some SAS work remained unfinished, the majority of which was tracking down Germans wanted for war crimes. However, it was clear that the Allied governments of Britain and America were not keen on searching for the large numbers of Nazis still at large. Faced with a renewed threat from the Soviets, the Allies preferred to recruit their former Nazi enemies rather than to prosecute them for war crimes. The SAS had more backbone, however, and set up an organization to bring as many Nazis as possible to trial.

# Final operations

Major Eric 'Bill' Barkworth was the intelligence officer of 2 SAS. In May 1945 he was dispatched by his Commanding Officer, Lieutenant-Colonel Brian Franks, with a small party of 2 SAS to investigate reports of the discovery of the bodies of British troops in Germany. Barkworth's group, designated the SAS War Crimes Investigation Team, identified some of the bodies as those of members of 2 SAS deployed on Operation Loyton in August 1944. Captured by the Germans, they had been taken to a concentration camp at Rotenfels, in Germany, summarily executed and buried. Another mass grave was uncovered at Gaggenau near Baden-Baden: it contained the bodies of 28 captured SAS men who had been tortured and murdered by the Gestapo. Barkworth and his men continued their investigations, travelling to Moussey, in the Vosges mountains of north-eastern France, where they uncovered the remains of more men of 2 SAS. Despite the disbandment of the SAS in 1946, the group continued investigating the deaths of men from both SAS regiments whose fates were unknown until 1949. Several men identified as being responsible for the atrocities were tried by military courts sitting at Wuppertal and hanged – though some stories from the period suggest that some of those Nazi officers captured failed to make it to court, the SAS men preferring a slightly more direct and appropriate form of retribution.

# Chapter 8

# After the
# Regiment

*Learning to shoot, as taught by ex-SAS instructors.*

What do SAS soldiers do when they leave the Regiment? It mainly depends on how much service they have. A handful of the longer-serving soldiers will be selected for other government work, such as Customs and Excise or the intelligence services. However, it is fairly true to say that most soldiers who have passed SAS selection stay in Hereford for the rest of their military careers. This makes them highly skilled and very much in demand once they retire. But not every SAS soldier retires, and there are two exceptions: getting killed during service, and premature expulsion or Returned To Unit (RTU'ed).

# Death in Service

An average of three SAS soldiers die every year, on a bad year it can be as high as 20. The SAS is not a large Regiment and the death of an individual soldier is a great loss. It is an unfortunate part of SAS life that many soldiers do die, some while in training others during operations. One only has to take a look in the SAS graveyard at Saint Martins church in Hereford to see the cost. Here lie many young men, good men, men full of life and promise, dead before their time. It is not that the Regiment is careless or 'Gung-Ho', on the contrary, it is because these men dared to face foe and adversity head on – they 'Dared to Win'. Many have died since the Regiment was reformed back in 1952, just one example is Sergeant 'Geordie' Barker.

# 'Geordie' Barker

Geordie was one of the funniest and best loved characters ever to join the SAS, and like so many of his peers his deeds were not amplified by some outstanding media headline. Geordie joined the SAS from the Royal Engineers, passing selection in 1968. He was posted to G Squadrons Air Troop where he became a free fall expert, and a man who could raise everyone's spirits. Between 1971-75, he rotated with his Squadron through the Oman war as part of the BATT force (British Army Training Team) commitment. During this conflict, one of the major problems was to keep the enemy forces, the Adoo, from getting near the edge of the mountain escarpment where from such a vantage point they were able to bombard the town of Salala and the nearby RAF base below. In the end, the only solution was to build a series of small, defensive encampments along the escarpment. These positions became known as 'Dianas'.

On one tour, Geordie was stationed at Diana 5, a location that came under frequent fire from a small hill some 800 metres away. The only weapon the SAS men possessed which could effectively reach such a distance was the .50 Browning heavy machine gun. To compensate for this shortcoming Geordie decided it was time to use a bit of improvisation. His idea was that we should make a launch ramp out of a wooden pallet and attach five 66mm rockets to it at a 45 degree angle. Given that the effective range of the rockets is around 350 metres the

plan required that the launcher be carried and secured out in no mans land between the Diana position and the enemy hill. Cutting the fuses and re-wiring them to one central electrical detonator would make it possible to launch all the rockets through a single control wire back at the Diana 5 position.

The launch ramp was completed and under cover of darkness Geordie and a friend named Barry walked out to a spot where the adoo position was in range and set-up the rocket apparatus. Of course, there was always the chance that the adoo would spot the rockets, come down, dismantle the launcher and then use them against the Diana position. To prevent this, Barry set up several jumping mines around the launch site. The mines were particularly nasty bits of ordinance because, when triggered, they would pop up out of the ground attached to a cord. The cord was only waist high in length and once it had reached its limit, it would pull out the safety pin, instantly detonating the mine. The resulting damage to a human body was devastating. And to make matters worse, the mines they were dealing with were old and therefore rather unreliable. It was a tense, nerve-racking job removing the safety-pins.

Barry had just finished removing all the pins, thus arming the mines, when Geordie put his torch directly in his face and switched it on.

"Can you see OK?" he said jokingly to Barry who instantly lost his night vision. Not a desirable situation when surrounded by a whole mess of armed and extremely dangerous mines.

"I saw this First World War movie once where guys were blind and they had to put their hands on the shoulders of the man in front to go through the minefield. So come on, I'll save your life," Geordie grinned.

Despite the situation, Barry had to laugh. It was Geordie's way of creating a joke, one which he would be able to tell many times over, how he, Geordie, had led his friend from the minefield – neglecting to mention that he had caused the temporary blindness in the first place.

Some weeks later while in the base camp on R&R (rest and recuperation) Geordie regaled the story of the rocket ramp in great detail. By all accounts, the enemy had turned up at the hill and started firing, at which every man in the Diana 5 position had tried to pull the firing lever which Geordie had constructed to launch

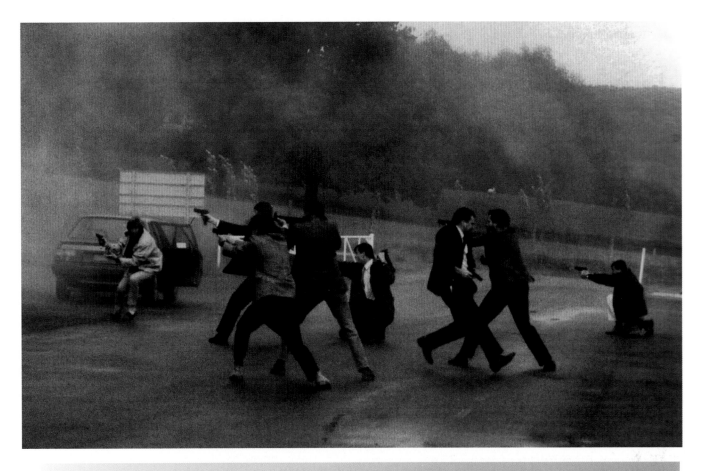

*The real thing: this photograph was taken at the SAS facility in south Hereford. All these men are now retired but many still continue to practice their skills.*

the rockets. Geordie got there first. The rockets went off, hitting the hill in a blaze of glory. Two of the adoo were killed and the rest driven away, never to return.

## Italy

Years later, in March, 1978, Aldo Moro, the leading Italian Christian Democrat politician was attacked in his car while driving down a street. The car was stopped by a blockade before gunmen opened fire with their automatic weapons, killing Moro's bodyguards. The attackers were members of the Red Brigade (Brigate Rosse), an Italian terrorist group. They took Moro and held him hostage for 54 days, all the time making demands of the Italian government. The demands were always refused. Realising they were not going to get anywhere, the terrorists executed Moro

with a shot in the head. His body was eventually found on May 10, dumped in the boot of a car in a Rome street.

While the Red Brigade were holding Moro, the Italian authorities decided on a crack down on terrorist activity. Raids were mounted on Red Brigade safe houses, suspected terrorists were arrested with a great deal ammunition and weaponry being seized. However, they found nothing that would tell them of Moro's location. By a coincidence, also during this time, an SAS four man team was in Italy trying to gather information on the Red Brigade; Geordie Barker and his friend Barry were two of the team members. Obviously, in the interests of operational security, no details about their task can be given, but what happened to them vividly illustrates what occurs when there is lack of communication between intelligence services.

On this particular occasion, the SAS men had been led

to a small hut on the side of a wooded hill. It was a safe house used by the Red Brigade and it was thought that some contact might be made. The SAS men only moved around at night, but on that particular morning they were late and were spotted in the early dawn by an over-vigilant villager. Suspicious of their motives, the villager called the police. At around 10 in the morning, the SAS men had just settled down to get some sleep when the door burst open to reveal a fat, sweating Carabinerei (Policeman) waving a pistol. He seemed as surprised to see them, as they were to see him. As the SAS men jumped to their feet all the policeman could manage was a muttered "Good morning. What are you doing here?" all spoken in Italian.

The men, not speaking Italian, replied in English. This, as well as the scene around the hut: sleeping bags and half-eaten food, seemed to unnerve the policeman and he ran for the door and back down the hill. Not

*Skills learned in the Regiment are very much in demand around the world. These ex-SAS soldiers are teaching counter-terrorist entry methods.*

thinking much of it, the men had a laugh and then went back to sleep.

Two hours later, Geordie went outside the hut, needing to relieve himself. He wasn't gone long before he burst back into the room announcing that there were armed policemen surrounding the hut. Upon hearing this, the rest of the men went outside to take a look and were met by a hail of bullets from more than one sub-machine gun. Instinct took over and they all made a run for it, not stopping until they had put as much space between them and the armed policemen as they possibly could. Once they were clear, the SAS soldiers made contact with their controllers and were quickly placed in a safe house and from there returned to England. The breakdown in communication between the Italian intelligence groups had almost cost them their lives. Before returning to England the four were held in a store room for security. After several days this became a bit much and the SAS men demanded to be let out on the town for a couple of hours. It was agreed, however they were to leave in two's and return very quietly not to blow the cover of the safe house supplied by the Italian agency responsible for the SAS operation. Needless to say Geordie and Barry paired up and left the building, making it not further than the first bar 100 metres away. Within the hour Geordie was drunk and insisting that British footballers were brilliant and the Italian's crap and proceeded to give a demonstration of ball control with a plastic football. So funny was his act that the Italians gathered in the bar bought Geordie and Barry beer all night. Some short hours later the pair staggered back to the safe house singing 'Just one cornetto' at the top of their voices.

Sadly, Geordie Barker died in Oman, not from a bullet but when his parachute failed to open. It was a great blow for everyone, and Barry, in particular, found his death difficult to come to terms with. He is often in Barry's thoughts and now he continues to tell the tale of the rocket ramp and the rest of Geordie's antics. Those who remember his cat-like grin and wicked sense of humour will think of him not just for his work in the SAS but also for his affect on the human race. Without doubt, the world would profit greatly if we had a few more Geordie Barkers.

## Returned To Unit (RTU)

The other premature way of leaving the SAS is through being RTU'ed. Anyone, officers, NCOs and soldiers alike can be RTU'ed for a number of misdemeanours, but generally the soldier in question must have made a serious error of judgement. For example, there was a sergeant who had served with the Regiment for around 10 years, his error of judgement was getting caught. At the time, the guy was operating in Northern Ireland and being one for the ladies had taken up with a local Catholic girl. He had used one of the covert operational cars for his first date, driving her out into the countryside. His chat-up line had been 'naff', actually indicating that he was an undercover spy, the real James Bond bit etc. The conversation progressed from the undressing stage through to the relaxing cigarette afterwards. This incident may not have come too light other than for one small detail. All the covert cars were fitted with miniature press to talk buttons hidden around the car. The operators press these in order to talk to the base unit. On this particular car, there was a presser switch hidden by the foot of the passenger – and the girl had somehow locked it down. Unfortunately, while our erring sergeant was having his wicked way, a full-blown operation, involving the several security agencies was taking place, the communications for which were trafficked through the SAS base station. The rogue transmission blocked out the entire operation and was heard by everyone; additionally it was recorded on the master back-up system. Result? RTU the moment he arrived back at base.

## Surviving the SAS

Those that spend several years in the Regiment begin to fully understand its workings, which I might add are complex, and therein lies another dimension. Many SAS solders rise through the ranks to the point where they are offered a commission. Those that take this, and many do, make excellent officers, although their employment is normally restricted to the role of training or stationary command positions. Those that serve out their time, which is at the completion of 22 years military service, leave with three attributes: SAS expertise, mystique and confidence.

Armed with these attributes the retired soldier goes looking for work. Imagine you were a 40-year-old squadron Sergeant Major with all the privileges and responsibility the rank carried. Suddenly you find yourself in a suit applying for a job and the interviewee is half your age. Luckily, that scenario is a rare one, as most SAS soldiers have guaranteed employment before they leave. It is difficult for the SAS soldier to do any other that military type work, but some do. They have become publicans, postmen, professional gamblers, private investigators, adventures and smugglers.

Then there are the mavericks. Mavericks are those soldiers who choose to go it alone. One such person left the SAS to work in Saudi Arabia. He set up a company dragging the scrapped cars from the side of the road and fitting new tyres to those that had suffered a blow out. That failed so he went to work for a security company protecting a British High Commission in some African state. He married the commissioner's daughter, but both the marriage and job failed. He next found employment as a bodyguard, protecting a woman millionaire who owned half of a Dutch oil company. He married her (at her invitation I might add) and the last I heard they were happy together.

In some cases ex-SAS soldiers have attracted criticism about such employment, yet in reality, ex-SAS members are only providing a service based on their skills learnt while in the Regiment. Many ex-SAS soldiers went back to Oman working in a training capacity for a company called KMS. Oman is extremely friendly to Britain, thus such training was in the country's own interest. Some years later, also with the blessing of the British Government, the same company sent a team to Sri Lanka. What happens if a blue chip company had one of its diamond mines overrun with rebels in some remote corner of the world, who do they turn too? Likewise, oil is a commodity on which the western world is reliant, and what happens when rebellious villagers hijack the company helicopter and hold several senior oil workers hostage in Nigeria? The blue chip companies call for expert help, and lo and behold a few days later a couple of casual looking guys will turn up and assess the situation. Their solution to the problem will not normally advocate the use of arms, more likely they will negotiate a peaceful and lasting settlement with the rebels or malcontents. That's not to say that all these security companies are whiter than white, indeed many become actively involved in the military and political situations of smaller countries. For helping to establish a more settled situation in these emerging countries they are usually repaid in the form of mining and drilling concessions. For good or bad, if corporation and commercial interests are threatened you can be assured that ex-SAS personnel will be involved in resolving the problem – its what they are trained for.

As for the mystique... Mystique is what the media sell, in reality the SAS only has secrecy. If the SAS are deployed to Bosnia, then everyone will know about it. What they will not know is how or where the Regiment is operating. Therefore, the answer is to look back at past encounters and fabricate a story. As the years go by fabrications are built on fabrications, and so we have mystique. Who has benefited from this mystique? A handful of SAS authors maybe, but they are few in number.

Confidence is a different matter all together. For example, many SAS soldiers can pick a lock, make home-made explosives using a variety of items found in any kitchen cupboard, and shoot the eye out of a rabbit at one hundred metres. These skills are not very handy in civilian life, unless you are a crook, and yes, the SAS has had a few of these. All the same, these attributes and length of service, breed confidence into every SAS soldier. It remains with them for the rest of their lives. This virtue has always been a characteristic since the formation of the SAS way back in the early 1940s. It is bred from working with men who are undaunted when faced with indomitable and life-threatening problems. It is linked to the discovery that you are as capable as the next man, and that includes heads of state, Prime Ministers, and millionaires. The confidence comes from facing yourself, a process that starts when any soldier volunteers for SAS selection. It is this confidence which helps many adapt to civilian life once they have left the SAS – and that is difficult.

# Private Military Companies (PMC)

One of the first PMCs to emerge, WatchGuard International, was founded by David Stirling, founding father of the SAS. WatchGuard was to become the model for all future PMCs. In 1967, the company, which employed mainly ex-SAS soldiers, trained the militaries of the sultanates of the Persian Gulf. This training involved raising and instructing personal bodyguards and special forces units for the sultanates. The company rapidly expanded to provide Military Advisory Training Teams to foreign governments, predominantly in the Middle East, but also in Africa and South America. In 1986, Stirling went on to form KMS Enterprises (Keenie Meenie Services) with the retired Major Ian Crooke. One of their operations involved anti-poaching operations in Southern Africa, which was carried out with the support of the World Wildlife Federation. KAS also had a subsidiary, Saladin Security, which took on a military role in Sri Lanka and the Middle East.

Defence Systems Ltd (DSL), was founded in 1981 by Alastair Morrison, who, like Ian Crooke, had been Second-in-Command of 22 SAS. Having previously served with the Scots Guards, Captain Alastair Morrison joined the SAS in 1968. He was first placed in command of G Squadron's Mobility Troop, but before long was made acting Squadron OC because of difficulties with the current commander. In this role, he and his unit went to the assistance of the beleaguered BATT team at Mirbat. His reputation grew and he became Second-in-Command of 22 SAS.

After a full army career, Morrison retired from the SAS in 1979 and went to work for the German weapon manufacturers Heckler & Koch. After a spell with them, he set up his own company, Defence Systems Limited (DSL) which has evolved into one of the largest private security companies in the world.

DSL was taken over by Florida-based American Body Armour and Equipment, makers of bullet-proof vests, flak jackets and equipment for detecting drugs, for £20m. Morrison set up DSL with fellow SAS officers, including David Abbott, who spent 20 years in the SAS, becoming its Regimental Sergeant-Major. They have been joined by Sir David Ramsbotham, a former Green Jacket who now heads DSL's United Nations Division, and the Hon Richard Bethell, a Scots Guard who did four tours of duty with the SAS, including the Falklands War. Bethell, who was involved in the TWA hijack at Beirut, was decorated for bravery in 1978. Many British companies use DSL to protect their staff from kidnapping and robbery in Russia, for example. Major city banks such as BZW, Morgan Grenfell and Kleinwort Benson operate in Moscow alongside industrial companies such as British Gas. DSL is also active in Colombia, where BP and PowerGen have operations. The company has gained a reputation for professionalism and reliability, with most of their 'managers' being drawn from the ranks of ex-SAS.

Most of the larger PMCs operate legitimate business ventures, albeit in difficult areas, but it would be wrong to call them mercenaries. However, certain individuals have committed themselves to undertake what can only be described at mercenary work.

## Mercenary?

One story to emerge in recent years tells of an ex-SAS non-commissioned soldier training young men and women in tactics which would allow them to occupy commercial farms in Zimbabwe. The purpose of the training was to be able to overcome white farmers who were armed and replace them with locals who had fought in the war. Although not established it is believed that the training took place in Kariba, Victoria Falls, and Nyanga. Many of the white farmers found it incredible that a former British soldier could bring himself to teach such tactics – but some people will do anything for money.

Nevertheless, for every bad egg there is always a good one and the following individual is renown throughout the SAS. Peter McAleese had joined the Parachute Regiment in 1960 and a year later volunteered for service with 22nd SAS Regiment. Posted to D Squadron, subsequently seeing action in Aden and Borneo, he became one of

**During his time with the SAS, Major Alistair Morrison took part in the rescue of 91 passengers from a hijacked aircraft. On leaving the SAS, he started Defence Systems Limited (DSL). It has grown to be the largest Private Military Company in the world.**

*The SAS bodyguard course taught in Hereford is without doubt the finest in the world. Once soldiers have retired, these skills are put to use protecting foreign dignitaries around the world.*

the most colourful soldiers the Regiment produced. In 1969, he left the Army and returned to civilian life. In 1975, however, he was recruited as a mercenary to fight with the FNLA guerrillas against the Cuban-backed forces of the MPLA government in Angola. A year later he returned to Britain but shortly afterwards returned to Africa where he joined C Squadron Rhodesian SAS, subsequently 1st SAS Regiment, with whom he served until 1980, taking part in a large number of cross-border operations in Mozambique.

Rhodesia having fallen to the communist government of Robert Mugabe, McAleese left for South Africa where he joined the 44th Parachute Brigade in which he reached the rank of warrant officer. He was soon on active service again, returning to Angola on cross-border operations

against the guerrillas of SWAPO. Eventually he retired and returned to Britain in 1986, but shortly afterwards made his way once more to Africa, working in Uganda in the employ of a security company. Subsequently he travelled to South America and Colombia where he was hired to lead an attack on a communist terrorist base deep in the jungle. The operation was, however, aborted but McAleese's employers then contracted him to mount an operation to assassinate Pablo Escobar, the head of the Cali drug cartel. McAleese assembled and trained a 12-man force to carry out the operation but disaster struck en route to the target in helicopters. Flying in mist, one of the aircraft struck a mountainside and the operation had to be aborted. Thereafter, McAleese returned to Britain where he has since been employed in the security industry. There has never been a finer SAS soldier.

Some ex-SAS soldiers have set up shop providing training in the UK, and one such firm is Stirling Services. The company specialise in providing services and training in all aspects of personal and corporate security. Most of the instructors are ex-SAS with years of experience, and a whole range of skills. Their courses involve Global Risk Protection, Counter-Terrorist Training and Survival Training. The training facilities at Stirling Services are extensive, with the possibility to carry out full room combat drills.

# SAS Authors

There have always been authors who write about the SAS. Philip Warner published *The Special Air Service* back in 1971 while Tony Geraghty wrote *This is the SAS* in 1982. Geraghty not only had permission from the Regiment but they also provided him with endless photographs of SAS soldiers on operations, the faces of individuals were clearly visible. A year later, Peter Dickens wrote *The SAS: Secret war in South East Asia*, describing in minute detail the operations in Borneo. These works, both of which made excellent reading, passed off without any derogatory mention from the SAS. Likewise, there have been books by Colonel Tony Jeapes, and General Peter de la Billière. Then in the early 1990s a non-commissioned soldier going under the pseudonym Andy McNabb wrote about his experiences in the Gulf war. The book was an immediate hit and ranks as one of the best military books ever written. It was at this stage that the SAS decided that 'SAS authors' were to be sent to Coventry, or as the regiment put it, PNG. The Regiment claim that such publications only serve to provide an insight to SAS operational methods and techniques. While this may be true, the SAS does little to curtail the activities of the PMCs whose soldiers teach operational methods and techniques. In reality, the culprit is the British syndrome of knowing your place, and more than a little jealousy that ex-NCOs can actually write. The Regiment tried to curtail any further publications by insisting that all members sign a confidentiality clause which would prevent them from writing after they left the army. It was handled, not with finesse, but with a fist of iron – sign or leave the SAS. This further embittered many serving soldiers when some of those senior NCOs

that enforced the signing, slipped through the net and thus were able to write books themselves. Barry Davies, a serving soldier of some 18 years with the SAS, had this to say about being an author.

"I cannot comment on what other SAS authors write, that is for their conscience. As for myself, I like writing, unfortunately the publishers see me as some form of historian on the SAS, and I have become entrenched in this role. I enjoy writing and tried to break the mould by writing fiction, but the public demand for SAS material is very strong. While it is true that I write for monetary gain, we all have to work, and I am proud of being an author. This in part is due to the SAS, for I came to the Regiment with no scholarly qualifications. It was the SAS which sent me back to college, whereupon I achieved 2 A levels and 4 O levels. While I appreciate the Regiment's position on security, they are very much in the public domain. Their policy of non-disclosure is working as very little new information is emerging. That said, I think it's important that the SAS history be recorded. Perhaps they should consider having their own official author; at least that way they could control the flow of information."

# The Adventures

There is adventure in every SAS soldier, both past and present. They have crossed seas, climbed mountains, and set numerous world records. An example would be Corporal Michael 'Bronco' Lane and Sergeant John 'Brummie' Stokes. These two friends had climbed together for many years when they were selected, in 1976, to be part of a team put together by the Army Mountaineering Association to climb Everest. The idea had been conceived five years earlier but it had taken time to get everyone fit enough and for the Government of Nepal to give their consent to such a venture. The team spent this time in preparation and honing their climbing skills. One such undertaking was an attempt on the 7,804 metre (25,850 ft) high Nuptse, which is the lowest peak in the Everest triangle. The peak is difficult and on this occasion cost the lives of four of the original climbing party. This early disaster did little to inhibit the team's morale – all of them had been chosen not only for their climbing skills, but also for their ability to work under the adverse conditions found on Everest. The team was led by Lieutenant-Colonel Tony Streather and was part of a joint venture with the Royal Nepalese Army and a group of sherpas. The team consisted of 27 service personnel, with a high percentage from the Parachute Regiment and, considering its size, the SAS. These two regiments also formed the final ascent party in support of Stokes and Lane who had been chosen to be the summit pair due to their extreme fitness.

The combined endurance of Stokes and Lane had been naturally forged from 10 years of climbing together, and it was this endurance that was needed to conquer Everest. The world's highest peak does not fall easy to humans – it requires a continuous chain of food and oxygen to be ferried up in support of the summit team, and even then luck plays a large part. Battered by high winds and blinding snow, there are hidden dangers at every turn. At one base camp, around 6,705 metres (22,000 ft), one of the party simply walked out and fell down a deep crevasse – such was the instability of the mountain. However, despite the continual hardships and growing dangers, by May 14, the support party and the summit team had climbed up to Camp 6 at 8,229 metres (27,000 ft) where Stokes and Lane were left alone to carry out their attempt the next day. Bad weather suddenly closed in, delaying their departure from Camp 6 for 36 hours. The pair patiently waited. Their patience was rewarded and finally they were able to tackle the summit. However the weather was still not perfect and it took them from 06:30 in the morning until 15:00 in the afternoon to cover the 425 metres (1,400 ft) to the top.

Standing triumphantly on the summit and looking down on the rest of the world, the two men quickly took some photos and decided it would be best to make the descent as soon as possible. The weather looked as if it would turn again at any minute and they wanted to make it back to camp before it got dark – at 18:00. Getting back down was less easy than they thought and visibility started to fail; they were running out of time to make it back to camp. By sheer coincidence, they stumbled across some oxygen bottles which they had cached there on the way up. This helped to reveal their location – about 300 metres (1,000 ft) above Camp 6, but darkness was now falling fast and they knew it would be sheer folly to try and carry on in the dark. The cold was intense and there was only one thing they could do to save themselves.

Using the sparse equipment they carried and their bare hands, they scooped out a hole in the snow, huddling together in it to conserve body heat. The night seemed endless, and the cold slowly reduced their ability to talk or even think. The one plus was the oxygen bottles which helped them to survive the long, freezing night. At some stage Stokes became completely blind, the result of removing his goggles earlier in order to see better in the darkness. When morning finally arrived both men were unable to walk, or even to move. They knew that their only chance of survival now lay with the support team at Camp 5, 750 metres (2,500 ft) below them.

Luckily for them the weather had now improved and the sun was shining. The alternative summit team reached their location at 09:00 and arranged for their rescue. Even then the ordeal was not over, for it took four days for the party to reach base camp where a helicopter could fly in. Four days of enduring the extreme pain of frostbite and blackening toes and fingers. Both men were flown out of the base camp to the hospital at Kathmandu to be treated for the results of their unscheduled night on the bare mountain. Due to the effects of severe frostbite, Stokes lost several toes, while Lane had to have several fingers on his right hand amputated.

# Back for more

In 1984, both Stokes and Lane returned to the mountain that had nearly claimed their lives. This time, the team they led was made up solely of SAS soldiers, drawn from the Regiment's various Mountain Troops. It was a well-planned expedition, with fit and experienced men and the first part of the climb went extremely well. The summit pair had already reached 6,950 metres (22,800 ft) when tragedy occurred. On April 3, just after dawn, falling ice started off an enormous avalanche. Base camp was directly in its path and men and tents were swept down the mountainside. When everything became still again, one man lay dead and several of the men were seriously injured.

Today these SAS veterans, inseparable buddies and conquerors of Everest, are fundraising and have their sights set on a mountain of money – £1m. They are inviting local companies and their employees to join them in a club with a difference; one that will take them on an ascent of achievement. It was Bronco's idea, seeing

it as a way to raise money for Brummie's brainchild – the nationally-renowned 'Taste for Adventure Centre' at Credenhill. This wonderful facility teaches a wide range of outdoor activities to disadvantaged young people. Since 1991, Brummie Stokes and his team of instructors has introduced more than 4,000 children to outdoor adventure activities.

## The Men

Like most people on retirement, deciding what to do with the rest of their working life can often be a difficult one. With the Regiment, very much like the police force, the problems come because most members tend to retire active enough to want a second career, but often too old to start one. Most will have known only one way of life – the military. They will have served with either their parent regiment or the SAS for most of their active life. Most are trained for only one thing, the army. Some regiments, such as the Royal Engineers, will train their serving officers and men to do a variety of jobs, preparing them well for the outside world. Most regiments, including the SAS, won't. Although on retirement they move into a variety of work, one former hero of Mirbat for example, joined the Post Office and now works happily as a postman. The kind of work most former troopers are drawn towards however, tends to be limited to the security industry. Before the Iranian Embassy siege this was true of former members of the SAS, and after it, when the view of serving members of the Regiment was that of some kind of supermen, it became almost fashionable to have a former SAS trooper working for you, or acting as your bodyguard. Suddenly for many film and television personalities they became a necessity. The trouble with fashion accessories is that they tend to change with the tide, and the 'celebrities' are the first to change their image, and lose their protection (which they probably didn't need in the first place, but it made them look more important than they were) when it no longer serves their purpose.

Despite their superhuman image in the papers and on television, former SAS members still have to live in the real world. They have mortgages to pay, families to support and debts to service. To this end they, like everyone else, prefer the idea of a long-term and reliable income. Although some find long-term work in troubled

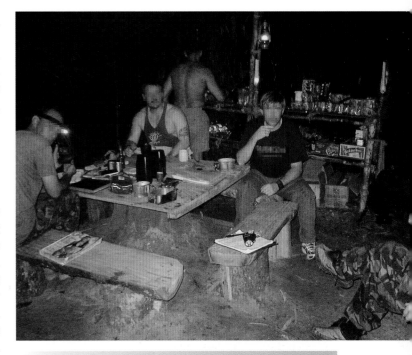

*These men are all ex-SAS, although not all British. The television series SAS-Are You Tough Enough, had retired SAS soldiers from Britain, Australia and New Zealand. They were all used to the jungle living conditions.*

areas like Algiers and more recently Iraq, most of the security industry is based on short term contracts, so former members of the Regiment find themselves having to move continually from contract to contract, relying on word of mouth or recommendation for their next job. Several former members who have pulled away from the security circuit to try their hands at other types of work, often find themselves pulled back into security work through sheer necessity.

## John Mcaleese

Better known to the rest of the world as 'The Man in Black' and one of the Regiment's most famous sons, without anyone knowing who he really is. John Mcaleese was the man the world saw during the Iranian Embassy siege, telling the journalist Sim Harris to get down, before leaping from one balcony to the other, placing a bomb against the embassy window and then jumping back

*Selling arms and military weapons is a restricted business but there are those that are prepared to risk the odd consignment in exchange for financial rewards.*

to safety seconds before the bomb exploded and the attack commenced. The photograph of John dressed entirely in black and entering the Iranian Embassy through a blown out window was flashed around the world, appeared on the front page of every major newspaper in the world, and was seen by billions. During his 17 years with the Regiment John was also decorated with the Military Medal for other outstanding acts of gallantry. A highly intelligent former Royal Engineer, Mcaleese epitomizes the image of the SAS soldier. A strong, compact man, distinctive by his Poncho Villa moustache. He is highly intelligent (more than capable of completing the *Times* crossword in a very few minutes), thoughtful and calm, but with an air of menace that most members of the Regiment seem to possess and retain.

John retired from the Regiment with the rank of WO2 in 1992 after serving 17 and a half years. During an interview with John he told the author that he knew that SAS was for him when he first visited the camp in Hereford and saw soldiers drinking beer while basking in the sun on old settees. Not that he passed selection first time, he failed to complete the final fitness test by only a few minutes, which was probably due to him breaking his ankle half way around the course. The Regiment very sensibly kept him on, and he completed selection second time around.

On leaving the Regiment John was quickly picked up by the security industry and he worked as a bodyguard for several years, as well as helping make a series for Carlton TV on some of his experiences while serving with the Regiment. The sight of John's amazing physique with his shirt off turned many a girl's head and he received a number of inviting letters. His acting ability was also of a surprisingly high standard. After marrying for a second time, John decided to try something a little different and became a pub landlord. He took over the Ship Inn in Hereford. 'The Ship' was a notoriously difficult pub and one not taken over by the faint-hearted. John is anything but faint-hearted and quickly established his presence on the place, removing all the unsavoury aspects from the pub very quickly and making it more inviting to families and a better quality of clientele. Despite all John's hard work however, and due to a number of natural disasters including two severe floods, John was eventually and reluctantly forced to give up the pub. For a while he struggled for work picking up bits and pieces of security work where he could. Finally he was taken on by Stirling Services, a company who specialize in air ball games, but are rapidly diversifying into other specialist areas. Having John as one of their executives must have been a bit of a coup. Through Stirling Services John has found an area of work that he enjoys and is working hard for the company. After all, who would not want to be trained by the Man in Black?

# Don (Lofty) Large

Don Large is a big man in every sense of the word. Even in later life he is still an impressive figure, and in his day he must have been awesome. Behind the large frame Don conceals a sharp, intelligent mind, which is quick to react, quick to understand, and quick to learn. He became a legend within both his parent regiment the Gloucester's and later the Special Air Service. Don joined the Gloucester's young and was posted to 'B' company. He travelled with his Regiment to Korea and saw action with them on the Imjim River. The Glouster's, then under battalion strength, were attacked by thousands of Chinese troops on the Injim River. The Glouster's mowed down wave after wave, but bravely the Chinese troops still kept advancing. Lofty can't remember how many of the enemy he must have killed and wounded that day, but it must have been in its hundreds. Eventually, despite a desperate and outstanding defence, the Regiment was overrun and Lofty, together with hundreds of other members of the Regiment, was taken prisoner.

Despite having two machine gun bullets in his shoulder and no medical assistance, he, along with the rest of the Regiment, was forced marched over 600 kms (400 miles) into captivity. Here Lofty remained with the rest of his friends and colleagues for over two years. It wasn't until the end of his captivity that one of the bullets was eventually removed from his shoulder by a Chinese surgeon. Although the surgeon was good, the conditions were basic, and the operation was conducted with only a local anaesthetic and light from several torches which were held over the wound by nurses while the surgeon operated. To add to the problems, while the operation was taking place, an allied air raid was going on outside. Despite probing around, the surgeon never discovered the second bullet. In the absence of an exit wound, as far as Lofty is aware, the bullet is still there to this day. During Lofty's captivity his parents were informed that he was missing in action presumed killed. It wasn't until months later and with the arrival of several letters from Lofty, that they finally realized that their son was still alive. The Ministry of Defence was less convinced however, and his parents had to persuade them that it was indeed Lofty's handwriting on the letters before they finally accepted that he wasn't dead and was in fact a prisoner of war. Internment was grim, and besides malnutrition the camps were rife with dysentery, bery bery, as well as a variety of other unwelcome and disabling diseases. When Lofty entered captivity he was a little over fifteen and a half stone, when he was finally repatriated he was a little under nine stone ten.

# Back from the brink

A shadow of the man he was when he had fought so gallantly on the banks of the Injim, and expecting to be retired from the army at any time, the military, in its wisdom, kept Lofty on (certainly one of their better decisions). After four years in hospital and recuperation, Lofty passed selection for the SAS in 1957. After training he was to see action in Malaya, Borneo, Oman and Aden as well as eventually becoming an instructor in no less than eight specialist subjects. As with the Glouster's, he quickly established a reputation as a tough, resourceful soldier. Lofty learned quickly and became a first class tracker indispensable on jungle patrols. He also became involved in some of the most famous SAS actions ever, including the celebrated Koemba Ambush. Lofty led a four-man patrol (including his great friend Peter Scholey) onto the Koemba River and destroyed a CT troop ship, causing hundreds of CTs to be pulled out of the jungle to protect their supply lines. It was a remarkable achievement.

Lofty finally retired in 1973 with the rank of WO2 after serving 16 years with the Regiment. Lofty came out of the army at a very difficult time. It was the era of the three-day-week, power cuts and redundancies. He decided to go into transport and began to drive HGV 1 articulated lorries all over the world, including taking aircraft parts from Jeddah to Muscat, where he often lost the road to sand storms and had to manoeuvre his way out of trouble miles from nowhere, all on his own. With work getting tighter and harder to find Lofty found security and bodyguard work with Lloyds. Lloyds had a lot of security jobs including high-profile work for Cartier's the jewellers, and wanted an SAS team for the job. They considered the French but they wanted to be armed and that was out of the question. The former SAS troopers were trained to do the work effectively without having to carry firearms and were the perfect solution. Lofty continued with the security work until he finally decided, due to family commitments, to settle down as a driving instructor in Hereford. He was a first class and popular instructor and many people now driving the streets of Hereford and the local area have Lofty to thank. As Lofty once mused he could have written another book on his experiences as a driving instructor as some of his pupils were a lot more dangerous than the CT.

Lofty finally decided to retire in 1995.

Since then Lofty has continued to be active, writing a book on his experiences (*Soldier Against The Odds: Infantry to SAS*) as well as appearing on several television programmes about his experiences. He has also become a first class bowls player. Lofty is still a formidable man and is still a great presence in any company. He has also lost none of his charm or humour but like with every other former special services man I have met, the air of menace at the back of his eyes is still present. Despite retiring, his mind is as sharp as ever and he remembers his military experiences as sharply now as he did the day they happened. A remarkable and charming man with a life that any military man would envy.

# Peter Scholey

Peter Scholey is without a doubt one of the Regiment's great characters. Unlike Lofty or John, Peter is not at all as one might imagine an SAS soldier to be. Its not that he wasn't a first class soldier or SAS trooper, he was. He also saw a great deal of action and performed some outstanding acts of bravery, commitment and sheer determination. There is no menace in Peter. Just a twinkle in his eye and a compelling smile on his face. He can spout more jokes than Les Dawson on a good day and will have you in hysterics for hours. Peter has a very quick and active mind and is considerate to a fault. A career soldier, Peter saw service with both the RA and the Parachute Regiment before being selected for the SAS in 1963. Peter served in Borneo, Aden, Oman and Cyprus. Borneo impressed Peter and he spent most days amazed at the diversity of life that he saw. On one occasion Peter came across a remote village inhabited by an isolated tribe. As he entered the village he saw what at first he took to be a native women feeding her child, when he looked harder however, he realized that the woman was actually breast feeding a monkey. She was in fact fattening the ape up for the slaughter and it was due to go into the pot that night. Peter was also involved in the Koemba Ambush together with his great friend Lofty Large. He remembers the action vividly. As a small flotilla of boats came around the bend their first decision was which of the boats to destroy. If they were to have any chance to escape the attack, then retreat was going to

have to be quick and decisive. After selecting their target and preparing to fire, they noticed a beautiful young women in a white dress standing at the head of the boat together with what appeared to be a very senior communist commander. None of them had the heart to kill her so they waited for the next boat to pass by and attacked that one, making their escape clean and quickly after the attack. Some 12 years later and after things had calmed down, Peter and Kevin Welsh – another member of the patrol – were invited out by an SAS group then based in Chelsea. There they were introduced to a man named Mordani, formerly an area commander and now an important figure in the Indonesian government. Mordani had been the senior officer they had seen on the boat next to the women in white they had seen all those years before. They never discovered who the woman was, but had their suspicions. Even Mordani had been impressed with the operation, and the raw courage of the SAS patrol. Most people who worked with Peter during his career make the same point, not only was he a first class comrade but he always saw the funny side of things and kept morale high on even the most daunting of patrols.

# Moving on

After serving over 20 years with the Regiment (two years with the territorial battalion), Peter eventually retired from the Regiment in 1986. Struggling for work and with only his army pension to support his family he knew something would have to be done and done quickly. As resourceful as ever he borrowed £50 from his wife and made his way, like a latter-day Dick Whittington, to London. There he called in on Eric Morley who was running the Miss World competition and asked to see him. Eric Morley was one of the most important people around at the time and people didn't just walk in off the street to see him, but Peter being Peter did and got an immediate interview. He explained his situation to Morley and asked if there was any security work going covering the Miss World competition. Peter didn't have to tell him he had formerly been with the SAS – the fact that he had been in the military and was from Hereford was enough: Eric Morley hired him at once. Peter's typical bravado had paid off yet again and he had managed to get himself a first class job. For the next five years, as well as Miss World, Peter worked on the Miss UK and Miss Wales competitions. He became firm friends with both Eric and Julia Morley, people he still speaks of with kindness and the deepest respect. Amongst some of the celebrities Peter guarded was Halle Berry who later went on to win an Oscar in the film *Monsters Ball*. Peter still retains several scrapbooks full of signed photographs and letters from the many girls he looked after, all of whom clearly held him in the greatest esteem.

While performing his bodyguard duties with the Miss World competition Peter had to find himself work between various competitions he was working on. As an instructor, Peter also found work with Team Dynamics working on search and rescue scenarios. He also taught survival courses while picking up bodyguard work where and whenever he could. After retiring, Peter doesn't let the grass grow under his feet and spends his days working for a variety of charities as well as giving talks and lecture about his experiences. He is not, surprisingly, one of the most popular people on the circuit, lending a wit and a charm to his talks that only Peter is capable of bringing to a lecture. Peter probably proves more than any other SAS soldier that I interviewed of the sheer diversity of the men that line the ranks of the Regiment. Not at all what you might expect, but every inch the soldier.

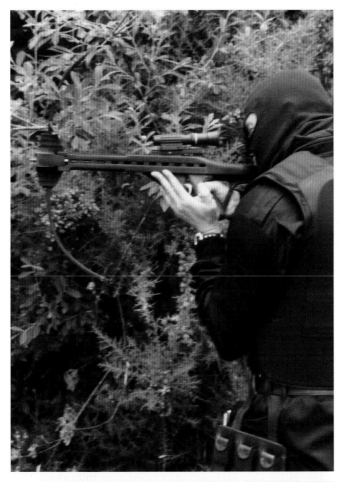

*Just a few retired members of the SAS go into manufacturing equipment for Special Forces. They have developed many interesting items from powered parachutes to this remarkable crossbow designed for use against terrorists.*

# Epilogue

In the play *Hassan*, written by modern British poet James Elroy Flecker, one of the characters, the Master of the Caravan, questions a group of travellers with the words:

'But who are ye in rags and rotten shoes,
You dirty-bearded, blocking up the way?'

The reply, given by The Pilgrims, is emblazoned on the SAS memorial at Hereford:

'We are the Pilgrims, master; we shall go
Always a little further; it may be
Beyond that last blue mountain barred with snow,
Across that angry or that glimmering sea...'

No matter what avenue an ex-SAS soldier takes or what attribute he exploits it is done so in the knowledge that he has survived life in the Regiment – for many do not. From time to time ex-SAS will meet another 'pilgrim' and for a brief moment over a pint, the light of their adventures is rekindled.

# Weapons of War

Members of the SAS are trained to be able to use as wide a variety of weapons as possible and they will source weapons from wherever they can if they need to. The weapons can come from all over the world and familiarity with them is essential.

## Colt M203

*Designed by the AAI Corporation and manufactured by Colt, the M203 was designed as a grenade launcher that could either be fitted underneath an M16 rifle, or used as a weapon on its own. It is a single shot, breech-loading weapon which works like a pump-action shotgun.*

## GPMG

*This classic general-purpose machine gun has been in service with the US Army since the 1960s, despite many problems. It was awkward to use with a permanently attached bipod and when the barrel had to be changed, asbestos gloves were needed! The Minimi has now replaced it.*

## MP5. Heckler & Koch

*The weapon of choice for many of the world's anti-terrorist units, including the SAS. It was the weapon used by the SAS during the Iranian Embassy siege. It's closed bolt mechanism makes it the most accurate sub-machine gun currently on the market. There are many variations of this gun, the most popular probably being the **MP5N** retractable stock version or the silenced **HKMP5SD3**.*

## SIG Sauer P226

*Developed by SIG in the 1980s. Costly but effective, it passed every required spec in the US joint services pistol trials. One of the best performers of the pistol world, it has now largely replaced the Browning High Power within the SAS.*

## Enfield SA80

*The current assault rifle in service with the British Army. Made by Enfield, it is of a 'bullpup' design. Short, accurate and well designed for urban combat it is also equipped with a 4x optical sight. However, it falls down on reliability, with magazines falling out unexpectedly as well as a number of other faults. For this reason the SAS tend not to use this weapon.*

### Accuracy International L96A1 PM 7.62 sniper's rifle
Calibre: 7.62mm x 51 NATO Match
Weight: 6.5kg with sight
Muzzle velocity: 850 metres per second
Magazine capacity: 10-round box

The current favoured sniper rival of the SAS. The PM is designed and manufactured by Accuracy International and has a reputation for great accuracy in any conditions, giving head shots at 300–600 metres. The rifle can be fitted with different sights, according to what is required. There are also various versions of the model, including one that can be used in Arctic conditions without freezing up. The PM is a bolt-action 7.62 rifle with a stainless steel barrel. The rifle is very comfortable to fire and the head need not be moved during bolt operation, allowing for continuous observation.

### AK-47 assault rifle
Calibre: 7.62mm x 39 Soviet
Weight: 4.3kg
Muzzle velocity: 710 metres per second
Magazine capacity: 30-round box

The Avtomat Kalashnikova was developed by the Soviets in the late 1940s and was designed for close range combat. Robust, easy to mend and reliable, with a fully automatic capacity, it became a popular weapon in the Warsaw pact countries. By 1959 it had been largely replaced by the AKM and later, the AK74. However, the AK47 has remained one of the most widely used weapons in the world and is often found in the hands of conscripts in Third World armies and guerrilla forces.

### Ammunition
In addition to the standard British Army 5.56mm and 7.62mm ammunition, the SAS also uses a variety of specialist ammunition, particularly in counter-terrorist and hostage rescue situations. In these scenarios the most important point is to neutralise any opposition quickly and efficiently, with the least risk to any hostages or other SAS members. In counter-terrorism strikes the SAS normally use 9mm calibre weapons, but normal 9mm bullets don't always stop when they hit a target; they will pass on through the body and may hit an innocent party.

To lessen this risk, a number of different rounds have been developed, which stop dead when they hit the body. There are two main types of rounds which have this property: accelerated energy transfer (AET) rounds, which flatten on hitting their mark, and frangible rounds which break up in the target's body.

AET rounds can be divided into three types. The 'equalloy' is a bullet made from an aluminium alloy, making it relatively light. The 'Geco' is a hollow bullet with a plastic core. On firing, the bullet and core separate. When it enters the target's body the hollow bullet then tumbles, causing massive tissue damage. The 'THV', a French bullet, has a concave front which also causes massive tissue damage on impact.

Frangible rounds include the British 'Spartan', which is made up of polymer mix and lead dust and breaks up on impact. A further development of the 'Spartan' is the 'Splat' where the lead dust is replaced by a non-lead metal. This has the same effect as the 'Spartan', but will also go through a certain amount of cover first, without breaking up until it reaches the target's body. A more deadly, although more costly, frangible round is the US Glaser Safety Slug. This is basically a plastic cap fitted to the front of a small shotgun cartridge. When it hits its target, the impact causes the shot to fly out of the cartridge causing death, mainly through shock. Because of the risk to hostages, should they be inadvertently hit, it is used with great caution.

As shotguns are also used by the SAS counter-terrorist team, various shotgun rounds are also employed, especially buck-shot, armour piercing and high explosive rounds. Hatton rounds are used to blow hinges and locks off doors.

### Arwen
The Arwen is a 37mm gas-, smoke-thrower and baton round propeller. It is basically an anti-riot weapon that has been adapted for hostage rescue. It has a five round rotating magazine, which is part of the weapon and works in a similar way to the cylinder on an old fashioned revolver. The baton round will cause immobilising damage up to 100 metres, although the accuracy is not all that good. The CS gas rounds vary, some are capable of penetration, though either light wooded doors and glass, before discharging.

### Heckler & Koch
Three former Mauser employees, who used their skills to develop a new type of sub-machine gun, founded Heckler & Koch in 1947. The company had its

first big break when, in 1959, the West German army adopted their G3 assault rifle. The MP5 was developed from the successful G3 rifle and shares many similar characteristics. Unlike most other sub-machine guns, the MP5 fires from a closed and locked bolt, using the same delayed blowback action as the G3. This makes the weapon expensive to produce, but the increased safety and accuracy compensate for this. Heckler & Koch now have factories worldwide.

### Heckler & Koch G3
Specification.
Calibre: 7.62mm
Length: 1,025mm
Weight: 4.40kg
Muzzle velocity: 790 metres per second
Magazine: 20-round box

The Gewehr 3 has its origins from a Mauser design which curiously found its way through Spain, Holland and eventually back to Germany where Heckler & Koch took on the task of perfecting the G3 into the weapon we know today. The weapon is robust and reliable which is why so many armies around the world have chosen it as the standard infantry weapon. The G3/SG1 comes with a telescopic sight and bipod and has an adjustable hair-trigger which the SAS use for the snipers on the anti-terrorist team.

### Heckler & Koch MP5
Calibre: 9mm x 19 Parabellum
Weight: 2.55kg
Muzzle velocity: 400 metres per second
Magazine: 15- or 30-round box.
(See page 209).

### Heckler & Koch PSG1 sniper rifle
Calibre: 7.62mm x 51 NATO (.308 Winchester match)
Weight: 9 kg with sight
Muzzle velocity: 820 metres per second
Magazine capacity: 5- or 20-round box

Heckler & Koch produce a range of sniper rifles, all adapted from the basic G3 model. The type considered the most accurate is the semi-automatic Prazisionsschutzengewehr 1 (or PSG1). This weapon has silenced working parts, a heavy barrel, adjustable butt and trigger and a x6 zoom telescopic sight. It is in use with German Special Forces and police, as well as other police forces worldwide.

### Ingram Model 10
Calibre: .45 ACP or 9mm x 19 Parabellum
Weight: 2.84kg
Muzzle velocity: 280 metres per second
Magazine capacity: 16- or 32-round box

Also known as the MAC 10 after the original promoter of the weapon, Military Armaments Corporation, this model was designed by Gordon B. Ingram in the US. The weapon has a high rate of fire, which can compromise its control and accuracy. This problem was improved by adding a suppresser that is covered in heat resistant material, allowing it to be used as a fore-grip, enabling greater control over the weapon. The SAS trialed the Ingram in Northern Ireland during the early 1970s where it met with some approval. Unfortunately, the Heckler & Koch MP5 appeared on the scene and completely eclipsed the Ingram. Since its fall from military favour the weapon has become a firm favourite with the drugs cartel.

### LAW 80 light anti-tank weapon
Launcher length: 1,500mm when ready to fire.
Weight: 10kg
Warhead diameter: 94mm
Warhead type: HEAT.
Effective Range: 20–500 metres.

A British derivative of the American 66mm, this disposable, one-shot weapon is capable of destroying most targets. It is only one metre long (collapsed), and its light weight means that it is able to be carried in addition to a soldier's kit and personal weapon. It is reliable and easy to use, requiring little preparation. It contains a spotting rifle which fires tracer rounds to enable aim correction before the main round is released.

### LAW rocket 66mm
Specification.
Warhead Calibre: 66 mm
Weight: 3.45kg
Length: 980mm
Range: 220 metres
Velocity: 200 metres per second

The 66mm LAW rocket is capable of penetrating 275 mm armour and is extremely effective, as was demonstrated in the Falklands War. Although designed for tanks, the SAS have used it successfully against caves, bunkers, and other enemy fortified targets. In an unconventional method, the SAS used batches of the 66mm rocket to protect the outer limits of the Diana defences during the

Oman War. The firing mechanism of the rockets was interrupted so they could be triggered electrically from a distance.

Like all such rockets, there is a back-blast danger area, which must be clear of friendly troops, equipment or close solid obstacles. Once fired, the launcher tube may be discarded, although it is common, time permitting, to destroy the tube.

### M203 40mm grenade launcher
Calibre: 40mm
Weight: 1.63kg
Muzzle velocity: 75 metres per second
Magazine capacity: belt-fed
(See page 208).

### M60 general purpose machine gun
Calibre: 7.62mm x 51 NATO
Weight: 11.1kg, 17.9kg with tripod
Muzzle velocity: 853 metres per second
Magazine capacity: belt-fed

### M79 grenade launcher
Calibre: 40mm
Weight: 2.95kg
Muzzle velocity: 76 metres per second
Range: 350 metres
Also called the 'bloop gun' due to the sound it make when fired, this predecessor of the M203 grenade launcher saw extensive service with US forces in Vietnam. Although it has a high trajectory, it can be very accurate in the right hands. It is now in use mainly in Korea and several Asian and South American countries. It was a weapon widely used by the SAS during the Oman War and remained in service until the M16 arrived with the 203 attached.

### Mark 19 40mm automatic grenade launcher
Calibre: 40mm
Weight: 34kg
Muzzle velocity: 240 metres per second
Range: 1,600 metres
This grenade launcher is belt fed, leading to it actually being designated as a machine gun. The later models have overcome the earlier problems with reliability and now provide a real source of heavy firepower at a low cost. The rounds are effective against personnel or light

armour and are unusual in that each link stays with the cartridge and is ejected with it. Its versatility means that it can also be used mounted on vehicles and used with day, night and laser sights. The SAS used this weapon during their missions in the Gulf War.

### Milan Wire guided anti-armour missile
Launcher length: 900mm
Launcher weight: 27.7kg
Missile length: 796mm
Missile weight: 2.98kg
Warheat: HEAT.
Range: 2,000 metres.
The Milan has been in service with the British Army since the mid 1970's. Built by Euromissile, a Franco-German consortium, it is one of the world's leading anti-tank weapons. Milan is simple to fire and has a very high accuracy rate, both by day and night. It can be fired by a two-man infantry team or attached to a vehicle. During the Gulf War the SAS used the Milan mounted on a roll bar attached to one of the open topped Land Rover 110's. When fired, a small charge forces the missile from the launcher before the main rocket motor kicks in. The missile is kept on target by using the optical sight which guides the missile to its target by sending commands and corrections down the command wire. By night the Milan relies on the powerful MIRA night sight which clamps to the top of the weapon.

### Minimi
Calibre: 5.56mm x 45 NATO
Weight: 6.85kg
Muzzle velocity: 965 metres per second
Effective range: 600 metres
Magazine capacity: disintegrating link belt, 200-round belt or 30-round M16 type box
Made by Fabrique National of Belgium, this gas operated weapon has been chosen as the squad support weapon for the US Forces. With its greater firepower and range capabilities it has proved itself to be the natural partner to the M16. The SAS have also adopted the Minimi, and it proved its worth during the Gulf War in many contact situations, allowing those in the ill-fated patrol 'Bravo Two Zero' to escape.

## Mortar L16 81mm

Calibre: 81mm
Barrel Length: 1,280mm
Weight: 36.6kg
Weight of bomb: 4.2kg
Types of bomb: high explosive, illuminating, smoke, practice and guided anti-armour
Maximum Range: 5,650 metres

The standard infantry mortar of the British Army. Sturdy and portable, with a good rate of sustained fire, the 81mm performed well in the Oman War, providing fire support when the BATT became short of artillery. Most SAS outposts would have a mortar as their main support weapon, which they would also use on some of the larger patrols. Their favourite trick – one not recommended by the army – was to pour a pint of petrol down the barrel to increase the range. This somewhat unorthodox method of firing the mortar achieved the desired results, but also proved expensive as it destroyed the mortar baseplate.

## PPSh-41

Calibre: 7.62mm x 25
Weight: 3.64kg
Muzzle velocity: 488 metres per second
Magazine capacity: 35-round box or 71-round drum

A Russian designed sub-machine gun which was extremely popular in the Second World War due to its durability, accuracy and light recoil. Thereafter, China took up the design and the PPSh-41 became its main weapon in the Korean War. Although it was slowly phased out in the Warsaw Pact countries, some models are still in use by some rebel groups in Africa.

## RPG-7

Warhead diameter: 85mm
Launcher Length: 950mm
Weight: 8.6kg
Velocity: 300 metres per second
Effective range: 300 metres

The Reaktivniy Protivotankoviy Granatomet-7 is a rocket propelled grenade launcher that has become one of the most popular and widely used anti-armour weapons in the world. In use with former Soviet and Warsaw pact armies, it is also in wide distribution with many third world armies and in many of the world's hot spots.

It was introduced into service in 1962 with Soviet forces and saw action with the Egyptians in 1967 during fighting in Sinai. North Vietnamese forces used it during the street fighting in Hue in the Tet Offensive of 1968. Both sides in the Iran-Iraq and Afghan wars used RPG-7s. The RPG 7 has also proved a favourite of terrorist groups. In September 1981 German terrorists from the Red Army Faction fired an RPG at the armoured staff car which was carrying General Kroesen, Commander of US Forces in Germany. The SAS encountered the RPG-7 in the Oman War when it was widely used against them by the 'Adoo.' An Iraqi RPG killed one of the few British casualties in the Gulf War in 1991. Today the RPG 7 is being replaced by the RPG 16.

## SA80 assault rifle

Calibre: 5.56 mm x 45 NATO
Weight: 3.8kg
Muzzle velocity: 940 metres per second
Magazine capacity: 30-round box
(See page 209).

## SIG Sauer P226

Calibre: 9mm x 19 Parabellum
Weight: 750g
Muzzle velocity: 350 metres per second
Magazine capacity: 15- or 20-round box
(See page 209).

## Vickers K

Calibre: .303
Weight: 9.5 kg
Length: 1 metre
Velocity: 745 metres per second
Range: 1,800 metres

Discovered in an aircraft hanger by David Stirling and apparently unused by the RAF, the SAS married the Vickers K to the new American jeeps thus producing a formidable mobile fighting machine. The weapon was originally designed for aircraft and would fire a mixture of ball, tracer and armour piercing ammunition. They proved their worth during the great jeep raid made by the SAS in July 1942.

# Chronology

It is sometimes difficult to follow the various units which make up the Special Air Service family, especially during World War Two, where units were constantly being re-designated. The following chronology should help readers understand the basic historical order of events which have governed SAS history.

## The Special Air Service Family

**1941** The Special Boat Section carried out its first raid on the night of June 22; prior to this it had been known as Floboat Section.

**1941** Lieutenant-Colonel David Stirling was given permission in July to raise the SAS from members of 'L' Detachment. The SAS was stated to be a Brigade; however, there was at that time no SAS Brigade: it was a ruse to deceive the Germans.

**1941** On the night of November 16-17 the SAS carried out their first raid, which was not successful.

**1943** In January David Stirling, founder of the Regiment, was taken prisoner and sent to Colditz Castle in Germany. Lieutenant-Colonel R.B. 'Paddy' Mayne took over command, by which time the SAS had developed considerable water-borne raiding skills, and at the conclusion of the African campaign 1 SAS was renamed SRS (Special Raiding Squadron). The Special Boat Section became the SBS (Special Boat Service) and was under the command of Lieutenant-Colonel the Earl Jellicoe. While the SBS operated in the Aegean and Adriatic, the SRS carried out commando-style raids in Sicily and Italy.

**1943** 2nd SAS regiment was created by the founder's brother, Lieutenant-Colonel W.S. Stirling.

**1944** By January the SRS units, less SBS, were re-formed into the SAS Brigade, under the command of Brigadier R.W. McLeod. It comprised:

**1** SAS (Lt. Col. R.B. Mayne), the former SAS and SRS.
**2** SAS (Lt. Col. B.M.F. Franks)
**3** SAS (French) Lt. Col. J. Conan.
**4** SAS (French) Lt. Col. P. Bourgoin.
**5** SAS (Belgian) Lt. Col. E. Blondeel.
**F** Squadron from Phantom (GHQ Reconnaissance Regiment)

**1945** Following the end of hostilities in Europe, in July 1 and 2 SAS (British) were disbanded, with 3 and 4 SAS (French) going to the French Army; likewise 5 SAS went to the Belgian Army.

**1945** The SAS Regimental Association was formed in November.

**1947** 21 SAS (Artists') (TA) formed under command of Lieutenant-Colonel B.M.F. Franks.

**1950** 2 SBS was formed from a detachment of the Amphibious School attached to the Royal Navy Rhine Squadron in West Germany.

**1950** Malayan Scouts formed under the command of Lieutenant-Colonel J.M. Calvert. Joined by volunteers from 21 SAS (Artists') (TA).

**1951** In March the Southern Rhodesia Far East Volunteer Unit was raised for service in Malaya. The unit was designated C (Rhodesia) Squadron Malayan Scouts (SAS). A and B Squadrons were already in existence, A Squadron having been formed from volunteers from units in Malaya and B Squadron from volunteers from 21st SAS Regiment (Artists') (TA). 264 (SAS) Signals Squadron's origins also date back to 1951 when as a signals troop it was attached to the Malayan Scouts (SAS).

**1952** The Malayan Scouts were officially re-designated 22nd SAS Regiment (22 SAS).

**1952** C Squadron (Rhodesia) returned to Rhodesia where it was disbanded shortly afterwards.

**1957** NZSAS Squadron returned to New Zealand and was disbanded.

**1957** The Australian SAS unit formed.

**1958** The SAS are sent to Oman where they assault Jebel Akhdar.

**1959** SAS leaves Malaya. Settled temporarily in Malvern but then transferred to permanent camp at Hereford (1960).

**1959** The New Zealand Squadron was reformed. In May 1962, a detachment was deployed to Thailand where its two troops assisted US Army Special Forces. In 1963 the Squadron was re-designated 1st Ranger Squadron New Zealand SAS.

**1959** 23 SAS (TA) formed in London, but later transferred to Birmingham.

**1962** A small team from Rhodesia was sent to train with the SAS, enabling its members to restart the Rhodesian SAS.

**1962** Regimental Headquarters transferred from Duke's Road, Euston, London, to Centre Block, Duke of York's Headquarters, Chelsea, London SW3.

**1963** 22 SAS were committed to Borneo.

**1964** The Australian Special Air Service Regiment (SASR) was formed on September 4.

**1964** The Regiment had a permanent squadron operating in Aden.

**1966** In July of that year 264 (SAS) Signals Squadron was formed as a fully independent unit co-located with 22 SAS in Hereford.

**1966** In June an Australian SAS squadron (SASR) was deployed to South Vietnam.

**1967** The SAS withdraw from Aden.

**1968** In December a detachment, designated 4 Troop, of 1st Ranger Squadron NZSAS was deployed to South Vietnam on attachment to the Australian SAS squadron based at Nui Dat in Phuoc Tuy Province.

**1969** SAS troops are committed to Northern Ireland, albeit in a small way: by 1971 a whole squadron was operating throughout the Province.

**1970** The Oman War begins with two squadrons leading the main assault on to the Jebel Massif.

**1971** In February the New Zealand SAS was withdrawn from Vietnam. Subsequently, the 1st Ranger Squadron NZSAS was re-designated the 1st NZ SAS Group.

**1971** The Australian SASR withdraw from Vietnam.

**1974** The SAS anti-terrorist team was raised in Hereford to counter the growing international terrorist threat.

**1977** Two SAS anti-terrorist team members assist the Germans with a hijacked aircraft.

**1978** 1 Special Air Service Regiment (Rhodesia) officially renamed.

**1980** 1 Special Air Service Regiment (Rhodesia) is disbanded; many members went on to join the South African Defence Force (SADF).

**1980** The SAS are called in to deal with the Iranian Embassy siege.

**1982** Two or more SAS squadrons are sent to the war in the Falklands, which cost the Regiment 21 men.

**1989** As part of a joint Anglo-American effort to defeat the drugs barons, a squadron of SAS is sent to train the Colombians in anti-terrorist tactics.

**1991** Three SAS squadrons are sent to fight in the Gulf War, where they operated for the full duration of the war deep inside Iraq.

**1994** SAS soldiers are sent to Bosnia. The Regiment prepares to move to its new base in Credenhill, Hereford.

**2000** Assisted by 1st Battalion Parachute Regiment, an SAS team rescues members of the Royal Irish Regiment being held captive by the West Side Boys militia in Sierra Leone.

**2001** In September, the Regiment commits three full squadrons to the war in Afghanistan.

**2003** The SAS fight side by side with America's Delta Force during Operation Iraqi Freedom.

# Roll Call 22 SAS

## Malaya

| | |
|---|---|
| Tpr T. A. Brown | 1950 |
| Pte G. A. Fisher | 1950 |
| Tpr F. G. Boylan | 1951 |
| Sgt O. H. Ernst, Rhodesian SAS | 1951 |
| Cpl J. B. Davies, Rhodesian SAS | 1951 |
| WO2 W. F. Garrett | 1951 |
| Tpr J. A. O'Leary | 1951 |
| Tpr A. Fergus | 1952 |
| Cpl V. E. Visague, Rhodesian SAS | 1952 |
| Cpl K. Bancroft | 1953 |
| Major E. C. R. Barker, B. E. M. | 1953 |
| Lt P. B. S. Cartwright | 1953 |
| 2/Lt F. M. Donnelly-Wood | 1953 |
| Tpr E. Duckworth | 1953 |
| Cpl P. G. R. Eakin | 1953 |
| Lt J. C. Fotheringhan | 1953 |
| Tpr J. A. S. Morgan | 1953 |
| Lt (QM) F. S. Tulk | 1953 |
| Tpr B. Watson | 1953 |
| Tpr F. W. Wilkins | 1953 |
| L Cpl C. W. Bond | 1954 |
| Lt G. J. Goulding | 1954 |
| Tpr A. W. Howell | 1954 |
| Tpr B. Powell | 1954 |
| Tpr W. R. J. Marselle | 1956 |
| Tpr A. R. Thomas, New Zealand SAS | 1956 |
| Cpl A. G. Buchanan, New Zealand SAS | 1957 |
| Lt A. G. H. Dean | 1957 |
| Tpr R. Hindmarsh | 1968 |

## Oman (Jebel Akhdar)

| | |
|---|---|
| Cpl D. Swindells, M.M. | 1958 |
| Tpr A. G. Bembridge | 1959 |
| Tpr W. Carter | 1959 |

## Malaysia

| | |
|---|---|
| Tpr. N.P. Ollis | 1967 |

## West Malaysia

| | |
|---|---|
| L Cpl R. Greenwood | 1969 |

## Borneo

| | |
|---|---|
| Cpl M. P. Murphy | 1963 |
| Maj R. H. D. Norman, BE, MC | 1963 |
| Maj H. A. I. Thompson, MC | 1963 |
| Sgt B. Bexton | 1964 |
| Tpr A. Condon | 1964 |
| Pte G. H. Hartley | 1964 |
| Tpr W. E. White | 1964 |

## South Arabia

| | |
|---|---|
| Capt R. C. Edwards | 1964 |
| Tpr J. N. Warburton | 1964 |
| Tpr J. Hollingsworth | 1966 |
| Tpr M. R. Lambert | 1966 |
| L Cpl A. G. Brown | 1967 |
| Tpr G. F. F Iles | 1967 |

## Ethiopia

| | |
|---|---|
| Cpl I. A. Macleod | 1968 |

## Oman (Musandam)

| | |
|---|---|
| L Cpl P. Reddy | 1970 |

## Oman (Dhofar)

| | |
|---|---|
| Capt I. E. Jones | 1971 |
| Tpr C. Loid | 1971 |
| Sgt J. S. M. Moores | 1971 |
| Cpl T. Labalaba, B. E. M. | 1972 |
| Tpr M. J. Martin | 1972 |
| L Cpl D. R. Ramsden | 1972 |
| Tpr T. P. A. Tobin | 1972 |
| Capt S. Garthwaite | 1974 |
| L Cpl A. Kent | 1974 |
| Sgt A. E. Gallagher | 1975 |
| Tpr C. Hennessy | 1975 |
| L Cpl K. Small | 1975 |

## Brunei

| | |
|---|---|
| Sgt E. Pickard | 1973 |

## France

| | |
|---|---|
| Maj R. M. Pirie | 1972 |
| Cpl F. M. Benson | 1978 |
| Sgt S. H. Johnson | 1978 |

## Northern Ireland

| | |
|---|---|
| S-Sgt D. J. Naden | 1978 |
| Capt H. R. Westmacott | 1980 |

## UK

| | |
|---|---|
| Cpl K. Norry | 1962 |
| Tpr J. Hooker | 1965 |
| Tpr P. C. O'Toole | 1965 |
| Cpl R. Richardson | 1965 |
| L Cpl J. R. Anderson | 1967 |
| Cpl R. N. Adie | 1968 |
| L Cpl A. C. Lonney | 1968 |
| Tpr C. P. Martin | 1968 |
| WO1 E. T. Nugent | 1968 |
| WO2 J. E. Daubney | 1974 |
| Maj M. J. A. Kealy, DSO | 1979 |

## South Atlantic

| | |
|---|---|
| Tpr R. Armstrong | 1982 |
| Sgt J. L. Arthy | 1982 |
| S-SM M. Atkinson | 1982 |
| Cpl W. J. Begley | 1982 |
| Cpl P. Bunker | 1982 |
| Cpl R. Burns | 1982 |
| Sgt P. P. Currass, QGM | 1982 |
| Sgt S. A. I. Davidson | 1982 |
| WO2 L. Gallagher, BEM | 1982 |
| Capt G. J. Hamilton | 1982 |
| Flt Lt G. Hawkins, RAF | 1982 |
| Sgt W. J. Hughes | 1982 |
| Sgt P. Jones | 1982 |
| L Cpl P. Lightfoot | 1982 |
| Cpl D. McCormack | 1982 |
| Cpl M. McHugh | 1982 |
| Cpl J.Newton | 1982 |

| | |
|---|---|
| S-Sgt P. O'Connor | 1982 |
| Cpl S. Sykes | 1982 |
| Cpl E. T. Walpole | 1982 |

## Northern Ireland

| | |
|---|---|
| Cpl T. Palmer, MM | 1983 |
| L Cpl A. Slater, MM | 1984 |

## Belize

| | |
|---|---|
| L Sgt L. Cobb | 1983 |

## Nepal (Mt Everest)

| | |
|---|---|
| Cpl A. Swierzy | 1984 |

## UK

| | |
|---|---|
| Sgt R. Abbots | 1985 |
| Sgt A. Baxter | 1985 |
| S-Sgt J. Drummond | 1986 |
| Tpr G. Worrall | 1990 |

## France (Mt Blanc)

| | |
|---|---|
| Tpr R. P. Arnott | 1986 |
| Tpr S. J. Windon | 1986 |

## Botswana

| | |
|---|---|
| S-Sgt K. J. Farragher | 1986 |

## Far East

| | |
|---|---|
| Cpl P. Hill | 1988 |

## Iraq

| | |
|---|---|
| Tpr R. Consiglio, MM | 1991 |
| Tpr D. Denbury, MM | 1991 |
| Tpr S. Lane, MM | 1991 |
| Sgt V. Phillips | 1991 |

## Bosnia

| | |
|---|---|
| Cpl F. M. Rennie | 1994 |

## Sierra Leone

| | |
|---|---|
| LCpl B. Tinnion | 2000 |

## Kenya

| | |
|---|---|
| S-Sgt M. Halls | 2000 |
| Tpr A. M. Powell | 2000 |

## UK

| | |
|---|---|
| Sgt A. Pugsley | 2002 |

## Oman

| | |
|---|---|
| Tpr K. Butterton | 2002 |
| Tpr L. Tandy | 2002 |

# Index

All page references in *italics*
refer to pictures

21 Squadron 80, 146
22 Squadron 11, 12, 14, 37, 46, 84, 147, *159*
264 Squadron 11

## A

A Squadron 11, 37, 41–6, 126, 148,
    161, 184
Accuracy International L69A1 PM 7.62
    sniper's rifle 210
Acuna, Carlo Giusti 51
Aden 116, 117, 123, 136–41, *139*
Adoo *see* People's Front for the
    Liberation of the Occupied Arabian
    Gulf
Aegean Sea 173
Afghanistan 26–33, 80
African National Congress 16
Afrika Korps 163
Agedabia 166–7
Ageila 172
Ailey, David 123
AK-47 assault rifle 210
Akache, Zohair 117, *118*
al-Badr, Mohammed 123
Al Jouf 40
al-Qaeda 22, 25, 27, 28, 29, 32
al-Tikriti, Watban Ibrahim Hasan 29
Alba 176
Ali, Ghalib bin 157
Ali, Nadir 25
Alison, J. 144
Alpha Three Zero 38–41
Andrade, Fernando 48
Anne, Princess 141
Anti-Terrorist Team 17
Antrim, HMS 69, 70
Aoki, Morihisa 48
Aquabat al Dhafar *159*
Arabistan 56, 58

Armagh 53, 78, 111
Arthurs, Declan 79
Arwen 210
Asad, Saeed 25
Ascension Island 75
Auchinleck, General Sir Claude 164, 165
Australian Special Air Service Regiment
    127
Azahari, Sheikh 125
Azzam, Abdullah 22

## B

B Squadron 11, 37, 77, 98, 146, 148, 152
Baader, Andreas 119
Baader-Meinhof 112, 119
Baghdad 28
Bagnold, Major Ralph 166
Bahrain 112
Bakau 64, 66
Baker, Corporal Paddy 137
Bani Shihoo 87
Banja Luka 51
Banjul 63, 64, 65, 66
Barker, Sergeant 'Geordie' 194–6
Barkworth, Major Eric 191
Bateman, Lieutenant 184
Baxter, Andy *75*, 76
Belfast 55, 110
Belize 106–8, *106, 107*
Bell, Corporal 105, 106
Bergé, Commandant 167, 168
Berka 167–8
Berry, Sir Anthony 77
Bessbrook Barracks *109*
Billière, Lieutenant-General Sir Peter
    de la 37, 38, 75, 84, 130, 152, 156, 161,
    201
Bimrose, Captain Charles 187–8
Bin Laden, Osama 22, 25
Bishop, Private Thomas 173
Black September 16
Blaxland, Gregory 152

Bogota 36
Bojang, Usman 64, 66
Bolden, Corporal 190
Bonnington, Lieutenant 166
Borneo 123–36, *124, 153*
Bosnia 47–8, 51
Bradbury Lines 15, 62, 112, 121
Bravo Two Zero 38
Brecon Beacons 13, 14, 88
Briggs, Lieutenant General Sir Harold
    146
Brighton Bomb 76–7
Brilliant, HMS 70
Briquemont, General 47
British Army Training Team (BATT) *90*,
    98, 99
British Empire Medal 114
Brize Norton 62, 85, 106
British Airways 37
Broadsword, HMS 71
Brooke, Colonel Oliver 150
Brown Mountain 71
Brown, Trooper 128–30
Browning .5 heavy machine-gun 38
Browning hi-power pistol 17, 81
Brunei 125
Buck, Captain Herbert 167
Bucket Force 187–8
Bullig, David 66, 115
Bury, Lieutenant Bob 174, 175

## C

C Squadron 12, 146, 148, 152, 184
Callaghan, James 108, 112
Calvert, Brigadier Mike 81, 146, 147, 150,
    188, 191
Camp One 16, 56
Canepo, Joseph 81
Castleford 111
Castro, Fidel 50
Central Intelligence Agency (CIA) 28, 29
Challen, Sergeant 'Tanky' 177

Chapman, Freddie Spencer 144
Charles, Prince 15, *62*, 141
Chigley, Corporal 123
Chile 75
Chin Peng 144
Christian, Ian 144
Clandestine Communist Organisation
    (CCO) 125, 131, 133
Cleary, Peter 108
Cobra Committee 60
Colditz Castle *171*
Cole, Barbara 12
Colt M203 208
Columbia 35–6
Communist Terrorists (CT) 144, 145, 146,
    148, 150, 151, 152–4
Connell, Brian 157
Cooper, Johnny 123, 147, 152–3, 157, 161,
    182, 190
Counter-Revolutionary Warfare
    (CRW) 141
Coventry, Major Dudley 152
Cramer, Chris 59, 60
Crater 139, 140–1
Creasey, Major General
Credenhill 11, 17, 21
Crete 168–9
Crisp, Lieutenant 184
Crooke, Major Ian 62, 63, 65, 66, 67–8,
    198
Cross-Border Scouts 126

**D**

D-Day 181, 182
D Squadron 37, 69, 71–2, 74, 126, 130, 131,
    133, 148, 152, 156, 158, 159, 161
*Daily Telegraph* 29
Dakar 65
Darrell, Sergeant Porter 174
'Dave' 25–26
Davies, Barry 8, 84–5, 102, 112, 114, 201
Deane-Drummond, Lieutenant-Colonel

    Anthony 155–6, 161
Defa 103, 104, 105
Defence Systems Ltd 198
Delius, Captain Charles 105, 106
Delta Force 25, 38
Delves, Cedric 71
Denton Bridge 66
Diana, Princess 15, *62*
Dickens, Peter 201
Dorman, Sergeant 123
Drljaca, Simo 51
Dubai 112, 113, 115
Dudgeon, Captain 176

**E**

Earls Court 56
Edwards, Captain Robin 136, 137
Edwards, Major John 126
El Alamein 170–1
*Elite, The* (Cole) 12
Endurance, HMS 70
'Endurance March' *13*, 14
Enfield SA80 209
Enniskilllen 79
Ensslin, Gudrun 119
Equipment
    Huey helicopter *91*
    Type 110 Land Rovers ('Pink
        Panthers') 27, 28, 38, 41, 122–3
    Rigid Raider 22–3, 74
    Unimog 39
    Willys Jeep 166, *167*
Everest, Mount 75–6

**F**

Fajura 66
Falklands War 18–19, 68–75
    Chile 75
    invasion 68–9
    observations 69

    Pebble Island 71–3
    Port Stanley 74
    South Georgia 69, 70–1
    surrender 75
    Wireless Ridge 74
Farafenni 66
Farran, Major Roy 178, 179
Farrell, Maraid *53*, 80, 81
Federation of South Arabia 123
Felon, Peter 66
Fenwick, Major Ian 184
Fermanagh 77
Fijians 122
Finn, Corporal 156
Firqat A'asifat 91
Firqat Kalid bin Walid 88, 89, 92, 94
Fleming, Lance-Corporal Tony 105, 106
Fort Brooke 152
Fortuna Glacier 69, *70*
Franks, Lieutenant-Colonel Brian 179,
    186–7
Fraser, Major Bill 167, 182, 189
FRELIMO 12
Front for the Liberation of Occupied
    South Yemen 123
Fujimori, Alberto 49, 50

**G**

G Squadron 11, 19, 55, 69, 73, 74, 98, 100,
    102, 127, 138, 141
Galic, General Stanislav 51
Gallagher, 'Lofty' 71
Gambia 62–8
Gaz 69 *39*, 40, *41*
Geary, Sergeant 'Tanky' 174–5
Geraghty, Tony 201
Ghotzbadeh, Sadegh 58
Ghurkas *130*, 133
Gibraltar 80–1
Glamorgan, HMS 71, 72
Gorazde 48
Gormley, Michael 79

Gowrie, Lord 77
GPMG 208
Grand Hotel (Brighton) 76–7
Greaves, Corporal Sidney 173
Greece 187–8
Grenada 37
Grenadier Guards 55
Greville-Bell, Major Anthony 146
Grey, Dusty 56
Grytviken 70
GSG9 113, 114, 115, 118–9
Guards Independent Parachute
    Company 126–7, 141
Guatemala 106–8
Guinea-Bissau 68
Gulf War (1991) 14
    A Squadron 41–6
    Alpha Three Zero 38–41
    Bravo Two Zero 38
    commendation for SAS 46–7
    human shields 38
    invasion of Kuwait 36
    Scud missiles 38, 46
    United Nations task force 36–7
Gumla 87
Gummer, John Selwyn 77
Guscott, Sergeant 190
Guzman, Abimael 49

## H

Hamilton, Captain John 69, 72, 73–4
Hamood, Sheikh Baraik Bin 84
Harding, General Sir John 146
Harris, Sim 59, 203
Harrison, Captain Derrick 186
Head, Major L.G.S. 127
'Hearts and Minds' policy 125
Heckler and Koch G3 211
Heckler and Koch MP5 sub-machine
    gun 65, 209
Heckler and Koch PSG1 sniper rifle 211
Hermes, HMS 71, 72, 73
Hibbert, Captain Grant 178
Hill, Lietenant Michael Sinclair 147
Himyar, Suleiman bin 157
Hogg, Trooper 128–30
Hoi, Ah 155–6
Holmes, Captain 113
Hopkinson, Major-General Gerald 180
HQ Squadron 11
Huey helicopter 91
Hughes, Antony 79

Hughes, Lance Corporal J. 150
Hussein, Saddam 29, 38
Hussein, Uday 29

## I

Ibri 160
Illman, John 49
Indonesia 123, 125, 126–7, 131, 136
Ingram Model 10 211
International Criminal Tribunal for the
    Former Yugoslavia 51
Intrepid, HMS 73
Iranian Battle Group 103
Iranian Embassy Siege 13, 56–62, 57, 58,
    59, 61, 65, 203–4
Iraq
    Gulf War (1991) 14, 36–47
    invasion (2003) 33
Irish Republican Army (IRA) 53, 54, 55,
    76–9, 80–1, 83, 108–12
Israel 46
Italy 175–80

## J

Jawara, Sir Dawda Kairaba 62, 64, 65, 66
Jeapes, Colonel Tony 161, 201
Jebel Akhdar 157–61
Jebel Ali 98
Jebel Aram 88, 95
Jebel Dhofar 88, 90–1, 95
Jett, Dennis 48
Joseph, Sir Keith 77
Jumla 85

## K

Kalimantan 125, 126
Kallay, Foday 22
Kandahar 27
KAS Enterprises 198
Kayan, Anak 155
Kealy, Captain 98, 99, 100, 101, 102
Kedah 151
Kelabit 153
Kelly, Patrick 79
Khomeini, Ayatollah 56
Khormaksar Airport 116
Khuzestan 56, 58
'Killing House' 15, 56

Kinnevane, Corporal 185
Kota Bahru 154
Kovacevic, Milan 51
Kunduz 25
Kuwait 36, 37, 115

## L

Labalaba, Trooper 98, 99, 100, 122
Lamonby, Lieutenant Kenneth 173
Lane, Corporal 'Bronco' 75, 201–3
Lapraik, Major Ian 173
Large, Don 204–6
Lassen, Major Anders 173, 174
LAW 80 light anti-tank weapon 211
LAW rocket 66mm 211–12
Laycock, Brigadier Robert 164
Layforce 164
Lea, Lieutenant-Colonel George 152, 154
Lebanon 81
Lee, Clive 65, 66
Lees, Major Michael 190
Leith 69, 71
Letts, Captain Robin 128–30
Lewes, Lieutenant 'Jock' 165, 166
Lexham Gardens 56
Libya 64, 81
Life Guards 157
Lilley, Corporal 168
Lillicoe, Sergeant Geordie 133–6
Lima Embassy Siege 48–51
Lock, Trevor 56
Logan, Jock 97, 140
Long Jawi 126
Long Range Desert Group (LRDG) 166,
    168
Loughall 77–9, 78
Lufthansa Hijack 112–19
Lynagh, Jim 79

## M

M Squadron SBS 18
McAleese, Peter 199–201, 203–4
MacBride, Tony 77
McCann, Daniel 53, 80, 81
McDonald, Lieutenant 169
McGillivray, Captain Malcolm 131–3
McGonigal, Eoin 166
McIntosh, Lieutenant-Colonel 181
McKenna, Sean 108
McLean, Brigadier Fitzroy 155

McLean, Trooper Tom 141
McLeod, Rod 146
McNabb, Andy 201
Maktab al-Khidamet 22
Malaya 12, 81, 123, 144–57
    Operation Hive 150–1
    Operation Termite 151–2
Malayan Scouts 81, 146, 147
Massoud, Ahman Shah 80
Mayne, 'Paddy' 164, 166, 167, 168, 169, 173
Mazar-i-Sharif 25
Menendez, Major General Mario 75
Mercenaries 199–201
Merebrook Camp 121
MI5 111
Milan anti-tank missiles 39, 212
Military Cross 42, 55, 74, 130, 161
Min Yuen 144
Minimi 27, 212
Mirbat 94, 97–104, *100, 101*
Mitchell, Lieuteant-Colonel 141
Mobility Troop 45, 138
Mogadishu 56, 66, 114, 117–19
Montesinos, Ivan Vladimiro 50
Morley, Eric 206–7
Moro, Aldo 195
Morrison, Major Alistair 85, 87, 101, 103,
    112, 113, 115, 119, 198
Mortar L16 81mm mortar 213
Mount Kent 73
MRTA 48–51
Mugabe, Robert 12
Muirhead, Major Alec 182, 189
Mulcahy, Trooper Jerry 156
Müller, Irmgard 119
Munich Olympics 16
Muslim Brotherhood 22
*MV Nisha 19*

**N**

Nadan, Dave 111–12
Nairac, Captain Bob 109–10, *110*
Nassau 106
Nasser, President 123
National Liberation Front 123, 137
Negri Sembilan 150
Newell, Major Dare 81, 144
N'Gom, Abdourah-man 65, 66, 68
Niet, Ah 157
N'Jie, Lady Chilel 66, 67, 68
North Africa 163–75, *178*

North Atlantic Treaty Organisation
    (NATO) 47, 48
Northern Alliance 22, 25, 26-27
Northern Ireland 53–5, 77–9, 108–12
Norway 190–1

**O**

Oan 58–9, 60
O'Callaghan, Gerald 79
Oman 24–5, 83–106, 197
    Jebel Akhdar 157–61
    Jebel Dhofar 84, 90–1
    Mirbat 94, 97–103
    Operation Jaguar 90
    Operation Taurus 95–7
    Saudi invasion 157–61
    Shirshitti caves *102,* 103–4
    Straits of Hormuz 84
    Taqa 88–9
Omar, Mohammed 25
Operation Apostle 190–1
Operation Archway 188–90
Operation Barras 21
Operation Bulbasket 184–7
Operation Chestnut 175–6
Operation Claret 126–8
Operation Corporate 69
Operation Derry 186
Operation Dickens 186
Operation Favius 80–1
Operation Helsby 148–50
Operation Hive 150–1
Operation Houndsworth 182, 184
Operation Jonquil 177–9
Operation Kipling 186
Operation Loyton 186
Operation Tango 51
Operation Taurus 95–7
Operation Termite 151–2
Origins 164–6
Oyster Creek 66

**P**

Pagoda Team 17
Pantoja, Moises 48
Papa, General 21
Parachute Regiment 21, 77, 152
Parachute Regiment Squadron 152, 155
Parsons, Alfred 77
Patterson, Major Ian 187, 188

Pea Green House 130–1, *131*
Pebble Island 71–3
People's Front for the Liberation of the
    Occupied Arabian Gulf (PFLOAG)
    84, 89, 91, 92–3, 94, 95, 97–106, 194–5
Perak 151
Percival, General 143
Peru 48–51
Peterhead Prison 79–80
Phantoms, The 180–2
Pinckney, Captain 175, 176
Piper, Larry G. 65, 66
Pirie, Commander 'Duke' 98
Poat, Major Harry 188
Point 985 103, 104
Polay, Victor 48
Popular Front for the Liberation of
    Palestine 112
Port Howard 73
Port Stanley 18, 74
Portadown 79
Power, Major Peter 189
Price II, Charles H. 77
Prijedor 51
Private military companies 198–9
Punta Arenas 75

**Q**

Qaboos, Sultan 84, 85
Qadhafi, Colonel 64
Qala-i-Jangi 25–26, *30,*

**R**

R Squadron 14–15, 47
Radfan Mountains 136, 138
Rakyut 103
Raspe, Jan-Carle 119
Rawes, Sergeant 178–9
Red Brigade 195–6
Reddy, Paul 87
Reese, 'Ginge' 98, 101
Reeves, Michel 141
Rennie, Major Frank 152
Returned To Unit (RTU) 197
Rhodesia 12
Riccomini, Lieutenant 190
Richardson, Trooper 123
Rigid Raider 22–3, 74
Ritchie, Major-General Neil 164
Roberts, Corporal 132, 133

Rokel Creek 21
Rommel, General Erwin 163
Rose, Major General 'Mike' 47, 48, 62–3, 74, 75
Rowe, Lieutenant Ronnie 173
Royal Irish Regiment 21
Royal Marines 18
Royal Ulster Constabulary (RUC) 53, 78, 110, 111
RPG-7 213
Rumsfeld, Donald 28, 29

# S

SA80 Assault Rifle 213
Sabah 123
Sabrina 161
Sadoine, Captain 185
St. Mary's Island 63–4
Salalah 84, 85, 95, 97
Sallal, Colonel Abdullah 123
San Carlos Water 71
Sana 123
Sandilands, Sergeant 156
Sanguineti, Rodolfo Munante 48
Sante Fé (submarine) 70–1
Sanyang, Kukoi Samba 64, 66, 68
Sarajevo 51
Sarawak 123, 125
Saudi Arabia 39, 42, 157, 197
Savage, Sean 53, 80, 81
Saveski, Trooper 99, 100, 101, 103, 122
Schleyer, Dr Hans-Martin 112, 119
Scholey, Peter 206–7
Schumann, Captain 116, 117, 119
Schwarzkopf, General Norman 37, 44, 46–7
Scud missiles 38, 46
Seal Team 6 24
Seddon, Sergeant 178
Seekings, Reg 182
Selection process 13–14
Senegal 62, 64, 65, 66, 68
Serbs 47–8, 51
Shahait 92
Sharjah 87
Shirshitti caves 102, 103–4
Sierra Leone 21–22
SIG Sauer P226 pistol 18, 19, 209, 213
Simi 173–5
Singapore 123, 143
Skrzypkowiak, Andy 80
Slater, Al 77

Slater, 'Rover' 131–2
Sloane, Lieutenant-Colonel John 148
Small, Lance-Corporal Geordie 105
Smith, Lawrence 42
Somalia 117
South Georgia 69, 70–1
Soviet Union 123
Spann, Johnny Michael 29–30
Special Activities Staff 25
Special Air Service (SAS)
    Aden 123, 136–41
    Afghanistan 22, 29–32, 80
    Alpha Three Zero 38–41
    Belize 106–8, 106, 107
    Borneo 123–36, 124
    Bosnia 22, 47–8, 51
    Bradbury Lines 19, 62, 112, 121
    Bravo Two Zero 38
    Brighton Bomb 76–7
    Brunei 123
    Colombia 35–6
    Credenhill 11, 15
    Falklands War 18–19, 68–75
    Fijians 122
    Gambia 62–8
    General Norman Schwarzkopf 37, 44, 46–7
    Gibraltar 80–1
    Gulf War (1991) 36–47
    Iranian Embassy Siege 9, 56–62, 57, 58, 59, 61, 65, 203–4
    Jebel Akhdar 157–61
    Lima Embassy Siege 49–51
    Malaya 16, 81, 123, 144–57
    Merebrook Camp 121
    Military Cross 42, 55, 74, 130, 161
    Mogadishu 114, 117–19
    Mount Everest 75–6, 201–3
    Northern Ireland 53–5, 77–9, 108–12
    Oman 20–21, 83, 84–106, 157–61
    Operation Apostle 190–1
    Operation Archway 188–90
    Operation Barras 21
    Operation Bulbasket 184–7
    Operation Chestnut 175–6
    Operation Claret 126–8
    Operation Corporate 69
    Operation Favius 80–1
    Operation Helsby 148–50
    Operation Hive 150–1
    Operation Houndsworth 182, 184
    Operation Jonquil 177–9
    Operation Kipling 186
    Operation Tango 51

    Operation Taurus 95–7
    Operation Termite 151–2
    Special Boat Section 173, 187–8
Special Boat Service (SBS) 18-19, 33, 36, 74
Special Forces Briefing Course 13
Special Patrol Team 17
Special Raiding Squadron 173
Springles, Corporal 'Taff' 128–30
squadrons
    22 Squadron 11, 84, 147, 159
    264 Squadron 11
    A Squadron 11, 37, 41–6, 126, 148, 161, 184
    B Squadron 11, 37, 77, 98, 146, 148, 152
    C Squadron 12, 146, 148, 152, 184
    D Squadron 37, 69, 71–2, 74, 126, 130, 131, 133, 148, 152, 156, 158, 159, 161
    G Squadron 11, 24, 55, 69, 73, 74, 98, 100, 102, 127, 138, 141
    HQ Squadron 11
    R Squadron 14–15, 47
    Training Squadron 11
Stanley, Commander Ian 69, 70, 71
Stephens, Lieutenant Tom 184
Stirling, Lieutenant-Colonel David 12, 35, 62, 155, 164–8, 169–71, 169, 198
Stirling, Lieutenant-Colonel William 171, 175
Stirling Lines 62
Stokes, Sergeant 'Brummie' 75, 201–3
Storey, Private 168
Straits of Hormuz 20, 84, 157
Sudan 22, 24
Suharto, General 136
Sukarno, President 125, 136
Sun-Zu 144
Swierzy, Corporal 76
Swindells, Corporal Duke 159

# T

Taimur, Sultan Sadi bin 84, 157
Tait, Sergeant Bob 167
Taliban 25–32
Taqa 88–9, 89
Taylor, Eric 77
Tebbit, Norman 77
Tel Aviv 46
Templar, General Sir Gerald 125, 150
Tentera Nasional Indonesia 127
Terrorism 19, 20–1, 23, 48–51, 53–5, 56–62, 141, 195–6

Test Week *12*, 14
Thatcher, Margaret 36, 62, 65, 68, 69, 76–7
Thomas, Lance-Corporal 104
Thompson, Major Harry 156, 157
Thomson, Trooper Jock 133–6
Thumier 137
Tidespring, HMS 69
Tikka Findlander 17
Tobin, Trooper 101, 103
Tonkin, Captain John 184–5, *185*, 189
Tora Bora 24
Training 7, 12–3, 16–21
Training Squadron 11, 13
Trucial Oman Scouts 20, 88
Tudela, Francisco 48
Tupac Amaru 48–51
Turnbull, Sergeant Bob 155
Type 110 Land Rovers ('Pink Panthers')
   27, 38, 39, 122–3

## U

Ula Langat *145, 151*
Ulster Defence Regiment 111
Um al Gwarif 98, 100, 102
Unimog 39
United Arab Emirates 112
United Nations 29, 36, 37. 199

## V

Vickers K 213
Victor Two 43
Victoria Cross 173
Vidal, Kentin 49
Vietnam 37

## W

Wadi Darbat 90
Wadi Rhawdah 20, 87
Wakeham, Mrs John 77
Walker, Arthur 144
Walker, Captain Roderic 160, 161
Walker, Major-General Walter 126, 128,
   136
Walker, Sergeant 105–6
Walls, Peter 152
Warburton, Trooper Terry 136, 137
Warner, Philip 201
WatchGuard International 198

Watts, Colonel Johnny 83, 84, 90, 91–2,
   161
Weapons
   Accuracy International L69A1 PM
   7.62 Sniper's rifle 210
   AK-47 assault rifle 210
   Arwen 210
   Browning .5 heavy machine-gun 38,
   98, 167, 194, 209
   Browning Hi-Power pistol 17, 81, 109
   Colt M203 208
   Enfield SA80 209
   GPMG 208
   Heckler and Koch G3 211
   Heckler and Koch MP5 sub-machine
   gun *17*, 65, 209
   Heckler and Koch PSG1 sniper rifle
   211
   Ingram Model 10 211
   LAW 80 light anti-tank weapon 211
   LAW rocket 66mm 211–12
   Milan anti-tank missiles 39, 212
   Minimi 27, 212
   Mortar L16 81mm mortar 213
   RPG-7 213
   SA80 assault rifle 213
   Scud missiles 29, 38, 46
   SIG Sauer P226 pistol *14*, 15, 209, 213
   Tikka Findlander 17
   Vickers K 213
Weavers, Cyril 123
Wegener, Ulrich 65, 113, 115
West Side Boys 21–2
Westmacott, Captain Richard 55
White City 95
Whitelaw, Willie 60
Willys jeep 166, *167*
Wireless Ridge 74
Wiseman, Captain 182
Woodhouse, Major John 13, 126, 147, 148,
   152
Woodiwiss, Major Roger 134
World Trade Center 22
World War Two 163–91
   Bucket Force 187–8
   D-Day 182
   Italy 175–80
   North Africa 163–75
   Norway 190–1
   Operation Archway 188–90
   Operation Bulbasket 184–7
   Operation Houndsworth 182–4

## Y

Yemen 123, 136, 141
Yugoslavia 155
Yundum 64, 65, 66

## Z

Zakhir Tree 103, 104, 105
ZANU 12
Zimbabwe 16, 199–200

# Bibliography

Baker, W. D. *Dare To Win – The Story of The New Zealand Special Air Service*. Lothian Publishing Co. 1987.

Barber, Noel. *The War of The Running Dogs – The Malayan Emergency 1948–1960*. Collins 1971.

Benyon-Tinker, W.E. *Dust Upon The Sea*. Hodder & Stoughton 1947.

de la Billière, General Sir Peter. *Looking For Trouble – SAS to Gulf Command*. BCA 1994.

Bonds, Ray, ed. *The Vietnam War – The Illustrated History of The Conflict in South-East Asia*. Salamander Books 1979.

Bradford, Roy & Dillon, Martin. *Rogue Warrior of The SAS*. John Murray 1987.

Cole, Barbara. *The Elite – The Story of The Rhodesian Special Air Service*. Three Knights Publishing 1984.

Cole, Barbara. *The Elite Pictorial – Rhodesian Special Air Service*. Three Knights Publishing 1986.

Cowles, Virginia. *The Phantom Major – The Story of David Stirling and The SAS Regiment*. Fontana Books 1958.

Courtney G. B. *SBS in World War Two*. Grafton Books 1985

Davies, Barry. *The Complete Encyclopedia of the SAS*. Virgin Books 1998.

Davies, Barry. *SAS Rescue*. Sidgwick & Jackson 1996.

Draper & Challenor. *Tanky Challenor – SAS and the Met*. Leo Cooper 1990

Dickens, Peter. *SAS – Secret War in South-East Asia*. Greenhill Books 1991.

Farran, Roy. *Winged Dagger*. Arms & Armour Press 1986.

Farran, Roy. *Operation Tombola*. Arms & Armour Press 1986.

Generous, Kevin. *Vietnam – The Secret War*. Hamlyn Bison 1985.

Geraghty, Tony. *Who Dares Wins – The Special Air Service, 1950 to The Falklands*. Arms & Armour Press 1983.

Harclerode, Peter. *PARA! Fifty Years of The Parachute Regiment*. Arms & Armour Press 1992.

Harrison, Derrick. *These Men Are Dangerous – The Early Years of The SAS*. Blandford Press 1988.

Hoe, Alan. *David Stirling – The Authorised Biography of The Creator of the SAS*. Little, Brown & Co. 1992.

Hoe, Alan & Morris, Eric. *Re-Enter The SAS – The Special Air Service and the Malayan Emergency*. Leo Cooper 1994.

Horner, David. *Phantoms of the Jungle – A History of the Australian Special Air Service*. Allen & Unwin 1989.

James, Harold & Sheil-Small, Denis. *The Undeclared War*. New English Library 1973.

Kemp, Anthony. *The SAS At War 1941-1945*. John Murray 1991.

Kemp, Anthony. *The SAS – The Savage Wars of Peace, 1947 to the Present*. John Murray 1994.

Ladd, James. *SAS Operations*. Robert Hale 1986.

Ladd, James. *SBS – The Invisible Raiders*. Arms & Armour Press 1983.

Ladd, James & Melton, Keith. *Clandestine Warfare – Weapons and Equipment of the SOE and OSS*. Blandford Press 1988.

Langley, Mike. *Anders Lassen VC, MC of the SAS*. New English Library 1988.

Lassen, Suzanne. *Anders Lassen – The Story of a Dane*. Frederick Muller 1965.

Lodwick, John. *The Filibusters*. Methuen & Co. 1947.

Lorain, Pierre. *Secret Warfare – The Arms and Techniques of the Resistance*. Orbis Publishing 1983.

Malone, M.J. *SAS – A Pictorial History of the Australian Special Air Service 1957-1997*. Access Press 1997.

Parker, John. *SBS – The Inside Story of the Special Boat Service*. Headline 1997.

Pitt, Barrie. *Special Boat Squadron – The Story of the SBS in the Mediterranean*. Century Publishing 1983.

Pocock, Tom. *Fighting General – The Public & Private Campaigns of General Sir Walter Walker*. Collins 1973.

Ramsay, Jack. *The Soldier's Story*. Macmillan 1996.

Seligman, Adrian. *War in the Islands – Undercover Operations in the Aegean 1942–4*. Alan Sutton Publishing 1996.

Seymour, William. *British Special Forces*. Sidgwick & Jackson 1985.

Smith, E.D. *Counter-Insurgency Operations: 1 Malaya and Borneo*. Ian Allan 1985.

Warner, Philip. *The Special Air Service*. William Kimber 1971.

The publishers would like to thank the following sources for their kind permission to reproduce the pictures in this book:

**Barry Davies:** 8, 12, 13bl, 13br, 13tl, 13tr, 16, 17, 18, 19, 20, 21, 23, 24, 34, 40, 47, 50, 54, 55, 56, 63, 64, 67, 69, 73, 75, 76, 78, 86, 88, 89bl, 89tr, 90, 91, 92, 93tl, 93br, 96, 99, 100, 101, 102, 105, 106, 107, 108, 113, 117, 118, 119, 122, 127b, 127t, 129, 131, 133, 134, 135, 136, 137, 181, 192, 195, 196, 200, 203, 204, 207

**Colt:** 210bl, 210tl

**Department of Defense,** U.S.A. : 1l, 1r, 5, 5bl, 6, 11, 14, 22, 27, 29, 30, 33

**Heckler & Koch:** 211ml. 211tl

**Imperial War Museum:** 2, 10, 70, 72, 82, 120, 139, 142, 145, 147, 149, 150, 151, 153, 154, 156, 159, 160, 161, 162, 163, 164, 165, 167, 169, 170, 171, 174, 176, 177, 178, 179, 180, 185, 186, 189, 191

**Joseph Celecha:** 52

**Ministry of Defence:** 1r, 5m, 5br, 28, 210r, 211r

**Pentagon Picture Library:** 26

**Private Collection:** 37, 38, 39, 41, 43, 44, 57, 58, 59, 61, 62, 71, 74, 85, 110, 126, 140

**Sig-Sauer:** 211b

**TRH Pictures:** 123, 125, 130

Every effort has been made to acknowledge correctly and contact the source and/or copyright holder of each picture, and Carlton Books Limited apologises for any unintentional errors, or omissions, which will be corrected in future editions of this book.